MW00412323

New Beginnings

From Behind the Iron Curtain to America

Antonina Duridanova

Fulton Books, Inc.
Meadville, PA

Published by Fulton Books 2020

ISBN 978-1-64952-109-5 (paperback)
ISBN 978-1-64952-110-1 (digital)

Printed in the United States of America

Contents

Memories

Introduction

My name is Antonina, and I am not a writer. It was on the day of my retirement party at the Internal Revenue Service when I promised an agent, an employee of mine, to write a book about my life, and since I always keep my promises, I sat down at the computer to pour out my soul to people about my long journey. I had colleagues, students, and employees who knew certain episodes of my life and were curious if one day I would write a book. Their comments were that I lived an incredible and, by some, extraordinary life, which I should share with the world. My story is exceptional because of my background and the difficulties I had to overcome to live a brighter and fuller life. You are about to discover the meaning of courage, sacrifice, endurance, perseverance, and love for family and friends. You will learn the truth about life under communism and capitalism through my experiences at an early age to retirement.

For some, my writing will provide awareness as I will take them out of their comfort zones in unknown lands, and for others, it will be a motivational source inviting them to act and change their lives for the better. I expect my readers to be from all walks of life. For some, this will be an educational material; for others, a guide designed to provide them with life-surviving tools. My intentions are to challenge my reader to understand the value of freedom, to know the truth about justice and honesty, and to awaken in him/her the desire to live a decent and free life. I would like to give people hope and inspire them to follow their dreams no matter how steep the road is and to always pursue happiness. My intentions are to reach out to individuals who have no clue how precious freedom is and how privileged they are to live in America.

My reader will be a young adult from the inner city who needs to understand that there is a way out of their impoverished neighborhoods, a suburban kid in search of their own identity, a kid who may have suffered the cruelty of life and needs a direction of how to suppress the past and move forward, or a middle-aged person feeling cornered with no future. As a high school teacher, university instructor, tax advisor to foreign governments, and manager at the US Treasury Department, I influenced a lot of individuals in improving their lives and achieving their goals. This writing is designed to fire up the young and the old to follow their dreams. By sharing very intimate and personal moments of my life, I would like to empower the weak and the poor, the ones who feel forgotten to persist and never give up. This book is not a diary but rather a capture of important moments from my childhood to the date I retired. The reader will witness events that steered me in unexpected directions, gave me energy, and energized me to move forward. Some happenings were under my control, and a lot were not.

Having said this, I believe an introduction is in order, so here I am, a Bulgarian American who immigrated to the States in 1970 at the time of the Cold War, when it was difficult for even birds to fly over the Iron Curtain. I was born in 1949 in Sofia, Bulgaria, when there was still turbulence in the Balkan Peninsula after the end of the Second World War. Bulgaria was left in the Eastern Communist Bloc alongside with other Eastern European countries, adopting a regime of subordination to the Soviet Union.

You will observe my actions. You will feel my pain and happiness as I take you from the carefree days of a young child to the different levels of schooling in Communist Bulgaria. I will share the most intimate and true experiences of what growing up was behind the Iron Curtain. You will watch me escape a life of deceit and oppression and follow me every step of the way as witnesses to my struggle for personal freedom and growth. You will enter the life of an immigrant and learn the process of becoming a resident and an American citizen. You will learn about the greatness of the American people and the reason why a sincere person wants to be a part of the American society.

You will see me as a teacher first at a Catholic high school and then in the inner city of Detroit, where I grasped opportunities to make a difference. You will witness my restless personality, wanting to achieve more and more, as I earn my business degrees, BBA and MA in international trade and Spanish, as well as a BA with majors in Russian and French. I will take you to the scenes of my life as a high school teacher and a lecturer at the University of Michigan to my days of employment with the US Treasury as a Revenue Agent, an International Examiner, a Tax Advisor, and a manager. During my career with the Service, I encountered unexpected twists and events, which I am going to let you discover on your own.

I will also let you have a glimpse at some of my personal experiences. For one, I have three children, a boy and two girls, all grown up and living well. I am also a happy grandmother with six grandchildren. There will be a brief reference to their fathers without any juicy stories. You will not see unpleasant scenes of my personal or professional lives because in my journey, I always moved on, leaving destructive people and unpleasant situations behind.

As a closing remark, I would like to say that this book is not a fairy tale; it is a true and honest portrayal of my personal struggles and achievements. Writing it, I felt that I fulfilled my desire to reveal a story of victory over all difficulties that life might serve. There is a lesson to be learned behind every episode; some are explicit, and others are for the reader to interpret and discover. Having said enough, I will let you submerge yourself into my life and discover truths you probably never heard of or knew about. I hope you enjoy my journey.

Early Childhood in Bulgaria behind the Iron Curtain

We all remember the carefree, happy days as children, and I am not an exception. My memories go back to the times when I was about four, but the big games in the neighborhood were a few years later, maybe when I was six or seven. Born in Sofia, Bulgaria, and growing in the city center, I had friends with whom I played *narodna topka* (*dodgeball* in English), explored secret tunnels of basements in the apartment complexes, and jumped over fences. Every day after breakfast, I'd look out the kitchen window at Gavril Genev Street, and if there were a couple of kids with a ball in the street, I would fly out of the apartment building to join in the games. There could be ten to fifteen kids in the neighborhood playing dodgeball, and that could entertain us for the entire day.

Some days we were more adventurous and explored the basements. I distinctly remember a basement at an apartment building to the side of ours which had tunnels leading to other basements. We all crawled fearlessly to find the end of the tunnels, which I am still sure that most adults, including my family, were not aware of existing. Perhaps these tunnels were dug out during the war, but as children, this was not something to preoccupy us. We were all seeking adventures after reading Tom Sawyer and Huckleberry Finn stories. We climbed over fences, getting into yards of different apartment buildings, where we searched for unusual things. There was nothing special about them; they just had different shapes or landscape. Some had flowers, which I adored, and bushes. Others, just dirt, but they all had benches and a stand on which people hung their carpets and pound on them with a special stick to clean them (there were no vacuum cleaners in those days). I would come back home with bloody knees, and Grandma would silently wash the wounds with iodine. I never cried or complained about getting hurt and never interrupted my playing because of blood dripping down my legs and elbows.

My family consisted of my grandma (the most important person in my life because she took care of me for as long as I can remember), my grandfather, my mother, my father, and my aunt on my mother's side. We all lived in a two-bedroom apartment on the second floor at the corners of Gavril Genov and Asparuh Streets. My father kept an office at a different location on Rakovski Street, not far, maybe half an hour's walk away. Since he worked late into the night, there was also a bedroom set in his room. I did not see much of him as Mom used to take lunches to his study every day. He would come to the apartment with us for holidays and sometimes on weekends. Occasionally, Mom would take me to him, and I admired the tons of books neatly arranged up the walls and in stacks on the floor—it looked like a mini library. Dad's desk was a table with a typewriter and papers all around it. He would stand up and pat me on the head as we entered the room. Then Mom and Dad would whisper to each other. I remember asking them once why they were speaking in such low voices to which Dad responded, "The walls sometimes have ears, Nina. We don't want the neighbors to hear." All this made no sense to me, but I didn't question anything more. In my teens, I learned that people were spied upon, and the wrong word could get you in trouble, so even at home, people kept their voices down. When I saw Dad at home or when Mom took me over to him, I always tried not to do anything to upset him. My father was soft-spoken, never raised his voice, but he had a stern look and rarely laughed. I was not afraid of him as he never scolded me, but I did not want to do something where he could show me another side of his character. I was around five when I found out that he taught at the university and was an important scholar.

My aunt was my hero as she inspired me to love reading. She was a beautiful woman with long dark hair; piercing, beautiful eyes; and a body of a model. As a child, I slept with her in her king-size bed, and she read to me every night from the book of Andersen's fairy tales. I thought how wonderful it would be to be able to read by myself these miraculous stories. My father did not want me to read before I started school (in Bulgaria, that is at the age of seven). Later, I found out that when he was little, his father made him and his siblings read and study way before starting school until my great grandmother visited and, looking at the sad faces of the kids, said, "What is this punishment? Kids have to enjoy their childhood and play." All the kids darted out before my grandfather changed his mind.

My father did not want me to read before school because his thinking was that I would have a long life of reading and that I should play and enjoy my childhood. "There is plenty of time for Nina to read and study," he would say. But my curiosity and thirst for reading was already awakened. My aunt worked, so as soon as she got home and on weekends, I would run to her and follow her around. She took me visiting, and I loved going by her friends who always were happy to see me and treat me with sweets. Ah yes, sweets were something that we could not have outside the house, as every time we walked by a pastry shop, my mom would say, "No money, Nina." Soon I caught on that I could not have sweets, and instead of asking, I would say, "No money." Grandma was a great cook, but she did not believe in baking desserts every day; that was reserved for holidays, Christmas, Easter, and name days. She made the best pumpkin strudel, *banitsa* (cheese strudel), *kozunak* (sweet bread with raisins), and *kurabiiki* (Bulgarian cookies).

Mom was a high school teacher and sometimes took me to the school where her students would gather around me, telling me how pretty and cute I was. Mom was also beautiful, but her look was soft and kind, and her smile was like a sunshine, which used to brighten my day. I could tell that her students liked her a lot by the way they looked at her and talked to her with admiration. Spending time with Mom at the school where she taught was very special for me. I felt proud watching how students and colleagues were looking up to her. There was a funny happening that I still remember. Mom had to attend an important meeting and could not take me with her, so she asked a couple of the female students to watch me. The girls took me to their house and left me in the backyard, which was fenced, thinking that nothing would happen. I was lonely and started to look for things to do. There were small trees, so I tried climbing them. Not always successful, I would fall and try again. When Mom returned and the girls showed up, I was all dirty, with bloody knees and scraped elbows. "We are so sorry, *drugarko*" (in Communist times, everybody was addressed as friends/comrades, the Mrs. and Ms. did not exist). Mom examined me, and after determining that I was not hurt seriously, she told the girls it was all right and that I was okay. She never left me alone with anyone after that incident.

Mom also discovered a trait in my personality that everybody at home considered when disciplining me. I remember one day running and jumping in puddles after the rain and Mom becoming very upset seeing mud all over me. She ran after me. I got scared and tried to get away, but all of a sudden, everything turned black in front of my eyes. Ever since this incident, the adults at home knew that scolding and being talked to loudly would make me sick, and I was never again disciplined. Mom was in charge of my health and schooling; she watched over me to ensure that I had a happy, carefree life. When I was sick, she took me to doctors and took care of me until I got better.

It was mom who was in charge of my education. When I was six, my father told her that the future was in learning English, so she enrolled me in an English preschool class at Alliance (the name of the educational facility on Slaveykov Square). The teacher was an elderly lady with gray hair tucked in the back, but she was very energetic and lively. She spoke only in English with the idea that we could learn the language as we did our native tongue. This approach worked. She used pictures and objects for reinforcement, and it wasn't long before I started to say whole sentences in English. I remember even learning the days of the week and the months in English before in Bulgarian. Our teacher talked to us about what life was like in England for children our age. All this was fascinating, as I would picture this far land with beautiful cities and nature, with children running in the parks and the meadows speaking English and playing games similar to ours. A music teacher came every day with an accordion. I loved learning all the English children's songs. I still remember them: "My

Bonnie Lies over the Ocean," "Daisy, Daisy, Give Me Your Answer Do," and many more.

Then just before Christmas, I got sick with scarlet fever. I was only six, and I was terrified as they took me alone in an ambulance. Once in the hospital, they scrubbed me with disinfectants. A nurse with a mask on her face told me to follow her and took me to a room where there was another little girl, very pale, lying in bed and a woman with a small child lying in a bed next to hers. This was the first time I was away from my family, and I wasn't feeling well. The nurse pointed me to a bed. I walked slowly and sat on it, feeling very sad and scared. Tears started to roll down my face when the nurse said, "Go to the window. You can see your mom and grandma from there." Terrified, I walked with shaky knees to the window, looking down in the street below. Seeing my mom and grandma made me sadder, and I started to cry louder. "Nina, you need to be strong, child!" my mom was shouting out over my crying. "We will be here all the time waiting for you to get better. But you have to do your part. You need to eat all your food, take the medicine they give you, listen, and do everything you are asked to do." I calmed down, wiped my tears, and told them that it would be as Mom said because I missed them and wanted to go back home badly. I don't remember how long I was in the hospital, but I ate all my food and that of the child who didn't want hers. The first thing I did every morning was to run to the window. Mom and Grandma were there, and I was comforted just to see them, telling them that I was eating well and listening to the nurse. I still remember the day they dismissed me from the hospital. It felt like a big holiday.

It was also Christmastime, and as soon as Mom opened the door of the apartment, I ran in and saw a small wardrobe made of wood under the Christmas tree. My eyes lit up. There were no presents under the tree for any of the prior holidays that I remembered, and I was beaming with happiness. "It's from your class," Mom said. "The kids exchanged presents, and this is what you got from one of your classmates." Christmas was not an official holiday in Bulgaria at those times. Later, I found out that it was forbidden to celebrate Christmas in public, but Christian families like ours prepared special meals on Christmas Eve and Christmas Day, saying prayers at home. New Year's was the big holiday when everybody dressed up and celebrated openly with family and friends. My grandmother kept the tradition, and for Christmas Eve, she prepared the Bulgarian vegetarian dishes typical for this holiday—stuffed cabbage and vine leaves, bean soup, red peppers stuffed with beans, the famous round bread called *pogacha* with fortune writings drawn by each one of us, and *banitsa* (strudel) with pumpkin and cheese. There were twelve vegetarian servings, and everything was prepared by Grandma. Easter was another holiday we were forbidden to celebrate, but Grandma gathered the family each year for a big feast, the best part being the colored eggs, which, as a custom, my cousins and I, each with an egg in hand, knocked with the pointed ends to see which one could remain unbroken. And the *kozunak* (sweet bread), which she prepared for hours was the best bread anyone could taste.

Mom also snuck me with her into the church St. Petka by the St. Nedelya Square. Praying and going to church was not only forbidden but could have bad consequences, from losing a job to problems with the police, which I learned about when I was older. Nobody was guarding the entrances of the churches, but people knew from meetings at work or school that religion was not allowed to be practiced and that it was not recommended to be seen entering a church. St. Petka was a small building, where Mom used to take me and teach me how to light candles and pray. I was fascinated by the icons with paintings of saints and religious scenes. Mom lit candles for the living and the dead, kissed the icons of St. Mary and Jesus, and prayed. I followed her and did the same. Sometimes she talked to a priest, and he would say a prayer mentioning our names. There were other bold people entering churches, but nobody was looking at other people's faces, and there were no services. Then I had my best friend, my cousin Krum, who lived close by and with whom I met regularly in a neighboring small park on Patriarch Eftimi Boulevard. There was a church in the middle of the park, and we often snuck in there out of curiosity. I remember that the church was full of people at times when the priest was giving communion. That was intriguing for us children, so we would line up to get bread. I remember the priest asking us, "Are you baptized?" to which we nodded yes. Back home, Mom told me that I was baptized, so I knew it was true. But I got in trouble when I wanted to go with my cousin behind the altar. "That's only for boys. You can't go in!" the priest yelled out, which I thought was very unjust.

Ever since I was little, I tried to do the right things, but my judgment was not always good. I remember an incident when I must have been not older than four. It was a bright, sunny summer day. The backyard of the apartment complex in Sofia was small, surrounded by two tall brick walls with fading gray paint. Children were playing in the yard, inventing games and digging the dirt with spoons (sandboxes, play shovels, and buckets were not known to us kids then). I have recollections of that day being hot, knowing that my cheeks were bursting red from the heat, with messy long hair and a ribbon on the side, a red summer dress with white dots, and sandals, digging in the dirt and trying to build maybe a tunnel. All of a sudden, my aunt showed up at the window on the second floor of our apartment and yelled out in a very stern voice, "Nina, lunchtime, if you don't come home to eat, don't come at all!" I was not hungry and wanted to play more. I thought for a minute about my options and decided to keep playing. Since I took this decision and knew that I couldn't go home, I quickly figured out that after I was done, I would go to my cousin Krum's apartment.

After a while, the other children started to leave, and I headed out walking down the streets in the busiest and most commercial part of town. I was not scared, and none of the adults stopped me. They were too tall for me to see their faces anyway. I hurried crossing a big street with trams, cars, and occasionally, carts of gypsies. Now gypsies I stayed away from as my grandmother told me scary stories of gypsies stealing children and hiding them in their big sacks. I reached my cousin's apartment building, walked up to the fourth floor, and knocked as loud as I could. Aunt Seka, Krum's mother, opened the door and looked for my grandmother, but then she realized that I was alone. She pulled me inside the apartment and ran to the phone, which she frantically dialed. I knew something went wrong for Aunt Seka to be so upset. My grandmother answered, and Seka yelled,

"Gina, your naughty granddaughter is here all by herself! Come and get her." In my mind, I did nothing wrong as I had done exactly what my aunt said, but now I knew that I did something wrong.

I hid under a bed where I stayed until my grandmother arrived, all puffy and breathless. I heard my grandmother's voice, "Where is she?" And my heart sank. Grandma peeked under the bed, but I would not budge.

"Grandma, please promise not to be mad, and I'll come out." Grandma has never hit me before, but I just could not stand to see her upset. She promised not to say a word, and all ended well with us walking in silence back home. This is my first memory as a child that taught me a lesson to be careful of choices that people offered to me.

Another special person from that early age was my grandfather. Grandfather was a very soft-spoken, quiet, and sweet old man. He was tall and skinny and always looked at me with gentle and loving eyes. My favorite time was to sit by him and watch him draw horses in a drawing book with black hardcover dedicated for this purpose. This book was safely guarded as grandfather took it out only when he was drawing for me another of those beautiful animals with free manes, galloping or standing still, becoming alive in front of my eyes. Grandma and Grandpa did not talk much; they lived silently. Grandma went about her daily work of bringing coal from the basement for the stove, cooking, cleaning, and washing while Grandpa sat quietly. Sometimes he would go out, and Grandma would send me to tell him to come home as soon as he appeared across the street from our apartment. Then one day, Grandpa stopped getting out of bed. The doctor came and saw him once a day, and everybody kept silent. I wanted to have fun again with Grandpa, so one day, I dragged the big drawing book to his bed and plopped myself next to him. I was happy and started to bounce around him at which time my mother ran into the room and told me to get out immediately. Grandpa smiled and said, "Leave her. I am okay." And the day ended with another horse added to my collection of Grandpa's drawings.

Then Grandpa was gone. They said that he died and that he was taken to the graveyard. Mother took me to the church where he was lying in a wooden box called a casket. Grandma was by him; her face was stern and pale. She seemed tense, bent over Grandpa, dressing him in a shirt that mother just brought. All the family was present— my uncles, their wives, my aunt, my mother, and my father. I knew something bad happened as Grandpa was sleeping in a strange bed with everybody sad and crying. Then two men came and loaded the casket on a cart pulled by horses. Everybody followed on foot to a place with a hole on the ground. Mother screamed out in pain and pulled me aside as the men lowered the casket in the ground. I did not know why these people would put Grandpa on the ground and pour dirt over the wooden box. It seemed so cruel as I was gazing at the men throwing shovels of dirt in the hole, and all relatives were weeping and sad. This was the last time I saw Grandpa, and the image of his funeral stayed with me forever. Nobody at that time spoke to me about life and death and funeral processions, so I had to figure it on my own.

But my best memories as a child were discovering the country- side at my grandmother's village, where two of her brothers still lived, and my cousin Krum with his mother, Aunt Seka, would also join us in the summer months. We would take a bus and stop by a dirt road leading to the houses tucked in the hills. This place was called Rakelovci and was close to the village of Kovachevci. Grandma took me there in the most beautiful season of the year, when the meadows were green and wildflowers were spreading aroma of perfume in the air. Butterflies of all colors were flying from flower to flower, and we children would try to catch them. Birds were singing, making us all happy, as we were running up and down the hills. There were three houses in the yard—an old clay house with a hearth in the kitchen where I stayed with my grandma and two other houses belonging to my grandma's brothers. There was a well in front of the old house where we got water for cooking and drinking. The barn was next to the old house.

Our days were filled with games and chores we did on the farm. Almost every day, we took the cows out to pasture; other days, we would run in the fields and by the river, chasing butterflies, rolling down the stacks of hay, eating freshly baked bread and homemade cheese. In the evenings, we would return to the old house cheerfully laughing. We used to jump on top of the barn walls then run in the front yard and the orchard in the back, where we climbed trees to get janki fruit. My knees were always scraped, but I never stopped playing for a minute, not wanting to miss any of this good time. Here I learned that I should not disturb the bees in the beehives, as one day, after deciding to visit them, they buzzed all around me and got into my hair. I ran to Grandma, this time crying. Grandma did not say a word but started to get them out of my hair one by one. I still don't know how she was not hurt and how I survived. I had no clue that this was a deadly situation with my grandma remaining calm and getting all the bees out of my hair. I also discovered that I was afraid of snakes, as one day, bringing the herd home, my cousins yelled, "Watch out! There is a snake at the curve, probably a boa." That was all I remembered as I passed out. When I came to myself, my cousins were looking at me saying that the snake was gone and it was all right, that we could go home.

It was at the farm where I discovered that the horse is your best friend. There was an old horse in the barn that Krum and I decided to ride and explore the area. We could see at the distance houses scattered on the hills, which were difficult to get to on foot. We would hop on the horse's back without a saddle and ride off to visit neighbors. People were happy to see us and cooked us meals, sometimes with chicken from their chicken coop. It turned out that all families all over the hills and ravines were related, if not by blood, by marriage.

Then one day, as we were taking the cows to the pasture, a group of men came over, rounded them up, and took them away. I started to run fast up and down a steep path, falling several times, and finally arrived at the house with bloody knees and tears in my eyes, crying out to my grandma and to the other adults that they took our cows. The adults became mad and cursed the men but did not go after them. Later, I learned that the cows were taken to the cooperative farm of the village as farmers were not allowed to have more than one cow per family. This made me sad because I considered the cows my pets and was very attached to them. Each one had a name, and I talked to them as my cousin and I took them out to the pastures.

As days went by, I continued to observe with great interest the life on the farm. Women were making butter and cheese from the milk, and I joined in helping. Especially interesting was watching my grandma weave carpets (*chergi*) from the wool of the sheep. I was fascinated by the whole process of cutting the sheep's wool, placing it on a spindle, dying it, and finally making the carpets with a weaving loom, which my grandma had in the back of the house in an open field. I was sad every summer coming back to the city as I missed playing in the fields, rolling down hay stacks, and chasing butterflies and the freedom to roam the hills and the ravines all day long. I fell in love with life on the farm, and every summer, I was eager to return there. The country life enchanted me from an early age with its picturesque sights of hills and ravines, the beautiful colors and smells of the meadows and flowers, the sounds of animals and birds, the freshness of the air, and the simplicity and closeness between people. I liked the city life too because of the plays and operas and art exhibits that Mom took me to, but I could trade it in a heartbeat for the beauty and tranquility of the country.

School Years in Bulgaria— Elementary and Middle School

Turning seven was a big event in my life as I was going to start school and learn how to read the books from the children's library. September 15 is the first day of school in Bulgaria. On that date in 1957, Grandma made sure I was pretty, with a blue ribbon on my shoulder-length hair and dressed in a nice dark-blue pleated skirt and white embroidered blouse, which she sewed herself. I remember walking proudly down Asparuh Street with a schoolbag in my hand to the elementary school, Denkoglu, a couple of streets away located on Parchevich Street. There was a gathering in the schoolyard where I easily found my class. I wasn't at all anxious or nervous; I was happy to be at school, feeling like a bird finally flying on its own for the first time.

The kid across from our apartment was also starting school, and we happened to be in the same class. My teacher was a slim, short younger woman with round face. She seemed nice as she called our names and assigned us seats. Each desk had two seats with a compartment under to place our schoolbags. Following the instructions on how to behave in the classroom, we all settled down. I listened carefully to what we were going to study and what were the requirements for each of the classes. The next few weeks, I could not contain my happiness, running home every day and shouting from a distance at my grandma and mother, "I did all the work without any mistakes! I have all 6, which is an A!" I learned how to write cursive and enjoyed it as it looked like a drawing, which I liked a lot.

A couple of months later, my grades went down to 5s, which is B, without any corrections on my papers. It was difficult for me at this early age to understand what was going on. I remember one evening overhearing my mom talking to my grandma and aunt, "This teacher is taking bribes. The kid's father across the street is a pilot and has been giving her presents. I learned that from a friend who teaches the higher classes at the school. I will transfer Nina to the school on Rakovski and Patriarch Eftimi Streets."

"This is so ridiculous, a teacher taking it out on kids who do not provide favors for her," my aunt responded.

My enthusiasm for school vanished, although I was still eager to learn new things, both in Bulgarian language and in math. Shortly thereafter, Mom took me to the new school, where I was treated honestly. I was content, but the spark of love for school was gone. I also continued to study English with the same group of kids and learned how to read and write. I was very happy to see that our music lessons continued. I used to come home humming the new songs I learned, which my grandma liked a lot. She loved seeing me laughing and singing and especially telling stories of how my day went at both schools.

Then when I was in second grade, I got sick with a flu, which led to bronchitis and pneumonia. I was sick from October to May, attending school for a few days at the time. There were days when I had a hard time even walking; the fever made me so weak. Mom was by my bed all the time; she tucked me in at night and was the first face I saw waking up. There was a doctor on the fourth floor who gave me penicillin shots every day. Grandma fed me Bulgarian yogurt and oatmeal and cooked dishes with sauerkraut in the winter. After the complications from the flu, I got sick with mumps and had a very bad sinus infection with unbearable headaches. I pulled through, and sometime in May, I felt strong enough to go out for a walk to the neighborhood park. But I couldn't see well. Everything was foggy; there were floaters in front of my eyes. "Mom, I can't see!" I cried out to which Mom took me home quietly and made an appointment with an eye doctor.

"Nina's vision deteriorated because of the continuous fever and penicillin treatment" was the doctor's verdict. "She is not going blind. She needs glasses. I recommend taking her in the mountains or the village to relax her eyes."

Mom was teaching me at home and taking my homework to the teacher, so I passed second grade with excellent grades. On May 24, the Bulgarian schools celebrated the holiday of Cyril and Methodius, the brothers who invented the Cyrillic alphabet, and I was already well enough to be in the parade with my classmates. There was a year-end ceremony where each A student was recognized with a ribbon placed across the front of their shirt or blouse. I was startled to hear my name and turned to my mother who was smiling then slowly made it to the front of the class. "You did great, Nina. Even being sick, your work was excellent. Congratulations." I know my eyes were sparkling as the teacher handed me the ribbon. It was at this ceremony that we were all sworn in as pioneers. I don't remember any words said, but we all were given red scarves, which we were told to wear from now on every day in school.

After school dismissal, we spent a couple of weeks in the mountain, followed by a trip to the sea. My doctor recommended that after a long year of sickness, I spend some time at the seaside, so my aunt, who was a controller for the railways, booked tickets for the two of us for the sleeping car of a train to Varna. This is when I fell in love with the sea, amazed at the immense blue water disappearing in the horizon to reach the sky, the magic waves approaching the beach in a roar to disperse in silky drops resembling white lace. My aunt had me on a strict regime. We were at the beach by 7:00 a.m., and I sunbathed on each side for half an hour before we went in the water. But I didn't mind so long as I was there breathing in the fresh sea air and feeling the warmth of the sun.

I finished elementary school with recognition for excellence and was wondering where my middle school would be. At that time, Mom was teaching at a middle school at the outskirts of Sofia, a neighborhood at the foot of Vitosha Mountain. Her certification was for a high school teacher, but there were no openings when she returned to work after the divorce with my father. It was shortly after completing elementary school when I overheard Mom talking to Grandma, "I will enroll Nina in my school. I need to keep an eye on her considering our life lately." Mom and Dad's separation was painful as Mom was in court every day fighting eviction orders initiated by my father. I wanted to be with her and went along to her meetings with judges, watching her cry, which made me sad and cry in turn. Mom's decision to have me at the same school with her made me happy. I wanted to be close to her, and I already knew the school and some of the students. As a class teacher, she had to visit her students' homes and make sure they had good conditions to study. Mom took me along on her weekend visitations to her students' houses, so I met all of them and even became friends with a couple of girls. I also knew the school, a newer building with three floors, with a well-maintained schoolyard for fall and spring PE activities and an orchard in the front with a beautiful view of the mountain.

The transition from elementary to middle school was not difficult for me as I already knew from Mom that I was going to have a different teacher for each subject and that the teachers would come to our classroom rather than the students going to their classrooms, as in the States. From fifth to seventh grade, I had Bulgarian, math, Russian, history, geography, botany, zoology, anatomy, music, art, and PE. Those school years for me were unforgettable as they were filled with games, house parties, and hiking up on Vitosha Mountain with my classmates. They were mostly from blue-collar worker families with simple hearts and lives, taught to be nice to one another and respectful among themselves and with adults. There were meadows outside the schoolyard where we ran and played whenever the weather was nice. I excelled in all subjects; learning for me was easy and enjoyable as I was proud to recite to everybody at home what I learned. Everything fascinated me—the history of Bulgaria and the world; the location of countries, continents, rivers, mountains, oceans, seas; the study of flowers and plants, of animals, of the human body. I would look at the globe and compare countries and places with pictures, trying to visualize what life was there. My desire was to go to the equator one day and see what it was like on it. I wasn't particularly fond of going to places up north as I did not like cold weather. I also enjoyed sports, especially basketball. I still remember my PE teacher telling my mother, "Nina scored eight baskets today. She is unbelievable in this game." I probably took the frustrations from home to the basketball court and running in track. One thing I didn't like was dissecting a frog in a zoology class. I remember getting sick to my stomach and ready to pass out. I knew from that experience that I wasn't meant to be a doctor.

My last year in middle school came fast. One event though stood out. It was a day when the teachers lined us all up from each class and led us to the gym. It wasn't a voluntary participation, and nobody dared or thought of objecting to it or questioning it. There was a solemn ceremony where we were all admitted to the Youth Komsomol Organization, leading to becoming a member of the Communist Party after graduating from college. We accepted this as a normal event since we already knew that belonging to Komsomol was the only way we could attend the better high schools, have a job we liked, or simply live in Bulgaria without hassle. The ceremony was during the day, and there were no families present. Somehow, nobody, including my family, felt that they need to attend or feel bad about missing the event, and likewise, we kids did not expect family or relatives to be with us.

Life seemed to be regulated, and participation in activities was without questions asked. At this age, I did not dwell on the happenings in society, and I did what was expected of me. I loved studying and knowing all material inside and out in every subject. It made me feel proud of myself to know all answers and be recognized for that. However, I didn't keep all knowledge to myself and did not look for glamour. I remember helping classmates, after which we played games in the schoolyard. Thinking back on those years in middle school, I remember the sweet smell of lilac trees in the spring, the carefree playing with girls my age, the parties we started to have in seventh grade, dancing to rock and roll and the twist, something not allowed, but we loved the music and the beat. Somehow, "Come on twist again" penetrated in Communist Bulgaria and grabbed the hearts of the young people.

Studying at the English Language High School

The summer of 1963 was hot. I remember the times spent at the coast with my aunt after being at the countryside with my grandmother, but this summer, she was in Macedonia with her husband (Auntie married and lived in another apartment). Mother was in a desperate state, continuing to see judges at the courthouse and stopping eviction notices. One day, she came home with a man whom my grandmother immediately recognized. He was Lubo, a friend of my uncles from the neighborhood where the family first lived when they moved from the village. From that day on, Mom stopped crying. Her face was calm, and her eyes would light up when Lubo was visiting and having dinner with us. I liked him too because he included me in their conversations and taught me how to play soccer. Not long after that, I accepted him as a father and started to call him papa.

The day my aunt and uncle came back from Macedonia was like a family holiday. My aunt's husband had fled from Macedonia during the war, and this was the first time he went back to visit his family. Stepping off the train, he was singing from happiness, and from the platform at the railway station, the celebration moved to our apartment. My uncle Koljo liked to sing, and so did my aunt. Grandma had the table set with all kinds of yummy foods, and the festivity carried on into the night. I stayed up with the adults, feeling extremely happy that my family was so close and happy together. However, I had important tests in the next couple of days—entry exams for the English language high school, Bulgarian writing, and math. The lack of sleep did not affect my thinking. I wrote fast, my thoughts flowing freely, as if energized from the excitement of the night before.

The results from the testing were posted on a wall at the school a few days later, showing names of students selected for admittance. My name was not on the list, and I felt bad knowing that I did well on the tests. Mom did not stay with her arms crossed; she knew how to fight for me. In her investigation, she learned about the classifications of the candidates—those whose parents were considered big Communists, as former partisans or activists were ranked first, then those with 4.0 GPA (only with A grades from all classes in middle school) where I belonged. But that wasn't all. Further classification followed, looking into the parents—the last admitted candidate was a girl whose father was a professor like mine. Our mothers were both teachers, but her mother was a member of the Communist Party, and Mom was not. I was first on the waiting list. Not long after that, the add-ons were announced with my name appearing at the beginning of the list. That was when I learned about the privileged class in Bulgaria, which enjoyed admittance to schools and jobs based on their political standing. There were four elite schools at that time all located in Sofia, Bulgaria—English, French, German, and Russian high schools, with the English one being most popular. My admittance to the English language high school was not because of the social status of the environment where I was raised; it was because of a sign that from there on, I would have to follow a certain path.

The long-awaited first day of high school arrived, and Grandma made sure that I was dressed well, with a snow-white blouse and dark-blue pleated skirt. She braided my hair silently and crossed me, giving me a blessing. Then she ran in front of me with a cup of water, which she spilled for good luck. It's a Bulgarian custom meaning that your school, job, or anything you are undertaking will flow easily like water. I smiled at her, and Mom and took off for school, which was supposed to determine my destiny. The school was half an hour to an hour's walk, so I took the trolley. I felt uneasy and restless as I walked in the schoolyard full of students in uniforms. All classes were alphabetically numbered, and the students' placement was posted on a billboard. I was in class A, which was easy to spot as all classes were lined up, starting with letter *A*.

The first year was a breeze for me as I knew most of the one hundred new English words that we were supposed to learn daily. This year was called a preparatory year during which we were supposed to get ready to study all subjects in English in the following years. There were also lessons about London and its whereabouts, with pictures of landmarks we were expected to learn and talk about. Some of the students in the class had already been to London and shared photos with stories of their sightseeing tours and experiences. Life in London seemed to be wonderful as described by my classmates, contrary to what the Bulgarian press was reporting not only about England but also about the West. Capitalism was portrayed by the media as decadent, with only homeless people and as such traveling in the West, and any literature, music, works of art, and entertainment from there were forbidden.

These kids returning from England brought books, magazines, and records. I was eagerly reading articles about people's lifestyles and their way of thinking and was struck by the fact that it was possible for a person to express his or her feelings quite freely. It appeared to me that life in England was very attractive. And as a teenager, I fell in love with the Beatles, the Rolling Stones, and all American and English singers from other records that my classmates would bring to parties, which we had on weekends. Our English teacher was from England and often brought English newspapers and magazines from which he selected articles for us to read and answer questions. The classroom setting was like in my previous schools, with one desk each for two students lined in three rows, one behind the other, with the teacher's desk on a podium in the front.

I became friends with a girl who lived in my neighborhood, and we started to walk to school together when the weather was nice. Most students in the class were so-called privileged kids because of their parents' status as big Communists. This girl was no exception. We used to argue about the equality under Communism, which I knew did not exist as I had friends from my middle school who were extremely poor. A girl I used to play with in middle school lived with her parents and sister in one room, which was all they had. The average Bulgarian family lived with two or three other families in an apartment with an income of fifty to one hundred leva per month.

Later in the year, there was an incident that shook me up because of a created accusation against me. There was an event of going to the movies, which I did not attend. Shortly thereafter, my classroom teacher called me with a serious look on her face. "Nina, there will be a Komsomol meeting after school tomorrow at which you will be accused of not participating in Komsomol activities." I was stunned, my face froze, and I could not say a word. I knew that one of the requirements to attend the English language high school was to be an active member of the Komsomol. There was a girl sitting in front of me who was always frustrated, puffing and sighing, whenever I and not her knew the correct answers. She was the child of an important Communist family and considered to be one of the privileged kids, but she had a hard time memorizing the voluminous new daily words. At the meeting, that same girl raised her hand saying how I was not suitable to be in the Komsomol because I was absent from Komsomol events, referring to the movie. Only one of the guys stood up in my defense, saying that this accusation was ludicrous. I did not say a word, just sat in disbelief, watching the preposterous outplay of the meeting. I felt my blood rushing through my veins and my cheeks burning with frustration while the event played out to look as a big crime. I was stupefied and frozen, not feeling anything.

Soon it was over, with a decision to be made shortly thereafter about my Komsomol membership. I was distraught, feeling as if I had a lump in my throat, not completely aware of what happened. When I returned home, Mom knew something was wrong just by looking at me. She was not surprised to hear my story but was upset seeing me suffer. Ever since then, I hated to see Mom worried about stupid things, so I told her that I would be okay and went to do my homework. However, that night, I did not sleep at all. Lying in bed, I ran through my head a scenario of how I should have acted and what I should have said rather than sitting and taking it all. The next couple of days were very awkward as I did not feel like talking to anybody. The grim reality was that if somebody with a privileged status did not like you, they could put together the craziest of accusations against you, leading to grave consequences.

On the third day after this unfortunate event, Mom met me in front of the school and whispered, "Nina, I talked to the principal. You will be switched to class D. Let's go in together so I can introduce you to your new classroom teacher." I was introduced to my new classmates and assigned a seat in the back next to a tall, short-haired girl. She smiled at me and made me feel welcomed and relieved. Mom saved me because by transferring to another class, I was no longer in danger of being expelled from the Komsomol and from the school. During recess, I met the rest of the class and discovered that these people were very different from the ones in class A. For starters, they were not uptight and tense, but they also cared about their grades just as I did. I appreciated that nobody asked me anything. I was sure that they had heard about my story, but they did not seem to be people who cared about gossip.

The next few years were tough. The program was difficult with all subjects in English, except math, where testing was oral and written on all learned material from day 1. By our junior year, the class size shrunk from thirty-five to fifteen students, which meant more frequent oral testing. Math problems required knowledge from freshman year, and solving them used to take hours. At the end of the senior year, there was testing in core subjects, math being one of them, on all years of high school material, except for students with grades above B in all subjects. There were a lot of sleepless nights and early morning studying to keep my grades up. But it was also fun as my classmates had a motto of working hard and playing hard. Every Saturday, we all got together and danced to English and American music. We shared and exchanged records and tapes and talked about life in the West, and us girls talked about boys. The five boys in the class were very popular and busy dancing with the ten girls, not missing one dance. Toward the end of the senior year, there were graduation parties, and students from my old class invited me also to a few of theirs, where I was happy to see the guy who defended me at the crazy Komsomol meeting.

I knew my grade point average was above 3.5 (I had a couple of Bs), which meant that I would be exempt from the much-feared secondary school exit exams called *matura* in Bulgaria. Senior prom in Bulgaria at that time was not just for couples. All students went to it whether alone or with a girlfriend or boyfriend. I was alone and went with my deskmate and her date. Mom had my dress of sparkling golden color custom-made. I wore heels, which made my feet swell, but I didn't care. After the speech of the principal at the restaurant and a delicious three-course meal, we all danced till dawn. It was a true and well-deserved celebration of successfully graduating from one of the elite and most difficult high schools in Bulgaria at the time.

Our senior trip was to Macedonia, which for me was a very joyous occasion visiting relatives. I went and stayed with my uncle's relatives in Skopje and my cousin in Ohrid. I picked up on Macedonian language very quickly as it was close to the dialect spoken in my grandma's village in Bulgaria, and everybody was thrilled to hear me speak Macedonian with such ease. I felt a great pleasure and quite at home communicating with relatives in their language. My cousin's mother in Ohrid had passed away, but her father took us to the market and bought me shiny burgundy-and-white-colored high-heels, which were a precious gift for an eighteen-year-old girl from Bulgaria (stores in Bulgaria had dull-colored and limited styles of clothing and shoes). Yugoslavia was open to the world, with a variety of goods, music, art, movies, and food. People seemed to be relaxed and cheerful in comparison to the worried and tired faces on the streets in Bulgaria—worried and tired because of the daily grim reality of food shortages, low pay across the board from workers to doctors, and future uncertainty. Farmers lost their land and cattle; people's apartments were confiscated in the city.

Back home after the graduation ceremony, the family went on vacation at the Black Sea as usual. Even in the poorest of times, we used to go to the seaside, renting a cheap room and cooking meals like eggs and tomatoes at the house we stayed. This was, and still is I would say, a Bulgarian custom to find a way each summer to spend time at the coast. My aunt had acquaintances through her work as a controller for the railroad whom we visited quite often in Varna and Burgas, major Black Sea ports. Our vacations changed with my stepfather. One summer, we stayed at a tent in a state-owned camp when he came, and on the second day, he told us to pack, that we were going to stay at a hotel. My stepfather was the kindest and sweetest man on earth. He used to throw me from his shoulders in the water, which I enjoyed tremendously. We ate delicious dishes in restaurants, like julienne steak with mushrooms and cheesy sauce (before my stepfather, we had soups or watery stews with a few bites of meat on the bottom of the pot for the whole family). This summer was as enjoyable as the others—sunbathing, swimming, and playing cards on the beach with young people of my age. What made this vacation special was meeting a family from Liverpool. They were Mom's age, had no children, and had an advertising business in Liverpool. They also talked about life in England, where people could have their own business, live in a nice house, have cars—the lady's car was a Jaguar. Then she showed us pictures of their house with their guard dog, a beautiful white German shepherd.

When we returned to Sofia, Mom told me that the two of us were going on a special trip. She bought food like smoked kielbasa, cheeses, and canned vegetables to last us a month. We traveled by train to the main capitals of countries in Eastern Europe—Bucharest, Budapest, Prague, Warsaw, and Belgrade. I was impressed by the cultural monuments, the architecture, the varied history of the different countries. As a teenager, I remember that the stores were about the same everywhere; the food was somewhat different with sausages, dumplings with sour cream, and the way sauerkraut was prepared. What stood out in my mind was our stay in a bungalow on a hill in Budapest, where the manager of the place, a stout lady, spoke with animosity and a raised fist about how the Russian tanks killed people in the streets of Budapest in 1956, how the Hungarians hate the Russians, and how they would never back down from fighting against them. I remembered vaguely, those days in Hungary, how I overheard the adults at home talking about a possible similar uprising in Bulgaria. They were concerned because nonmembers of the Communist Party were identified with small black crosses drawn near their doorbells, and there was one at our door. This meant that if there was an uprising against the government, the police would arrest all people with marked homes as non-Communists and against the regime. Luckily, nothing happened. Mom washed with soap the drawing, and life went on as usual, people going to work and children to school.

Our last stop was Belgrade, and here I understood that the purpose of our visit was for Mom to enroll me at the University of Belgrade. By now, I was used to discovering things in the last minute as talking things out might reach the wrong ears and get you in trouble. We stayed with a family in New Belgrade, friends of my aunt's husband. They treated us as old friends and made us feel at home. It was a true Balkan hospitality, offering us meals and warm reception during our stay. Mom did not waste any time. She took me to the economics faculty, and I was admitted to start classes in the fall. This was all done after visiting the Bulgarian embassy and finding out that this semester about one hundred students from Bulgaria of Yugoslavian descent would be attending Belgrade universities. My father's side of the family was from Macedonia, and Mom and Dad lived in Skopje after the war for a few years. All my father's relatives were Macedonian as our ancestors moved from Shtip to Skopje. But Mom was Bulgarian, and Bulgarians were not looked upon favorably in Tito's Macedonia after the Second World War. My parents' best friends, who were Bulgarian and doctors in Skopje, were arrested one night and disappeared, which prompted my parents, my father's siblings, and my grandparents to move to Bulgaria. Based on my father's background, the Bulgarian consulate in Belgrade issued me a passport for students, valid only for Yugoslavia. I was a legal student in Yugoslavia, free to travel home and back as I wished.

Mom was extremely happy to arrange for me to study at Belgrade's Faculty of Economics. I became very good at math in high school, and Mom granted me my wish to study international economics. We returned to Sofia, and Mom organized a big farewell party with the family. I loved seeing my cousins, my uncles, and my aunts before leaving for Belgrade. Mom and Grandma prepared my luggage, a suitcase with a couple of dresses, a skirt, a couple of blouses, sweaters, and a pair of shoes. Grandma filled a travel bag with food, like *banitsa* (strudel with cheese), *kurabiiki* (cookies), yellow cheese, smoked meat, and apples.

Student Life in Belgrade

It was August 1968 when Mom and I arrived in Belgrade, two months before classes started on October 1. We took the train so we had a long time to talk about life and school. Mom shared her story as a student at the University of Sofia, which she attended during the Second World War and graduated after it ended. She studied political science, which, in the old regime, was a degree leading to a diplomatic career. Mom was the pride of the family being one of the first children to graduate from the university.

Her parents were from rural Bulgaria, coming from a region west of the capital, close to the Serbian border. Both families on my grandmother's and grandfather's side owned considerable acreages of land in the vicinity of the Kovachevtsi village, which was confiscated when Communists formed cooperatives in the villages. Education at that time was not important in rural Bulgaria, where people worked in the fields and took care of farm animals.

My great-grandfather on my grandfather's side was more progressive and sold most of his land with the idea of bringing the family to the city and providing better opportunities for his grandchildren. He bought a restaurant, and the family settled in one of the poorer sections in Sofia known as Konyovitsa. There was an unfortunate accident. My great-grandfather cut himself with a knife in the restaurant and, without a tetanus shot, died from infection. The family suffered a lot, especially after my great-grandmother, not being able to survive the loss of her husband, passed away shortly thereafter. My grandfather was devastated with grief, and my grandmother was forced to work hard labor with carrying in buckets of coal delivered on the sidewalks to people's basements. That's right, you heard it correctly. In those times, people had stoves that were heated with coal delivered in front of houses and apartment buildings. Basements were not like the basements in the States; they were cold storage units with dirt floors and brick walls. My grandmother was carrying buckets of that coal to the basement units of people who hired her. My mother's sister took bookkeeping classes and, at the age of sixteen, became a controller at a manufacturing plant, supporting the family and sending my mother and my uncle to attend the university.

After graduation, Mom became a high school history and geography teacher, as having studied in the former regime, it was unthinkable for her to pursue a career in diplomacy. On a positive note, she was glad because all her classes were accepted in the new regime, and she could graduate on time. She sighed and added, "You will have an opportunity to become what I couldn't. Studying economics in Belgrade will open a lot of doors for you."

Arriving at the railroad station in Belgrade, we took a bus to the dormitory, and Mom introduced me to the female student in charge of the building. The girl was of medium height with short black hair and round face. She was very friendly explaining the rules and showing us the rooms. It was an all girls' dormitory, no guys allowed to even visit. There were three beds in my room, a kitchenette on the same floor that was available to all, and a bathroom in the hallway. Mom helped me unpack, and we went out for a walk.

We noticed that there was more than usual commotion in the streets. People seemed agitated, talking loud and gesticulating with their arms, some holding newspapers in their hands. We bought a newspaper at the nearest stand and could not believe what we read. There was an uprising in Czechoslovakia, and Russian tanks invaded the country, crushing people on the streets of Prague. Another headline read that Bulgarian troops fired at Russians by mistake (this was never reported in Bulgaria or anywhere else that I know of). Tito, the Yugoslavian president, issued a decree that all Czech citizens who were in Yugoslavia at the time could remain free of charge for as long as necessary. Mom stayed for a week until things calmed down, and I started my student life away from home.

The Serbian language is Slavic, but there are words which sound and are pronounced differently from Bulgarian language, and the grammar is similar to Russian with cases (*padeži*). Since I had nobody to talk to but the girl at the dormitory (there were no other students at the time), I started to pick up the language and, in a couple of weeks, I could speak it fluently. She was from Kikinda, Vojvodina, and invited me to accompany her and visit her family. We took a bus and arrived in a village close to the Hungarian border. I recognized that people in the street were talking Hungarian, but they all knew Serbian. There was a church in the center of the square, as in other Serbian villages. Here I was immersed in the common life of ordinary people who gladly opened their home and greeted me as one of their own. The homemade food was just delicious, like Hungarian goulash with chicken and freshly baked bread. We stayed for the weekend at this picturesque village, breathing in fresh country air and enjoying the beautiful landscape of rolling green hills and meadows, before heading back to Belgrade.

October 1 approached rapidly, and a day prior to the start of classes, I headed to the university to take a placement test in Serbian language. A secretary met me in front of the office, and I started to talk to her in Serbian. I could tell from her face, and she even said that she was surprised to hear me speak so fluently. Soon the professor arrived and invited me to his office.

"How long have you studied Serbian?" he asked.

"I haven't studied it. I picked it up while staying at a dormitory."

"Can you read and write?"

"Yes, sir, I can."

He picked a textbook in economics and asked me to read the first paragraph. After finishing, he looked at me with a smile and said, "You are exempt from studying the Serbian language as a foreign student. Your Serbian is perfect." As I was leaving, I overheard him asking his secretary to forward the paperwork to the admissions office so I could start regular classes on the next day.

My first day at the economics faculty was exciting. I bought all the textbooks at the bookstore located inside the university for the first year classes of statistics, math, political economy, law, geography of Yugoslavia, and English. Then I headed to admissions where I picked up my schedule (I had classes in the afternoon from 1:00

p.m. to 6:00 p.m. every day except Thursday, when I had *vezbi*—workshops in small groups for practicing material from the lectures). Classes were scheduled to start, and I headed to the first auditorium listed on my schedule. There were at least one hundred students already seated, and I found a place somewhere in the middle. Most of the students appeared to know one another, but they were equally friendly with newcomers like me. First year students were called *brut-sosh*, something like a rookie if translated in English. And so my life began, and I thrived each day to go to my classes and be in this friendly environment where people greeted one another with hugs and kisses on the cheeks.

During break, we all headed for the café on the first floor. The air was thick with cigarette smoke. I usually ordered Turkish coffee and sat at a coffee table with students of all levels. It was then when I picked up smoking, as everybody was passing out cigarettes like candies. I learned about evening entertainment for students at Klub Omladina (youth clubs) where they played American and English dance music till midnight. I headed there the day I heard about it and became a regular visitor every evening after classes. It was a great place to unwind and dance all night after having lectures all afternoon. We usually left in groups and stopped at a café to have a bite before going to the club.

I felt so happy with the way my college life started. The students at the university were extremely friendly, very laid-back, cheerful, and fun to be around. Soon I settled into a routine of studying at the dormitory in the morning, then having classes in the afternoon, and afterward, swinging by a coffee shop where most of my new friends stopped after classes, dropping off my books back at my room, and heading to the youth club. I loved to dance all evening long, returning home bathed in sweat and crashing in bed after a hot shower. I didn't understand much from the auditorium sessions as the rooms were big and not all professors spoke loud enough, but I loved Thursdays when we had exercises in math and other subjects. I could solve any problem without even knowing the terminology, and as soon as the professor posted a problem, I volunteered to solve it on the board in front of the other students. I was amazed at how much I knew from high school; the math teacher there, feared by all students, did us a big favor.

I didn't care much about political economics, which was in essence Communist ideology, so before the tests, I went to the university library and asked students of upper classes for help. I remember a college student of a higher class spending all morning tutoring me a day before my final test the first semester just on goodwill. I passed the exam with a grade equivalent to C, which I was okay with. These people never ceased to amaze me as they all studied together and did not mind helping one another. I didn't care much about statistics, but I loved math. I liked law, and the geography of Yugoslavia was okay, except for studying about manufacturing and the economy of different geographical regions.

Almost every Friday, I hopped on the train after classes and spent the weekend home in Bulgaria. Mom bought a return ticket for me every time before I left, which helped me not to feel too homesick. I passed the remaining first semester final exams okay, but the subject I exceeded in was math. I went home for Christmas. Sofia was decorated for New Year's Eve, not Christmas. There were no church services or Christmas celebrations, but as always, my family celebrated Christmas Eve and Christmas Day. It was a tradition that my grandma kept, and I was happy to see my family gathered at the table sharing typical Christmas Eve dishes of stuffed cabbage and grape leaves with rice and spices, pumpkin strudel, bean soup and dry red peppers stuffed with beans, and freshly baked round bread with a hidden coin inside (the bread was ripped in pieces, and the person ending with it was supposed to be lucky for the entire year). A special meal with pork meat was prepared on Christmas. After Christmas, Mom came to Belgrade to spend the New Year with me. It was just the two of us having dinner and listening to the bustling noise of the city. Winters in Belgrade were very cold, with gusty, high-speed winds called *koshava*, bringing tears to eyes and piercing the body with freezing sensation. Prior to leaving, Mom moved me to a room in an apartment close to the university, and life resumed as I knew it.

I felt free and happy in Belgrade, surrounded by people who were always cheerful and joyful. There was nothing fake or superficial in the students relationships, and it was a tremendous feeling to be a part of this student life full of positivism and energy. I made friends with a third year student who came by to pick me up on those cold winter evenings for a glass of warm wine (*kuvano vino*) after delivering newspapers. I also enjoyed the cultural life in Belgrade, as I saw ballet and live theater performances. And I loved the Serbian folk music with songs played in Skadarlija, a cobblestone street area full of restaurants and cafés. The stores were so appealing with the latest fashions of clothes and shoes. Belgrade at that time was referred to as little Paris.

Spring was around the corner as the air was getting filled with a smell of perfume from all the blossoming trees and flowers all over the city. TopČider Park was my favorite place for walks and sometimes picnics after classes as the days became longer. I would walk intoxicated by the park's beauty, with forests in the upper parts and a hill overlooking a valley with a river and a railway that passed through it. I spent weekends there studying, especially when annual final exams were nearing. I met with study groups for all subjects, and again, students from higher grades came to the rescue. This was a very serious time for all students as the results from the finals averaged with those from the winter semester were going to determine promotion to the next grade in the fall. Math was the only subject that I didn't have to crack a book open; I even forgot how the cover of the textbook looked like. We were given a week to prep for the final exam session, and I felt that I had to go home the weekend before that. I had to hear Mom's encouraging words and get everybody's blessings for the finals.

Last Crossing of the Bulgarian Border behind the Iron Curtain

I woke up Saturday morning as always to the usual humming and buzzing noise of the Belgrade streets, feeling uplifted by the May fresh spring air but also getting anxious, not knowing why. It was probably because of the approaching exams, I thought to myself. I sprang out of bed thinking that this bad feeling was only nerves and it would pass away. I was going home for the weekend. "Mom will charge me with energy and confidence for the upcoming hard days of studying to pass my exams with flying colors," I said to myself. I dressed, packed a small bag, and quickly left the dormitory to catch the train for Sofia. I grabbed my favorite student breakfast, a wurst sandwhich, at the street stand in front of the building and headed to the familiar public phone cabin.

"Mom, I am coming home for the weekend. I'll arrive Saturday evening."

I could feel my mother's happiness in her ringing voice. "That's great, Nina. Papa will wait for you at the station."

I hopped on the train feeling uplifted and at the same time relieved. I always had a ticket on me for all the quick last-minute travel home that I decided to make. Grabbing a seat at the window, I enjoyed the changing scenes of fresh green meadows and blossoming flowers to the mountainous and pretty scenery of the Sićevo Gorge, with a soaring cliff covered with grass and rolling hills at the distance, and river Nišava's rumbling noise to complete the scene of nature's awakening from a long winter.

Images sprang to mind of last Christmas's travel to Sofia. I remembered how a tall, dark-haired, well-built, and good-looking guy with a very pleasant smile opened the door of my compartment before we left the Belgrade station.

"Zdravo, jel slobodno?" (Hi, girl, may I sit with you?)

"Be my guest," I answered.

He was a student going home to Niš for the holidays, and he invited me to spend a day with him in Niš on my way to Sofia.

"Why not?" I answered, and we happily headed down the small cobblestone Niš streets, covered with snow. My new friend gave me a sightseeing tour before heading for his house. I noticed that Niš was a typical provincial Eastern European town with squares and pedestrian walks, but it also had its memorable landmarks—a fortress, a cathedral, a nice park, a monument of the liberators, a skull tower commemorating the almost thousand Serbs decapitated by Ottoman troops in their fight for freedom, and the Red Cross Nazi concentration camp. I skipped visiting the last two as the sights were atrocious, making my stomach turn. It was a gloomy, cold winter day, and we cut our sightseeing short. Serbian hospitality was well-known, but what I remembered were this young man's piercing dark eyes and his goodbye hug.

"I want to see you in Belgrade. Where can I find you?" I rapidly jotted down my address and ran toward the platform to catch the train for Sofia.

The loud noise from the opening of my compartment door made me jump. Wrapped in my memories from last Christmas break, I did not notice that we were already at the border.

"Vous etes francaise?" It was a customs official.

"No, I am Bulgarian. I study in Belgrade, and I am going home for the weekend before finals," I responded in Bulgarian.

"Bulgarian? Do you know that you are not dressed properly?"

I froze. I knew what his words meant. In Bulgaria, girls or women in tight short dresses and skirts and tops with cleavage were arrested and shipped to labor camps. But I was dressed in long baggy black pants and a lightweight green sweater, nothing promiscuous that might get me in trouble.

"Get your things. You are coming with me."

I burst out in tears. Everything was twirling in front of my eyes as I was getting my bag with shaky hands.

"Don't cry. I'll come with you." I turned around and saw a slim, dark-haired young guy. "I am also a student, and I am going home." I was in a daze, and I couldn't catch his name and where he was from; it sounded Arabic.

We got off the train and headed to the waiting room of a small administrative building. The place was empty. The customs official was the only one at the border.

"You two wait inside," he grumbled.

We sat on a bench in anticipation of something bad to happen. I broke into a cold sweat, shivering next to my new friend.

"Don't worry. It will be okay." His calm voice and kind eyes gave me assurance and hope.

We spent all night on that bench—a night that seemed longer than any other night. At 5:00 a.m., the customs official walked in the waiting room. I froze and grabbed the guy next to me by the hand.

"There is a freight train for Sofia in a few minutes. I want you both on that train. Don't miss it, you hear me."

We both sprang to our feet and ran out, sighing in relief at the sight of the freight train. We arrived in Sofia early in the morning, totally exhausted. The wait at the border where anything could have happened, the worst being our disappearance, worn us out. The city was still sleeping with hardly any sign of life. There were no taxis, so we started walking hurriedly toward my home.

In about an hour, I rang the bell of our apartment. Mom opened the door; her face showed surprise and fear seeing me at that time of the day and not alone. Her eyes squinted, and she asked in a trembling voice, "What happened? Your papa went to meet you last night at the station."

Listening to my story, she held her face then shook her head, and her lips quivered. My new friend-savior and I felt alive after cleaning up and having breakfast.

"I need your help," he said. "I do not have a transit visa to stop in Bulgaria."

"We need to go first to your embassy and then to the police to get you a visa." Mom smiled at him, and we all headed out to arrange for the young man's visa and train ticket to continue his travel.

The weekend at home was usually lively and eventful, with aunts, uncles, and cousins visiting and my grandmother cooking the most delicious meals, like *guvech* (she knew I loved it), *pitka* (home-baked rolls), *banitsa* (Bulgarian cheese pie), and mouthwatering cookies. The family, as always, gathered for a dinner meal, with everybody chatting and laughing and my aunt and her husband singing old Bulgarian and Macedonian songs.

On Monday morning, Mom and I headed to the local police station to pick up my passport (every time I arrived home, I had to turn in my passport). The clerk at the station looked at us with a grim look on his face and hissed, "Can't give you the passport. You cannot leave the country." I felt like fainting, hearing Mom's distant voice. She was pleading to see the chief of police. To my surprise, he saw us, and Mom threw herself on her knees, crying and begging for his assistance to let me return to Belgrade and take my final exams. Tears went down my cheeks seeing my mother's desperation. I hated this guy who watched Mom humiliate herself.

"There is an order for the Bulgarian students to return home. They will be allowed to transfer their credits and continue their studies in Bulgaria." The man was speaking in an even and stern voice. We left his office, and Mom sent me home saying that she would see me later; she needed to locate some people, she said. I was in a daze, first the incident at the border and now being held back from going back to school. Mom returned home in the evening, her face swollen from crying, her eyes red, but she looked calm.

"I found a woman I knew from the Ministry of Education," she said. "This woman, through connections, found out the reason for bringing Nina back to Bulgaria and not allowing her to study in Yugoslavia," Mom continued in a calm voice. "It was written in her dossier at the police station that Antonina was at the Bulgarian embassy New Year's Eve behaving inappropriately."

I was with Mom on New Year's Eve, but nobody bothered to verify that there were two Antoninas and that the questionable Antonina was another person.

"Nina," Mom said, "this woman guaranteed personally that you will return after taking your finals, so for now, you can leave tomorrow. And you know what might happen to her if you don't return."

On the day of my travel, the whole family came to say goodbye and wish me luck for the finals. I was in a hurry to leave when I heard my grandma calling me. I turned around and saw her struggling to catch up with me. My god, I did not say goodbye to Grandma. I turned back and reached out to hug and kiss her. She knew before I did I was not coming back and that it would be the last time she could see me.

Life-Changing Decision—
Choosing Freedom

Back in Belgrade, I rushed to the university and went straight to the office of my math professor. I knew I had missed the final exam. My professor was a sweet elderly woman, I guess in her fifties, average height, silver hair, and glasses on her nose.

"What happened?" she asked. "You are one of my best students, and I couldn't understand why you missed the exam. You did not even call."

"They did not let me come back," I responded. "I went home to Sofia for the weekend, and the police held my passport. My mother had to pull strings for me to return for my finals."

"Stupid Communists," she murmured under her breath. Then she looked at me and firmly said, "Don't worry. I already gave you a 10 [the highest grade]. Have a nice summer."

I stood motionless, not believing my ears.

"Go on. You need to study for other tests," I heard the woman speak again. I thanked her and lowered my head. Leaving her office, I said *dovidenya* (bye) in a low voice. She winked and waved at me. I tried to understand what happened—Bulgaria and Yugoslavia. How could people from two neighboring countries be so different?

The next week, I had my nose in the books. Studying isolated me from the outside world, and the painful experience from the weekend started to fade away. This was it; after the last exam, I would go back to the dormitory in the student housing village. Most students had gone home after the finals. The buildings were empty and quiet. The usual laughter, music, and jokes could not be heard.

Emptiness and solitude overwhelmed me. I grabbed my purse and headed for the public phones.

"Mom, I need to see you. Please come on the next train," I whispered in the receiver.

"Of course. I will be there tomorrow." Mom's voice was dull.

"Thank you, Mommy. I will wait for you at the station." It sounded like she wasn't surprised to hear from me.

I hung up and started walking aimlessly. People were racing around me to get home. It was the familiar hustle and bustle at the end of the day. This night was one of the longest in my life. Tossing and turning, not blinking a wink till dawn, I thought of how different this time could be with Mom.

It was finally morning; the city was waking up with the few sounds of cars, trucks, and buses in the streets. The air was fresh, pleasantly caressing my face as I stood on the terrace of my room gazing, examining every detail of the place. This was my home for the last year, a students' town with its dormitories and libraries. There was the cinema, where I often went to see American and other Western movies; the theaters, where I saw the ballet *Swan Lake*; and the restaurant, where I made so many friends. Thoughts were rushing through my head in chaos. I was seeing familiar faces and hearing voices asking me to join them or to go out on a cold winter night for a glass of warm wine. I shook my head to chase all thoughts away, walked back in the room, dressed fast, and hurried to the bus stop.

I was at the railway station early, but that was all right. I could just sit and watch the people—the people who became so dear to me in the last year. Finally, the train pulled into the station, and I made my way to the platform to meet Mom. I greeted her and noticed how worn out her face looked, the sleepless nights and tension having taken their toll on her.

We reached the students' town not talking, and finally during lunch, I said, "Mom, I am not going back. I cannot go back home."

She did not utter a word as tears rolled down her face. Then she said in a soft voice, "Please come home. We will protect you. Papa [my stepdad] will support us. You won't have to work. We even saved money to buy you a car [Lada]."

I stood numb across from her. The scene was devastating. "Mom, you know I can't come back," I whispered, feeling an extreme pain tearing at my stomach.

Mom stayed with me for three days, our last three days together, as I knew I would not see her again.

Escape to Freedom

It was mid-June 1969 when I packed the few pieces of clothing I had in a carry-on suitcase and headed to the railway station. Mom left me enough money for a ticket to Vienna and a pocket money of one hundred dollars. *Am I going to make it?* I spotted a student I knew on the platform by my train. He was a tall, slim guy with dark hair, sculpted face, and playful eyes.

"Leaving on vacation?" I was afraid to respond honestly, so I shrugged my shoulders. "I am going to transfer to the University of Vienna," he continued.

Great, I thought to myself, *at least I will not travel alone.*

The train was packed with Serbians returning to Vienna for work. All seats were taken, and the corridors were crowded with people standing and leaning on their luggage. I managed to get my suitcase on the luggage rack in one of the compartments, remaining standing. More people got on the train at the next major stop in Zagreb. By that time, the train was packed, and it was impossible to walk with people leaning on one another in the hallway. An elderly couple next to me smiled, and soon we started to speak. Their work in Vienna was hard but worth it because they could save and return to Zagreb one day. They had two daughters, also working in Vienna. One was my age.

"You can stay with my oldest daughter and help her at the apartment building. She is the porter, responsible for locking the place at night and dealing with visitors. She also cleans the stairway once a week." I hugged the woman with tears of joy running down my cheeks. I had no idea where I was going in Vienna. My mother gave me her last one hundred dollars, which I knew would not last long. I felt as if these people were sent from heaven to help me.

"*Pasosi molim.* [Passports please.] And open to a page where I can stamp your visa," a Yugoslavian border patrol yelled out at the border with Austria. He hardly managed to squeeze in the crowd of people holding a stamp in his hand. I gave him my passport, opened to a visa page, feeling butterflies in my stomach, as I knew that if he looked through the pages, he would notice that it was valid only for Yugoslavia. Bulgaria and Yugoslavia had an agreement for Yugoslavia's border patrol to return to Bulgaria any Bulgarian without proper documents. And the punishment was known—imprisonment and/or camp. The man rapidly stamped all passports, including mine, at which I took a big sigh of relief. I was free, no more fear of the unknown, no more humiliation, no more threats or fear of jail and camps. I stood by the open window, breathing deeply the fresh summer air, exhilarated and relieved knowing that I was entering the Free World.

Life in Mozart's Country

How wonderful it was to be able to breathe freely in one of the most beautiful cities in the world, the city where Mozart lived and created ageless music. I was not paying for room and board in exchange for helping the Croatian girl with washing the staircase of a five-story building once a week. I also relieved her of porter duties at night. This schedule allowed me to pick odd jobs during the day. Being a seamstress in a factory, working on the line at a phone manufacturing facility, painting small ceramic gift objects, being a waitress and a dishwasher. But the weekends were magic as I would run out early in the morning to discover the city. I took the public transportation to all the twenty-three districts, finding out that they spiral out of the city's center—the first district.

I often visited St. Stephen's Cathedral, where I could pray for hours and attend Mass without worrying about being seen, reported, and arrested. I inquired of my hostess a list of all remarkable sights and dedicated my free time exploring them. I found myself staring in amazement at the beauty of Schönbrunn Palace. My heart stopped at the sight of the amusement park Prater with Vienna's Ferris wheel. I haven't seen anything like it before. I took in everything with great enthusiasm and joy, charmed with Vienna's impressive architecture of the opera house, Vienna City Hall, and the Austrian Parliament Building.

We lived on Mariahilfer Strasse, famous for shopping, which was an exceptional treat for me, providing me the opportunity to window-shop the most fashionable clothing and shoes or stare at the mouthwatering pastries, which I could not afford. The market in the back of the street was exceptional with fresh produce, meat, and Vienna sausages. As a nature lover, I soon discovered where to escape the summer heat—the Donaukanal by the river and Wienerwald (Vienna Woods), special places where I loved to roam. Weekends were special as I went with my new Yugoslavian friends to the market, planning the meals for the week. Once, I spotted a truck with grapes from Bulgaria.

"Hey, mister, I am Bulgarian. How much are your grapes?"

The man smiled. "Here," he said, "pick as much as you want. No charge. And what are you doing here?" He guessed right. I was alone. Then he shook his head and said, "You be careful. All cities are dangerous."

Weekend dinners were like holiday celebrations as the few Yugoslavian families in the area gathered to share traditional Balkan dishes, mostly *ražnjići* (skewers), *snicle* (breaded meat), *burek* (strudel dough with cheese), *juha* (soups with pasta), *hladetina* (head cheese), and bean soups. Yugoslavian music blasted, and people sang and danced traditional folk dances in a circle. It was a perfect world where everybody worked hard but was free to enjoy life to the fullest. I admired the Yugoslavian community for their unity, genuine cheerfulness, and the simplicity of their relationships. They welcomed me with open arms as an old friend, with no questions asked and no expectations, an experience that will stay with me forever.

There was one detail hanging like a cloud over the ecstatic feeling of my freedom. My passport was valid only for Yugoslavia and was expiring at the end of 1969. Every new resident at any location in Austria had to submit their passport to the police for registration. I thought of a very crazy idea. Why not run the passport through the washing machine hoping that the writing would be destroyed and I could ask for a new passport at the Bulgarian embassy? Being a very naive young girl, I followed through with my plan and appeared on the steps of the Bulgarian embassy requesting a meeting with the ambassador. The porter disappeared for some time and, upon returning, took me to the ambassador's office. A man in his forties, medium height, with pleasant-looking face, smiled and offered me a seat. I introduced myself as a student who intended to continue with my studies at the University of Vienna. Then I proceeded with my incredibly foolish story and handed him my passport.

The man glanced at it and said, "I understand your dilemma, and I will help you by issuing you a new passport valid only for Austria for six months." He also gave me the fee 1000 shilling for issuance of an international passport valid for one year. So I was safe for six months as I knew I could never earn and safe 1000 shilling. While I was in Vienna, Mom smuggled 500 shilling once through a man from a Yugoslavian company, but that was only one time. There was no banking for Bulgarians (with exception of the privileged ones) in the Western world. But the crazy thing was that stepping in the Bulgarian embassy, even in Vienna, I was in danger of being detained. I was too young at the time to know those international rules. Luckily, they let me go. The ambassador seemed a very nice man who shook my hand as I was leaving, and in a few days, I was granted a new passport valid for six months.

Six months were flying rapidly. I had my heart set on continuing with my studies at the University of Vienna, and I signed up to study German. A requirement for all foreigners was to pass a proficiency test in German before getting into the program of their choice. One November afternoon after class, I spotted an ad for a room rental at a very reduced price, available to a female student in exchange for helping a young mother with two small children. I grasped it as an opportunity to live with an Austrian family and practice German. The apartment was close to the center of the city. I gathered my courage and rang the bell. A very pleasant, attractive young woman in her late twenties opened the door. "Please come in. Let me show you the room and introduce you to the family, my husband, and the kids." They offered me to move in right away, which made me extremely happy. My face lit up as I shook their hands and agreed to be with them first thing in the morning.

"Wir sprechen kein Englisch," the man said, at which I smiled. I needed to practice German, but I also knew of the challenge I faced with communication without explanations in English. He was about the same age as his wife, of medium height, slim, with a boyish face. The children, a boy and a girl, four and three years old, were adorable—both fair-skinned, with sparkling blue eyes. The girl had golden curls, and the boy's hair was cut short. They smiled and greeted me then ran off giggling.

At the beginning, I talked to them with the help of a dictionary, and they tried to help by teaching me basic words around the house. In a few weeks, I could carry on a regular conversation in German, becoming a part of this wonderful Austrian family. I continued to work odd jobs and study German during the day, but my evenings were at the house helping with dinner and the children. Gathered at the big dining room table, we talked, while the children played nearby, always happy and laughing. Weekends were extra special as they took me along on family trips to the Alps and nearby Austrian towns. Sitting in the back of their station wagon, I was absorbing every detail of the scenery, entranced by the beauty of the majestic mountain slopes and peaks blanketed with snow. The serenity and austerity of the mountain ranges were captivating.

One of these trips was to the city of Graz, a jewel town with stunning architecture. I remember distinctly Hauptplatz and the town hall, a place reminiscent of the Middle Ages, with its narrow alleys, and the stunning stucco facade of the Luegg buildings from the seventeenth century. The monument fountain dominated the square, with figures of four women symbolizing the four rivers— Mur, Drava, Enns and San.

"Lunchtime," Greta said, and we headed to a biergarten for Wiener schnitzel and the famous Austrian beer.

It felt so good to be a part of a family; I eagerly embraced my new life, waking up every day excited to follow my daily routine. I was so happy to be included and to participate in all family activities, especially at Christmastime, picking up a Christmas tree and decorating the house for the holidays. Christmas with the Austrian family will always remain in my mind. What I remember most was the present I helped pick for the kids—an electric train. The children's faces lit up at its sight. They clapped their hands and ran toward it; you could hear the train whistle and their squealing and laughter for the rest of the day.

"Come play with us. It's fun!" they both shouted. I did not need more invitation. Getting caught up in the children's excitement, I did not waste any time and joined them.

There were a few evenings when I snuck out of the house to see the city lights during the holiday season. Stepping out in the street, I felt like a kid. I strolled through the Christmas bazaars with the stands of amazingly beautiful Christmas decorations and inhaled the smell of roasted chestnuts on every corner. These moments of carefree and delightful experiences were short-lived.

A few days after New Year's, Greta said she wanted to discuss something serious with me.

"Nina, dear, your passport expires in a couple of weeks. You need to have it extended, or there will be a problem for you and for us." I bowed my head and nodded in understanding. Then I looked at her, and my heart sank. I would have to leave them very soon, but I could not share the truth.

I returned to my room with tears in my eyes. I knew that I was losing this sweet family. I knew I had to turn myself in to the police to be transported to an immigrants' camp outside Vienna called Traiskirchen. This thought made me shiver, but it had to be done. At the same time, I ran out of money. After a couple of days on a water diet, I thought to myself, *What should I do?* I put on my coat and walked out in the cold winter evening. There were lights at the neighborhood pub. I approached it and opened the door, feeling very uneasy. A couple of middle-aged women were behind the counter. With my head down, I went straight to them, and I sat on a barstool.

"I am a student, and I need a job. I live nearby," I said timidly.

"We do not have anything here to offer, but we can use you at the other location in first *bezirk*. If you want to start tomorrow at nine a.m., here is the address."

It was January 1970, the beginning of a new year and a life full of uncertainties. I started work the next day in a café, serving light lunches, coffee, and other drinks behind the counter. This was the first time I had food in a while, and the bean soup tasted extremely delicious. In about a week, I had enough money for a cheap hotel. It was a gloomy, cold evening when I packed in a hurry. Greta was working nights, and her husband had gone to bed. I silently went to the living room and left a note on the dining room table, then I looked in the children's room. Both little angels were sound asleep.

I whispered goodbye, closed their door, picked up my suitcase, and left the apartment.

The freezing wind penetrated my body. I felt numb as I walked to the tram stop for Mariahilfer Strasse. I knew of an underground hotel that I could afford. This must have been a building used during the war because it was built all underground. The small room was clean, but the bathroom was in the hallway. Anxiety and exhaustion caught up with me as I immediately fell asleep. On the next morning, I woke up early and headed for the university, hoping to see some students from my German class. I walked in the café, ordered coffee, and sat at a corner table observing the crowd. It was a lively place. Students, cheerful after the holidays, were sharing stories of travel and events while away from school. Then two girls walked in with large backpacks speaking English. I was curious, so I approached them.

"Hi, my name is Nina, and I study German here. I heard you speaking English, and I will be so happy if you could spare some time talking to me."

Anna and Mary were from Ann Arbor, Michigan, traveling to Czechoslovakia in search of their family roots. They were both in their early twenties, graduates of the University of Michigan, and working on the Ann Arbor university campus. Their Midwestern American accent was very pleasant, as I thought that the English speak with an effort, their high-pitched voices with tones rising and falling to say simple things. By noon, we knew everything about one another.

My story affected Anna deeply, as she grabbed my hands and looked me in the eyes. "I will sponsor you to come to the States. You tell them that at the camp. Here is my address and phone number."

I was dumbfounded and could not utter a word. My face felt stiff, and my lips were trembling as I managed to only whisper, "Thank you."

The next day, I turned myself in to the closest police station. By now, my German was pretty good, and I could explain my situation quite accurately. The policemen handling my case were stern, and their faces showed no emotion. After completing the paperwork, they took me to the back of a police car. I felt nauseated and sick, doubled up in the seat, thinking in horror and despair what would happen next.

The drive felt extremely long, although it wasn't longer than an hour. There were high walls surrounding the grounds of the camp. A policeman at a booth at the entrance opened the barrier.

Immigrant at the Refugee Camp in Traiskirchen

Traiskirchen, a beautiful village in Baden District, is located twenty miles south of Vienna. Its rolling hills with vineyards, charming houses, and churches tugged between the hills created a captivating scenery, providing a feeling of serenity, peace, and hope. In January, the village was covered with a white blanket, and a smell of burning wood from the fireplaces lingered in the air. But I knew that in spring, nature would come alive with blossoming flowers and miles of Baden's beautiful green vineyards.

The camp was near a train station in the back of a small park. Upon arrival, the policeman escorted me to the police station at the camp. I had to tell my story from the time I grew up in Bulgaria to the moment I escaped. At the end, one of the policemen in the room explained, "This camp is transitionary. You can choose to immigrate to Australia, South Africa, Canada, or the United States. You will be interviewed at the embassy of the country you select, and upon acceptance, you will be able to leave as soon as the paperwork is completed, usually in a month's time. Which country would you like to immigrate to?"

I would have loved to go to Liverpool, to the English family from Liverpool, but England was not on the list of countries for immigration. I didn't hesitate in answering. "The United States. I have a sponsor. Here is her contact information." And I handed him the piece of paper Anna gave me.

The policeman who was questioning me took the paper and said that all this would be verified and that I was free to move into my new living quarters, a building for single women. Then he gave me a brief tour of the facility. The campgrounds resembled a students' town without a library, surrounded by tall walls. There were buildings for single women, single men, and married couples; a small clinic with inpatient facility; and a police station. The cafeteria was on the first floor in the single men's building. Meals were served three times a day and were quite decent, like meals in any other cafeteria. The week's menu, posted on a bulletin board, sounded good: *Wiener Frühstück*— rolls, jam, butter, coffee, goulash, bean soup, and *tafelspitz* (boiled meat with vegetables). Sausages were lunch and dinner dishes.

"The bedrooms in the single women building are on the second floor," explained the policeman. "Each room is occupied by girls and women from the same region. You will be in a room with three women from Bulgaria and a girl from Yugoslavia. The bedroom next to yours is occupied by girls from Czechoslovakia." He wished me a good evening and disappeared into the courtyard.

I walked slowly to the room that he pointed out to me. My roommates were all in. I stood in the doorway, holding onto my small suitcase, hesitant to walk in, when they all jumped up to greet me.

"I am Nadka."

"Petya."

"Irina."

"Rosa."

They all embraced me and helped me get settled, not much to unpack (contents of my suitcase were long pants, a sweater, two blouses, a couple of summer dresses, undergarments, a couple pairs of socks, and shoes). We all had single beds with clean white sheets, a pillow, a blanket and long narrow armoires for our clothes. They took me to the hallway to show me the bathroom, which was shared by all girls on the floor.

In the next couple of hours, I heard all their heartbreaking stories, except for Rosa's, as she was on her way to Australia to marry a boy from her village. Rosa, in her early twenties, was tall, big-boned, with shoulder-length light-brown hair and rosy cheeks. Irina, a woman in her thirties, with short wavy hair, plump figure, of medium height, was on a tour in Austria by herself. Her husband and son were in

Bulgaria as the Bulgarians did not let whole families travel. I did not ask for all the details of how she managed to be included in a tourist group to Austria, but at the end of the tour, she chose not to go back. She missed her family and started to cry, pulling pictures from her purse. Nadka, a young girl in her twenties, of medium height, with short blond hair and athletic figure, was in the camp with her Bulgarian boyfriend, but since they were not married, they had to be in the single housing facilities. The two of them escaped through Yugoslavia, where they were visiting family. Petya, a young woman in her thirties, was a registered nurse in Bulgaria. She was short, slim, with short straight dark hair. Petya's story was shocking; she and her fiancé crossed a river between Bulgaria and Yugoslavia at a time when there was low tide. They both carried poison with them to kill themselves if caught at the border. It was my turn, and I shared my story. They were all silent, nodding from time to time, and when I finished, Petya said, "It's okay. We are all safe now."

It was getting close to dinnertime, so we headed to the cafeteria. Nadka introduced me to her boyfriend.

"We are about forty Bulgarians in one room," he said. "This camp was used by Russian troops toward the end of the Second World War, and our room is a typical soldier's bedroom with bunk beds," he added.

During dinner, a couple of Bulgarian guys in their twenties joined us. They escaped, crossing the border between Yugoslavia and Austria on foot. As they were about to cross, a Yugoslavian border patrol yelled at them, and they froze in their steps. "You boys have a lighter?" the official asked, at which the Bulgarians heaved a sigh of relief. They smoked a cigarette with the Yugoslavian patrol guy who took them for Macedonians hitchhiking to Austria. Macedonian and Bulgarian languages are similar and easy to confuse for outsiders.

Petar was married and had a wife and a child in Bulgaria whom he missed tremendously and was trying to figure a way to smuggle them out. Nasko was a student and was hoping to continue his studies in America. We all became friends, and the guys looked out for us, which made life in the camp comfortable. The first month's room and board were free. From the second month onward, there were minimal charges, which meant that we had to work. Business owners arrived at the camp every morning at a designated location offering jobs and hiring those who qualified for them.

My first employer was the owner of a small motel in Baden. He was looking for a dishwasher. I started work that same morning. The motel was a typical Austrian decorated building with attractive painting and design. My workspace was small, with a couple of bigger-sized dishwashers and a counter with a window where waiters placed dirty dishes. It was a busy morning, and I was puffing and huffing, loading and unloading the dishwashers without a break. I hoped that at one point the morning rush would slow down, but it didn't. I couldn't figure out why there were crowds of people eating all the time and why the place didn't close between breakfast and lunch. I gave in as sweat was pouring down my face. Walking up to the owner, I apologized and added, "I can't keep doing this type of work. Could you please compensate me for the time I worked?" The man smiled, opened his wallet, and handed me the sum we agreed upon when he hired me.

I took the train back to the camp, and my new friends met me at the station. "We all had a bet of how long you would last," said Nasko.

Shortly after that, a French filming cast arrived at the camp. They were filming a movie called *Immigrant* and were giving auditions for small roles. I managed to get a role as a girl asking for her mail at the post office, and for that one sentence, I was paid a salary equivalent to working two weeks at a shop. They liked my fur coat, for which I negotiated a good price, and with the money from acting and the coat sale, I paid for my living at the camp for a few months. Nonetheless, I continued to work odd jobs. A man hired me to clean, together with my roommates, their new house from all the debris and paint. I remember lying in bed that night aching all over, but the pay was good, and it was worth it.

The following morning, after breakfast, I checked the wanted ad announcements on the bulletin board and spotted that there was a visit in the camp by women interviewing young women for modelling. I thought that this was probably a similar experience as with the French moviemakers, so I called on my roommates to join me in trying it out. Two women in their early thirties, dressed simply, both pale, with medium-length dark hair, met us at the interview room. They both eyeballed us from head to toe, and one started to explain the program.

"The modeling is in Italy. This offer is only for single women. We will provide you with passports to leave Austria. The pay is very good. You do not need experience. Modeling is all about posing in front of a camera. You are young and will be able to manage without difficulties. You can leave tomorrow."

I was only nineteen, but I knew that there was something wrong with this picture. Obtaining a passport overnight was not possible unless it was fake, and modeling in a different country offered only to single young women without families sounded very shady. I nodded at the girls to follow me in the hallway, and leaving the room, I glanced at the women. Their sleek, probing eyes were following all our movements and reactions. Outside, I told the girls that this job offer was fishy without knowing at this age that this was probably a trap for white slavery. My roommates trusted me and followed my advice not to leave the camp.

It was a cold February morning when there was a knock on the door of our room. It was a policeman. "I am looking for Antonina."

"That's me." I hopped up.

"Here, take this. It's an invitation for an interview at the American embassy. All the details are in this letter." And he left.

I stood speechless, not being able to utter a word or move. I hardly believed my ears. Finally, it was going to happen. I would be traveling to my new home. I slowly came to myself and read carefully the letter. There was detailed information for the interview date.

I arrived an hour earlier at the American embassy. A very pleasant and elegant-looking woman of middle age showed me to the ambassador's office. A tall man in his forties, I gathered, was the ambassador, dressed in a suit and a tie, clean-cut and shaven. He greeted me from behind his desk and then pointed to a seat in front of him, and we started to talk. He was very polite, but his voice was stern.

"I know some things about you and your family," he said. "Your parents are divorced, and you were raised by your mother, a high school teacher, who was not a member of the Communist Party. You graduated from an elite high school." Then he looked intensely in my face and asked, "Can you explain how schoolchildren become members of Komsomol?"

"It was simple," I responded. "One day, a teacher in my school assigned to a class in seventh grade gathered us, marched us to the school auditorium, and we were sworn in as members of Komsomol. It was not a voluntary program, and none of the children thought of raising a question."

"And how did you get to attend the English language high school? This school was reserved for children of big Communists."

I became a little confused, but I answered honestly, "I was a straight A student with recommendations from the principal of the middle school and my teachers for academic excellence and impeccable behavior. I was not accepted right away. I was first on an add-on list in case they had more openings." And I continued explaining the enrollment process for entering into this school.

He let me talk about my life as a child in Bulgaria, my studies in Belgrade, and the final episode at the border, which was the decisive factor for my departure or, more precisely said, my escape to Austria. I felt at ease talking with the man. Words were pouring out of my mouth about the life in fear behind the Iron Curtain, from my observations as a child and later as a student. Toward the end, the man took out documents from a folder.

"You were raised by your mother, who was not a member of the Communist Party. What was your relationship with your father?"

"Sir, I was nine when I saw him last. He took me to a restaurant and tried to convince me to live with him and a woman whom he was seeing at the time. I refused, so he took me back home to my mother, and since that day, he disappeared from my life."

"That's sad. Sorry, but I had to ask. Now on another topic, the girl Anna D. from Ann Arbor, Michigan, signed the necessary paperwork to be your sponsor. You will be traveling to her hometown. It will take a few weeks to complete the paperwork. You will travel first to New York City, where you will spend a couple of days. A representative from Tolstoy Foundation will meet you and assist you with getting a Social Security card. Tolstoy Foundation sponsors and assists immigrants of Eastern Orthodox religion to settle in the United States. You will be traveling with a white document on which your status will be *stateless* for description of nationality. If you leave the United States in the first two years, you will not be able to return to America. Upon the expiration of two years, you will be provided a permanent residence, and after another five years of life in the States, you will be eligible to become a citizen."

I was listening very carefully to every single word the man said, without missing any details. My face was red with excitement and happiness. I could feel the rush of blood through my veins and how fast my heart was beating. "Thank you, sir. This is a tremendous honor" was all I managed to utter.

Leaving the office, I was like a bird flying into the world of freedom. Once out in the street, I felt like a different person—a person whose boat has finally found its port. And Anna was sponsoring me, which meant I would not be working at a factory for matches in New York City, a work arrangement from Tolstoy for newly arrived immigrants, per rumor in the camp. Back at the camp, my friends were waiting to hear news of my interview at the café at the railroad station. And the celebration continued into the night.

It was March, and I could feel the arrival of spring, the crisp air and smell of blooming spring flowers intoxicating and energizing the body. One day after dinner, I walked out in the yard and noticed a big commotion, a man with a child on his shoulders and a woman next to him, all red in her face, crying and laughing at the same time, were surrounded by a group of Bulgarian men, all shouting bravo and hooray. Nadka joined me staring at the crowd.

"I can't believe they made it."

I looked, puzzled. "What are you talking about?"

"Didn't you hear?" she said. "He made fake passports for the three of them, snuck in Bulgaria, and smuggled them out."

I trembled as I knew that they all would have been dead if caught crossing the border. The festivities went on for days, but I was more concerned about covering my living expenses. A Czech girl offered me to join her to work at a small manufacturing facility not far from camp. At the small factory, I met the owner's wife at the offices of the shop, a woman in her early forties, with round face, sharp chin, wavy mid-length brown hair, medium height, who directed me to a spacious room with a huge table. Four women were sitting and wiring coil on boards then looked up at me with curiosity. The job was easy but tedious. At the end of the first week, I bumped into the owner's wife in the hallway and had a chance to talk to her.

"*Guten morgen*, Frau Bertha."

"*Guten morgen*, Nina. Come in my office. It's still early." She offered me a chair and continued, "Do you like the work here?"

"The work is fine," I responded. "But I am a student and would have liked to sign up for classes at the university. I studied economics at the University of Belgrade."

"Is that so?" she asked in a surprised voice. "I need an accountant in the office to help me with daily transactions and weekly payroll. Would you be interested?" I must have smiled with the biggest smile as she shook my hand and said, "Well starting today you are working in the office. Let me show you your desk and explain your duties."

I was overjoyed. In the days that followed, I settled into a very pleasant routine. Frau Bertha treated me as a friend rather than just an employee. We had coffee every morning discussing the daily tasks. She even invited me to their weekend villa where her son of my age proudly displayed his remote-controlled flying plane. I started to believe that I was finally having a normal life with a job I loved, working for an extremely nice lady. Not only could I cover my expenses but I could also afford some of the dresses I had been gazing at while window-shopping in previous months.

March and April went by fast, and then it was May, my favorite spring month. I breathed deeply the fresh air scented with the aroma of blossoming flowers. One morning in May, I was in a hurry as usual to catch the train for work when the police guard at the gate told me to stop at the police building after work. By the tone of his voice, I knew it was something serious and important. That day went faster than usual. I was in a daze, doing my office work mechanically. At the end of the day, I flew out of the building and ran as fast as I could toward the train station.

The policeman at the camp asked me to sit down and started to speak in a very solemn voice, "We received the official letter from the American embassy about your visa application. You have been approved to immigrate to the United States and will be flying first to New York, where you will be met by a representative of the Tolstoy Foundation. You will be flying to Detroit, Michigan, the next day, where you will be met by your sponsor, Anna. Any questions?"

"When do I have to leave?" I asked timidly. I was waiting for this moment for such a long time, but now I didn't feel I was ready for the far, unknown life on the other side of the ocean.

"In the next five months, latest toward the end of September," he responded candidly.

I wanted to learn more about the Tolstoy Foundation, so I asked, "And what exactly is Tolstoy Foundation?"

"This organization was founded by Leo Tolstoy's youngest daughter, Alexandra Tolstoy, and provides financial and other needed support to immigrants of the Orthodox religion. You were baptized in an Eastern Orthodox Church and will be contacted here in the camp by a Tolstoy representative."

I thanked him for the wonderful news and information, grabbed the letter, and walked slowly toward my building. My inner voice was telling me, *Now that you can travel, you should not rush. You could wait until September.* My life since I left home has been an upheaval. I needed to catch my breath. I was only nineteen, and I was going to leave Europe forever. America is so far.

I decided that night to travel at the last possible moment. I wanted to live the life I created for myself a little longer, after a very trying and eventful year. I truly enjoyed working at company Peschl, and I could not have asked for a better boss than Frau Bertha. I enjoyed working with numbers, and I learned all about keeping the books, banking, and doing weekly payroll for a small business. Some of my friends at the camp started to leave, but I did not feel that I should be in a hurry for a new adventurous life, not yet.

On the next morning, I went straight to the police station and asked for the last possible plane that I could take to America. The policeman looked into the schedule, verified my documents, glanced at me, and said, "September 30 at one p.m. Do you want me to book the flight for you on that date?"

"Yes, please," I answered quietly.

"Very well, I will book this flight for you. With such late departure date, there will be no problem."

The flight was confirmed that same evening, and I felt a weight lifted off my shoulders. I shared my news with all my friends at the camp, and we spent the evening talking about what we would do when we arrive in the States. People who left were writing how wonderfully they live in their apartments and how they already own cars. Nadka laughed and said, "I will make sure I have a TV, a radio, and a stereo. And I will have music from all turned on at the same time."

I left for work early the next day and waited in the yard for the owner's car to arrive. I needed to inform Bertha of my decision and my departure date. I met her with a smile and started to talk without stopping on the way to the office.

"It's far away, Bertha. I am not leaving soon."

Bertha took my hand. "Nina, you could work here part-time and study at the university. We could arrange the paperwork for you."

I felt uncomfortable. This woman had been extremely nice to me, treating me as her own daughter. I looked her in the eyes and responded with a sigh, "You can't imagine how difficult this is. Leaving this place and leaving you is extremely hard. I am in love with Vienna, with Austria, but I need to do this. I have dreamed for so long of going to America."

She embraced me, gave me a blessing, and said, "I understand you are young, and America is a fascinating country. I wish you all the best."

On the Saturday before my departure, there was a knock on the door. It was later in the morning. I jumped out of bed and peeked outside. A thin elderly woman in her fifties, with long face and black hair turning silver, asked for me. She introduced herself as a representative from Tolstoy, looked at me, and said, "Well, get dressed. We are going out shopping." I could not believe my ears. Grabbing my things fast, I was ready in no time, and soon we were on our way to town. She took me to a beauty salon, saying that I could not travel to America the way I looked. Then we went to a clothing store, and she bought me a red wool winter coat.

On the way to the camp, she told me about the way American women look like and behave. "Americans are neat and well-mannered. You need to get ready for your new life and look decent with a nice hairdo and new clothes."

I smiled at her, thanked her, and shook her hand. Then I went to the camp's office and settled my room and board account. I estimated that I would have twenty dollars left for pocket money. There were no goodbye parties on Tuesday, the day before I traveled. It took no time to pack. My clothes were stylish, but my entire wardrobe consisted of three or four tops, two skirts, a pair of pants, a dress, a couple of sweaters, and a pair of shoes.

Arrival in the Land of the Free

Wednesday morning, September 30, 1970, was the date marking the beginning of my new life. I joined at dawn the group of immigrants from the camp traveling to New York City. A policeman called out our names, and soon we were on our way to the airport. It was a gray, chilly morning, and I was wearing my new winter coat. This was my first time on a transatlantic plane. Arriving at the airport, I was amazed at its size as it looked huge. I nestled in a seat by the window, watching Vienna disappear below us. It occurred to me that I didn't know where Ann Arbor, Michigan, was, so I walked to the back and asked one of the stewardesses.

"Oh, it's north in the Midwest close to Canada," a pretty and tall stewardess responded.

I settled down again in my seat, reading magazines and newspapers. The served meals were delicious, and the stewardesses were extremely polite. It was a warm feeling thinking of my future life in this enchanted land. The excitement kept me awake, and upon arrival in New York City, I was utterly astounded at the grandiose sight which I knew only from pictures. New York City appeared from air with the Statue of Liberty and the famous skyscrapers, which I knew about from reading books and magazines. The sight was electrifying as the plane circled and landed. I felt like arriving on a different planet. Getting off the plane, I was absorbing every little detail of my surroundings, watching people communicate with one another, and noticing how happy they were chatting, laughing, hugging. Then I saw a lady holding a sign with my name, and I made my way toward her.

"Are you Antonina?" I handed her my paperwork. She nodded for me to follow her, and soon we were on our way to a hotel. I looked out the window of the bus, lowering my head in vain to see the tops of the skyscrapers. Looking around, I could feel the energy of the city, its charm and magnetism.

Upon arrival at the hotel, the lady checked me in, then turned to me, and explained, "I will be back in the morning. We will grab breakfast and head to the Social Security office."

I thanked the woman and headed toward my room. It was very noisy. There were people in the hallways; men and women were rowdy, yelling, slamming doors. It must be a hotel for immigrants, I thought, leaning a chair against the doorknob. I laid in bed listening to the sirens, hoping that the night would go by without any incidents.

In the morning, the lady arrived on time. We had breakfast at a fast-food restaurant, which was a new experience for me. She explained the structure and work of Tolstoy Foundation and how old immigrants of Orthodox religion donate back to help new ones. The Social Security office was within a walking distance, and on our way, the lady explained the function and importance of Social Security. Learning about it, I felt extremely proud to receive the card; it was my first American document.

Back at the lobby of the hotel, we sat down on the sofa across the reception desk.

"My work here is done," the woman said. She handed me an airplane ticket and continued, "This is your ticket for your flight to Detroit. You have some free time to explore New York. Your flight is in seven hours. You need to be in the lobby at 3:00 p.m. There is a shuttle that will take you to the airport."

I shook her hand and followed her to the street, feeling so happy that I was free to venture on my own in the greatest city on earth. I must have walked for hours when it dawned on me that I wasn't paying too much attention to the streets. Luckily, I had the address on me. Looking around, I saw an African American lady close by, very elegant and fashionably dressed. I smiled at her and asked her for directions to the hotel. She smiled back.

"It's very simple, dear. The streets and avenues in New York are parallel to one another and numbered in an order. This is Seventy-Eighth Street." And she proceeded by explaining exactly how to reach my hotel. She was extremely friendly and kind, which made me feel good. Smiling, I reached my hotel, ran up to my room, grabbed my suitcase, and rushed down to the lobby, where I waited impatiently for the shuttle.

My flight to Detroit was memorable to this day. I was so excited that I had a hard time staying in my seat, looking every minute at my watch, and calculating the time to my arrival. This was it, the road to my final destination. As the plane started to descend at the Detroit Metro Airport, I stared out the window anxious and happy and, I have to admit, also a little afraid. I immediately recognized Anna and Mary and rushed to meet them. They greeted me like an old friend coming back from vacation, and they both gave me the biggest of hugs. I could tell that they were excited as well.

"This is all you have?" Anna pointed at my small suitcase.

"Yes, I travel light." And we all laughed.

As we walked to Anna's car, my eyes opened wide. This was the biggest car I have ever seen, and it was a beautiful green color. I felt lost in the huge back seat, telling Anna and Mary details of my trip and even before of my life in the refugee camp. I didn't notice how we arrived in Ann Arbor, and Anna stopped in front of an apartment building.

"My parents live here. We are having dinner with them, and I will explain to you the arrangements I made for your stay."

A pretty woman in her forties, elegantly dressed, of medium height, with braided and picked-up brown hair, opened the door of the apartment. "Hello, Antonina, welcome to America. Come on in. We all have been very eager to meet you. This is Anna's father."

A man with glasses, brown hair, dressed in sports pants and shirt shook my hand enthusiastically. The dining room was decorated with a Welcome Home sign, and there were a few of Anna's friends at the table. They all stood up to meet me, and soon we were all seated at a very festive table with dishes which I saw for the first time. The main meal was beef stroganoff, and the desserts were delicious apple pie and cookies with milk. What struck me was that Anna's parents, who were married for over twenty years, were very affectionate with each other, holding hands. Anna's father was putting his arms around his wife gently and lovingly. My stepfather loved my mother, and when he spoke to her, one could tell that he adored her, but there was never such an exhibit of feelings. While watching this couple, I was so much impressed with this openness of expressing emotions in a relationship. And yes, for the first time, I saw a dishwasher at a residence.

My First Years in America

At the end of the dinner, Anna nodded at me, and we went to the living room.

"Nina, I made an arrangement for you to stay with a lovely family, free room and board in exchange for getting their preschool son and daughter ready for school in the morning and being at home in the afternoon to meet them after school. A school bus will pick them up and drop them off in front of the house. Their parents will be home around five, and you will have dinner with them. You will be free the rest of the time during the day and evening. I also signed you up for evening classes at the high school. You will be studying bookkeeping and typing. I will pick you up and drive you to school and back," she said all this in one breath.

I knew how much work and effort she must have put in setting me up, and I knew how much she was committed to help me in the future. I was completely astounded by the kindness and generosity of this girl whom I met only once in Vienna. I hugged her and whispered, "I don't know how to thank you."

"You can repay me when you start working as a bookkeeper. The classes cost fifty dollars and last two months. But now we need to hurry as the people at your new home are expecting us."

I gently squeezed the hand of Anna's mother as I said goodbye, thanking her for the warm welcome and delicious food. The look on her face was soft and warm. "I wish you the best of luck, Nina. Anna will make sure that you have a good start. Now give me a hug and go on to your new place. We will have you over again." I waved goodbye at the rest of the company and hurried after Anna.

While riding in the car with Anna, I looked out with curiosity, staring at the houses, the streets, and the people. I liked the wooden two-story houses painted in different colors—green, blue, purple. I saw mostly young people dressed in jeans and T-shirts with backpacks.

"Ann Arbor is a university town," Anna said. "The population is around sixty thousand, and forty thousand are connected to the University as students, faculty, staff and support personnel. The rest are somehow associated with the university as well. The house where we are going is close to downtown, and you can easily walk and get around. There are also buses to more remote areas."

Anna stopped the car in front of a big white house. I timidly got out with my suitcase and noticed my hosts standing on the porch, the two children next to them. They were young, I would think in their early thirties, and were both looking in our direction and smiling. The man was tall, with blond hair, and his face was radiant. The woman was about the same height, with long black hair and with a friendly face. The man shook my hand with a firm grip.

"We know all about you, and we admire you for your courage to escape from behind the Iron Curtain. I am Mike, and this is my wife, Nancy. We are both thrilled to have you, and we want you to feel at home. Children, let's greet Nina." He leaned over the kids, and they both said hi with big smiles on their faces. The kids reminded me of my little friends in Vienna, Austria. They were a little older; I would say four and five.

Anna left us, and I entered a new phase in my life, in my first home in the Land of the Free. Nancy took me to my room and then gave me a tour of the house. "Here are the kids' bedrooms. There are clean clothes in their closets if you can help them dress in the morning. This is your bathroom supplied with all toiletries. Let me show you the breakfast area and the cereal the kids eat in the morning. They need to be up at eight to catch the bus at nine, and the same bus brings them back home at three. There are snacks in the cupboard for them to have in the afternoon. But you are probably tired, so I will leave you to unpack, shower, and rest. If we do not see you in the morning, we will see you in the afternoon around five. Good night, Nina."

I walked in my room and dropped on the bed, drained from emotional exhaustion. Soon I managed to pick myself up and stroll into the bathroom to take a shower. Not long after that, I was sound asleep in a big and extremely comfortable bed. I winded my manual alarm clock, giving myself enough time before taking care of the children.

My Life by Nancy and Mike was carefree and full of joy. My hosts were a very loving couple, sweet and extremely nice, surrounding me with a lot of attention. They often barbecued hot dogs and hamburgers. That was the first time I had grilled marshmallows. The children always addressed me as Ms. Nina and did everything I asked them to do. They were cheerful and bubbly like the Austrian little kids and were very polite. I surprised Nancy a few times by cooking Bulgarian dishes, which made everybody happy eating a warm cooked meal at the end of the day. In the mornings, I vacuumed and straightened up the house after everybody was gone. My evening classes were interesting as I liked bookkeeping, and I knew I had to learn typing. I found a typewriter at the house, and I practiced in the mornings when everybody was gone. Typical of Europeans, until now I could type with only two fingers.

One weekend, Anna surprised me. "Nina, get ready. We are going to the store." That was when I discovered Kmart, a store with reasonable prices and clothing, which I found attractive. Anna bought me some basic necessities, and we headed back. On the way, she talked to me about her life and important things that I needed to remember.

"You will need a driver's license. Ann Arbor is an exceptional city. Most cities in America do not have public transportation. And you need to have a good medical insurance. When you work, you will receive it from your employer. Once you start working, you need to open a bank account and keep only a minimal amount of cash."

I paid attention to everything she said as I knew that she was teaching me life survival skills in America. I was impressed with Anna, being so young and already independent and successful. She had an administrative job at the university and lived by herself, owned a very nice car, and had a lot of friends. Most of all, she had a heart of gold.

Time was flying, and it was already November before I knew it. On my birthday, I felt sad being away from home. I missed Mom, Grandma, my auntie, and my stepdad. Mom sent me a beautiful green wool winter dress, and I felt bad because I knew she had to sacrifice to get it, but at the same time, it made me feel like a little girl getting a special present for my birthday.

Memories from my childhood were interrupted by the sound of a car stopping in front of the house. It was Anna. "Come on, Nina. Did you think that I forgot it's your birthday? Let's go." My jaw dropped, and I opened my mouth, but Anna did not wait for me to speak. She grabbed me by the hand, and soon we were at her parents' house.

"Surprise!" everybody shouted as we entered the door. The apartment was decorated for my birthday, and Anna's friends were all laughing and talking cheerfully.

After dinner and cake Anna shouted, "And now, everybody, we are going to see a play, after which, we will stop at my brother's house!"

I will never forget my first birthday in America. Anna made sure that it would be memorable and unforgettable. After that day, my life continued with my regular daily duties, but I needed to find a job to cover my expenses. I also wanted to check at the university for admission into business school.

A few days after my twentieth birthday, I was hurrying down the street, feeling uplifted by the thought of going back to school. Looking at the admission application, my eyes stopped at the tuition amount.

"Ma'am, is two thousand dollars the tuition for the entire program?"

She smiled. "No, miss. It's for one semester, and it is for nonresidents."

I was a nonresident and on probation in America with a white card for two years, which said stateless. In two years, provided I did not leave the country, I was going to become a resident and obtain the so-called green card for residents.

"How much is tuition for Michigan residents?"

The lady smiled again. "Five hundred dollars a semester."

My heart sank as my hope to continue with my studies just vanished. Even five hundred dollars a semester was out of reach for me. Back in 1970, you could buy a new midsize car for two thousand dollars, not that I dreamed of one. Education for me was far more important than material things, and now it seemed to be so out of reach.

I made my way from State to Main Street to look into the next item on my list for the day—finding a job. I spotted a Chinese restaurant, and my curiosity led me inside. I never had Chinese food before. The restaurant was empty that early in the day. A lady was sitting at a table in the back, cleaning peapods. I marched up to her, greeted her, sat down, and started to clean peapods with her. I introduced myself, giving a brief description of my life since I left Bulgaria. "And I need a job," I added.

"When can you start?" The lady was Chinese, tiny and pleasant but with a stern voice.

"I need to talk to the people where I stay. I will let you know tomorrow."

"If you come to work at the restaurant [she was the owner's wife], you can stay with us."

On my way back to the house, I was running through my mind different scenarios, and it seemed that it made sense to live with the Chinese family while working at the restaurant. There would be no salary as the room and board were free, but I could make money from tips. And I could still go to evening classes until the end of the program. What I did not account for was that I was going to work at the restaurant from early morning to closing, and the long hours wore me out. I could not endure the physical stress, so in a couple of weeks, I asked for a break after lunch.

Across the street was Sears, where I saw an ad for a job at the printing department as an assistant to the marketing director. It was a short interview, and I was hired on the spot. Back in the street, I said to myself, "Now for a room." I ran toward the university's international center, where I spotted an ad from a lady renting a room at a very reasonable rate to a foreign student.

Mrs. K lived near the university, and I arranged to move in by the end of the week. My roommates at Mrs. K's house were a girl from Puerto Rico and a guy from India. We all got along fine. The landlady was a tall, somewhat skinny, and bony woman in her forties, who lived with her teenage son who kept to himself. The house rules were simple: We each had a shelf in the refrigerator. Everybody cleaned what they used. No loud music or loud noise. And no visitors (except for Anna, who continued to take me to classes). On one of her visits, she looked at me differently. I could see in her eyes that there was something important that she wanted to talk about.

"Nina, Mary and I took new jobs in New York City. We will be leaving in ten days. You are finishing your classes this week, and you will be fine. Look for a bookkeeping job through an employment agency, and here is two hundred dollars to help you out in the meantime."

I mumbled, "Congratulations! A million thanks for your generosity, and thank you for caring." I wanted Anna to have her dreams fulfilled, but at the same time, I felt like I was losing a part of me. She was excited about her new job and started to tell me all about her plans in the Big Apple. At the end of her visit, I saw her off to the door. I hugged her gently and saw her off with teary eyes.

I completed both the bookkeeping and typing classes successfully about the time when Anna left for New York City. I felt so empty without her. There was this enormous feeling of void inside me. Nonetheless, I continued with my daily activities. At that time, working at Sears and pitching in with chores around the house, I knew I had to move on with my life. I could hear Anna's voice, "You need to contact an employment agency as soon as you finish classes." So there I was in front of an office with a sign Snelling and Snelling. I walked into the building and entered the reception area. A young lady met me with a smile.

"What can we do for you?"

"A friend of mine who is also my sponsor recommended your agency. I arrived from Europe a couple of months ago and just finished bookkeeping and typing classes. I studied economics in Belgrade, Yugoslavia. Now I am looking for a bookkeeping job."

"That's wonderful, because we have an opening for accounts receivable clerk at Follett's bookstore. I can set up an appointment for you to talk to the controller tomorrow morning."

I leaped with joy. "Of course, thank you so much."

Follett's was located on State Street and was primarily a college bookstore. I arrived for my appointment on time. Dorothy, the controller, met me at the door, and after introducing me to the administrative and sales personnel, she took me to the second floor where the accounting office was located. She showed me my desk, with a calculator on it, and explained my daily task of recording accounts receivable and performing additional duties with assisting her. Marian, the other bookkeeper, was also very friendly, as well as the remaining staff in sales and management. At last, no more manual labor. I was sitting at my desk caressing the calculator, so grateful to God for helping me all along.

"Tomorrow is a special day," said my landlady, calling us all to the living room. "It's Thanksgiving, and I expect you all to be here for early dinner."

I have not researched American holidays and I did not know the meaning of the word *Thanksgiving*. Showing up in the dining room at the time specified by Mrs. K, my jaw dropped at seeing the food on the dining room table. There was the biggest turkey I've ever seen, with all kinds of side dishes and desserts unfamiliar to me, except for the green beans casserole. Mrs. K was more than happy to tell us the story of the origin and reason for celebrating Thanksgiving. Each one of us shared what we give thanks for. I was thankful for all the good people I met on my way since leaving home.

The next morning, I had a call from the university's international center. An elderly Ukrainian man who spoke poor English needed help with house chores in exchange for free room and board. The house was on campus and a walking distance to the bookstore. I moved into Mr. B's place during the weekend. The house was on Jefferson Street, a short walk to the bookstore. The conditions were very agreeable, and I could keep my bookkeeping job. I would prepare dinner, shop and clean the house on weekends. Mr. B was a charming old man in his seventies. He was in high spirits but was suffering of poor health. Walking up the stairs from the basement where I cooked and we ate, he had to grab the tail of his extremely smart German shepherd dog. Mr. B spoke Russian, and soon I could speak it too without any grammar mistakes. I wasn't fond of learning Russian while in Bulgaria, but it was a mandatory subject from fifth to twelfth grade. I made sure I had excellent grades, but I forgot a lot after high school. Mr. B spoke all evening at the dinner table, and my Russian improved considerably. I learned about the tragedy in his life, losing both of his children. They were Ukrainian, and during the Second World War, he left the USSR with his wife and daughter. They made it to Paris, but the girl died from exhaustion and hunger. His son was drafted in the Russian Red Army, and Mr. B never heard from him again. The Red Cross could not come up with any leads. Mr. B told me that I was taking the place of his daughter, Manjusa. He'd say in the evening, "Let's listen to some Russian records. I like your singing."

I eventually settled down into a routine. Jimmy, the dog, walked me to work every morning and was waiting for me in front of the store in the afternoon. I learned how to drive and drove Mr. B's big black Impala to the store and, on weekends, to a Ukrainian park at Whitmore Lake. I loved this city. I loved the people who would greet you and smile at you even though you were a stranger to them. And okay, I gained a few pounds splurging on doughnuts, pies, and cakes. I remember walking in Dunkin' Donuts on Main Street in Ann Arbor and ordering one of each kind. Oh, they were all tasty, but I particularly liked was the French cruller.

A Miraculous Reunion
with Mom

Five years later, on a hot August evening, I was getting dinner when the phone rang. It was a man's voice. "My name is Ilia, and I work for the Voice of America radio in Washington, DC. President Ford recently signed an agreement for reunion of separated families. Since you are an only child, I could add your mother's name to that list. I know about you from my mother, who is a friend of yours."

I couldn't believe my ears, I would see Mom again. All this time, at least we could write, and she kept me up to date on their life in Bulgaria, letting me know that they were all okay.

"Ilia, are you for real? There is no mistake? I am going to see my mother?"

"Not only see, she will be granted permanent residency upon arrival. The only thing is that she will not be able to go back to Bulgaria. Write down my phone number. I will be in touch with details."

I hung up, looking into space, not believing that God was granting me such a wish. So much happened during the five years since I moved into Mr. B's. I married a Bosnian, and although we spoke Serbo-Croatian, the cultural and educational differences prevented us from communicating. We met in Traiskirchen, Austria, in the spring of 1970. It was a nice spring day, and I was sitting on a bench in the park just outside the immigrants' camp when a tall, dark-haired young man approached me, speaking in German. Soon I found out that he was from the Bosnia region in Yugoslavia, and we switched to speaking Serbian. He was two years older than me and had a techni-

81

cal background, told me about his life in France and Sweden before Austria. From that day on, we started seeing each other regularly until the day I left for the States. We stayed in contact off and on when six months later, he called me from LaGuardia Airport in New York saying that he was on his way to see me in Ann Arbor. That was a big surprise as he didn't mention about coming to the States in any of our calls. I walked over to Mr. B and told him what happened. Mr. B, Jimmy, and I went to meet the guy at the Detroit airport. I recognized him at once. He was dressed elegantly in a raincoat and casual pants, carrying a briefcase. Mr. B let him stay in one of the guest rooms, and I introduced him to friends, a few Bulgarian immigrants who came through the immigrants' camp in Italy, the ladies from my work, and some of Mr. B's Ukrainian friends.

I met the small Bulgarian community in a strange way. A lady called me at Mr. B's house just before Christmas in 1970 and told me that she heard about me and that she was Bulgarian. She invited me to their get-together on the following Sunday, and from then on, I spent my weekends in their company. It was a small group of people—a husband and wife, a young woman, and a guy. They told me their escape story through Trieste, Italy. Everybody made it over the fence on the border, except the married man. He was the last to climb the fence when a border patrol guy grabbed him by the feet. His wife started to pull him up, yelling at the patrol to let go of her husband. The man let him go, and they all ended up in an Italian immigrants' camp. I found in them another family as we had dinners together on Sundays, and for Christmas, they drove me around to show me how Americans decorate their houses for Christmas.

Going back to my visitor, he did not have proper documents to remain in the country, so the first thing I did was drive him to report his presence at the immigration office in Detroit. It all seemed so distant and foggy, but we ended up getting married. We had a small celebration at the house, and I remember seeing Mr. B wiping his tears. "Ah, Manysa, why did this happen?" This was the only thing he said.

My new husband did not speak English, so he worked odd jobs. I continued working at the bookstore until I got pregnant with my first daughter. Vanesa was born on Christmas Eve morning in 1971.

The night before she was born, I went shopping with Mr. B, and on the way home, we got into an accident. I went into labor a couple of hours later, and by morning, my daughter was born, three months premature, weighing only two pounds and two ounces. St. Joseph Hospital, where I had her, was connected to the university hospital by underground corridors, and Vanesa was transported while in incubator to Mott Children's Hospital. I went to see her the same day. She was so tiny, and there were so many wires attached to her little body. I went home happy to have a daughter and sad knowing that her chances for survival were slim.

From that day on for the next three months, I was at her side every day. Her father used to drop me off at the hospital on his way to work and pick me up at the end of his shift. I stayed and stared at her for hours, praying to God to give her strength to pull through. She was so fragile that I was startled by every movement she made. God heard my prayers, and after two months, Vanesa was out of the incubator, breathing on her own. I could finally hold her in my arms and take care of her, feeding her and giving her baths. She was discharged at the end of March 1972, which was the time she was supposed to be born. By then, we had moved out of Mr. B's house and stayed in a one-bedroom apartment across the street from him. I fixed the couch in the living room for my bed and spent day and night by Vanesa's cradle, watching her sleep. She was a sweet baby. At feeding time, she would look at me with her brown eyes as if wanting to say, "I know you have the bottle for me."

I was not lonely as Jimmy, Mr. B's dog, used to visit me every day. He would bark under my window and run to the front door, waiting for me to open the door. Jimmy assumed his job as a guard dog, spending the whole time sitting by Vanesa's cradle. By that time, Vanesa's dad learned English and was ready to start working at a better-paying job as a technician. Somebody from his work told him that Chevrolet in Plymouth, Michigan, was hiring, so we drove to the plant, and I filled his application—he still could not write well. He was immediately hired. The pay was good, so soon we could move to a new apartment complex in Plymouth, Michigan. We could afford a two-bedroom apartment, which was across from a small park with a pool.

I made friends with women who had small kids playing at the playground with Vanesa. We spent time together while the men were at work, sharing experiences and life stories, even doing art projects and taking sewing classes. That was when I got pregnant with my son and started to get ready for his arrival. We set the second bedroom for him, furnishing it with baby furniture, toys, and clothes. I planned to stay with the baby while my daughter and her father were going to be in the adjacent bedroom. Being in another room was fine with me as I could still hear if she needed something at night. My son was born a month earlier but was a healthy baby with the sweetest smile on earth. I had my alarm set up to feed him every three hours for the first couple of months, but I woke up before it went off, and every time I leaned over the crib, I saw his radiant face.

My daughter loved her brother. During the day, she played with us by talking to him and touching him gently. Still young at the age of twenty-four, I learned fast how to be a mother. The kids were the center of my life as I spent every minute of my time with them from breakfast to bedtime. It was fun and games as we arranged activities with the other women on where to go and what to do with all the children. I watched with admiration my children's expressions, the way they moved their little hands and feet, the first time they crawled, their first steps, the first words they said. My daughter could not pronounce her name and was calling herself Sasha, and my son started to make small three-word sentences like "I want cookie" when he turned one.

Their father worked long hours, and we saw him mostly around lunchtime. He did not complain about his work being hard since his job was to observe the lines of production, and if something went wrong, he had to replace the malfunctioning part. He used to take *Time* magazine and newspapers with him to occupy his free time.

Soon we saved enough for a house, and we moved to a three-bedroom ranch with a finished basement in Westland, Michigan. The house had aboveground pool, and we spent the hot summer days by it. I taught my daughter to swim when she was four. My son was ten months when we moved there, and I wasn't comfortable letting him in the water without floaties. The pool was seven feet deep at one end, and I was not a good diver.

I shook myself up to come back to reality and rushed to get the kids dinner, enough thinking of the past.

A week later, Ilia called again. "Hi, Nina, I have great news for you. Our mothers are arriving on September 6. Here are the details about your mother's flight."

On September 6, 1976, I was at the Detroit airport looking intensely in the direction of people arriving from New York. Vanesa and Erik were clinging on to me. My heart was beating fast, and my hands were trembling. And there she was, my mom, whom I hadn't seen in seven years. Her face was radiant, but it seemed to be also worn out. We ran to each other.

"Oh, Mom, I missed you so much." We hugged with tears rolling down our cheeks.

Then she let go of me and the kids, wiped her tears, and stepped back. "Children, you are so beautiful, but your mom is so skinny."

The next few weeks were filled with happiness beyond description. We talked a lot, catching up on everything that happened in our lives for the past seven years.

"Your grandma died, and shortly before her death, she kept saying, 'I hope the child is born.' I could not understand why she was saying that since you were not due for another three months. She passed away about the same time Vanesa was born and probably sensed that something was wrong."

I remembered the last time I saw Grandma. It was the day I left Sofia before my finals in Belgrade when she ran after me and we hugged. My grandma sensed that this was a goodbye hug, but the thought about leaving for good had not yet come to my mind. The idea of leaving forever materialized when I returned to Belgrade. Little did I know at that time that this was the last time I would see her. Now I wished I took more time to be with her. The news of her death was devastating because my grandma meant the world to me. Everything I became was because of her. I admired and worshipped her for the goodness of her heart and her ability to accept and forgive and to love unconditionally, never saying anything negative or complaining, just going silently about her daily tasks, and smiling when I liked her cooking.

"And you, what happened to you, Mom, after I left?"

Mom glanced to the side, didn't say anything for a while, and then started to speak without stopping, "The year you were in Austria, working and studying and even being in the refugee camp, was quiet. I continued to teach at the Chemical Technical School, but every time I left the house, I looked around me expecting somebody to tap me on the shoulder and tell me to follow them to the police. They called me in when you left Austria. As soon as I walked into the police chief's office, he immediately asked, 'Do you know where your daughter is today? She is flying to America. What kind of educator are you? You are fired as of today. Since you could not teach your own daughter correctly, you are incompetent to teach our youth.' With that, he waved his hand and signaled me to leave. The following day, the director of the high school called me to his office and handed me the discharge paper, saying that I was fired as enemy to Communism." Mom reached in her purse and pulled a paper. I saw it with my own eyes. She was fired because she was an enemy to Communism.

"'I am sorry, Mrs. M. The kids love you and will miss you. I will miss you as well. You are an exceptional, knowledgeable, and valuable educator, but this is an order from the Ministry of the Interior.'

"This was a big blow as I lost not only my livelihood but also my social status and my contact with my students and colleagues. From that day on, I expected to be deported and sent to one of their labor camps, so I had my suitcase ready by the door. I am in exile," Mom said. "I am not allowed to go back."

My head was spinning listening to Mom. I could envision those hard days of Mom being humiliated and threatened, but I had no idea that I caused her so much pain because of leaving. I realized at that moment that it was a miracle that they did not send her away, as people ended in camps of hard labor for stupid things like wearing tight pants. This accusation of Mom being an enemy to Communism was extremely serious. I know, for the freethinking democratic Westerner, this might be difficult to understand, but life under Communism was dangerous if you crossed the line by having ties to the West, especially America. Capitalism was described as decadent where all people lived in extreme poverty or being homeless. My cousin Krum, who was well-read, was also brainwashed as when Mom showed him pictures of us in the Westland house, he said that these pictures were taken in model homes since average people were homeless, living in the street.

Mom was becoming calmer every day, getting into the routine of our lives. I was not working, and we went to the stores at Westland Mall and Kmart by the house. Mom looked at the clothing stores with amazement. This was her first time at a mall, and I lost her. I was fussing over the kids, and when I turned around, she was gone. Getting security and running all over the mall, I found her. She was surprised that I was worried.

"Nina, I traveled alone from Europe finding my way around at Heathrow Airport. I am okay. Don't stress over me." What could I say? I just laughed and hugged her.

One afternoon in November, Mom looked at me and said, "There has been an epidemic with the swine flu. I heard that they are giving vaccinations. We should go and get vaccinated."

I was so busy with the kids and preparations for her arrival that I did not even know about the flu. I found a location where they were giving free vaccinations, and after standing in line for half an hour, our turn came. Mom and I only got vaccinated. I did not like vaccinating the kids except for the children's deceases prescribed by the doctor. Going back home, all of a sudden, I felt very weak. My heart started to race and would not slow down. I made myself coffee and lit a cigarette; I was still smoking at that time. I tried to calm down, but I couldn't. I felt sicker by the minute. My husband was at work, so I called an ambulance. They rolled me in the emergency room, asking the usual questions after taking my vital signs. The nurse and the doctor did not mention a thing about me getting sick because of the swine flu shot. My husband picked me up after work, but I was still weak; I wasn't well. I dragged myself for the next four months. My family doctor was giving me vitamin shots every day, which did not help. I was fading away, but I did not stay in bed. I went about doing what I was supposed to do at a slower pace. One day, I felt that my muscles were getting tight and stiff, so I cleaned the wooden paneling on the walls of the family room. I believe that pushing myself to move saved me because I learned of a few cases when people died after this vaccine. It wasn't until April of 1977 when we went to Florida for a week that I started to feel my strength coming back.

Holidays were approaching, and I introduced Mom to Thanksgiving. By this time, I knew how to prepare all the American side dishes, desserts, and trimmings. Mom kept shaking her head in disbelief at the food preparation for the big feast. She was still numb from the hardship and pain she went through since my departure and the miraculous work of God that brought us together. We had a lot to be thankful for in the year 1976, especially for our survival and our miraculous reunion.

Dreams Come True

Shortly after Thanksgiving, Mom brought up a topic that made me jump. "You know it is time for you to go back to school. Get your college transcripts from Yugoslavia and Austria. I will watch the kids while you are signing up for classes."

"Okay, Mom." I lowered my eyes so that my tears would not show. How much I missed school. I gathered all necessary documents, and the next day at dawn, I was on my way to Ann Arbor. I knew where the admission and counseling offices were. My heart was pounding in anticipation of starting the enrollment process. I picked up the registration forms and met with a counselor.

"What would you like to study, Antonina?" said a young man in his thirties, looking straight into my eyes.

"I studied economics in Belgrade. I'd like to work in the business world, but I also like studying foreign languages. I could not continue sooner because of financial difficulties."

"You had an interruption of six years. I recommend that you continue with foreign languages. Since you are Bulgarian born and you speak Serbian and Russian, I recommend that you meet with the chairman of the Slavic department. That would be in the LSA building. The University of Michigan is a prestigious university, and you will not have any trouble finding a job in business after graduating with a foreign language degree."

It was a pleasure to meet the chairman of the Slavic department. He was a slim, middle-aged, dark-haired man with glasses. He rose to his feet as I walked in and offered me a seat. My name intrigued him, and he inquired about my parents. His eyes lit up as he heard my father's name.

"Antonina, your father's books are in the graduate library. He is a globally recognized linguist. Now let's look at your transcripts. Just give me a few minutes to examine them." I waited anxiously while he was examining my college documents. "You studied in Belgrade, and you speak Serbian. You had eight years of Russian in Bulgarian schools. The courses you took at Belgrade's economics faculty are fully transferable. So are the classes in German from the University of Vienna. You will be accepted in the Russian program as a junior. The courses will be Russian classical literature in English. Fill in the necessary registration forms, and you can start studying in the winter semester."

I squeezed his hand and flew out of his office. By the end of the day, I was officially a student at the University of Michigan's Ann Arbor campus. I picked up my class schedule (three in Russian and one in English literature), applied for a scholarship, picked up some of the novels from the graduate library, and called home.

"Mom, I am a student again."

"God is merciful, child," Mom answered. "He will always help you. Just stay on the right path."

The next morning, Mom prepared breakfast, my favorite *palachinki* (crepes), but I was not hungry. The children were licking their fingers finishing up their meal and asking for more. I helped Mom, and after cleaning up, I rushed to her bedroom, where I stored all my novels and other books. I had to make a plan, so I started by looking at my curriculum and the number of novels, which amounted to reading 150–200 pages a day. Then I designed my daily schedule of attending classes, studying, and spending time with Mom and the children. Christmas was around the corner, and I wanted to benefit from the few days left to fully enjoy my family.

I peeked into the family room where Mom was reading. "Mom, we are going Christmas shopping now."

"What do you mean?"

"Well, for Christmas, I am Santa Claus. I buy gifts for the children and close friends. I wrap them and place them under the Christmas tree. We visit friends and exchange gifts."

I could tell that Mom liked the idea of giving and exchanging gifts. Her face lit up. She got up and was ready very fast. I dressed the children, and off we went to Kmart.

At the store, I took Mom and the children to the small coffee place for snacks, quickly loaded the cart with gifts, and put them in the car. Going back to the store I smiled as I saw Mom and the children waiting patiently for me. Mom self-taught herself English from my high school books and was managing to speak with the children. After lunch, with the kids taking a nap, Mom and I wrapped all the gifts, except for hers. Mom was like a kid herself admiring the packages, clapping her hands at the sight of the big toys—dolls for Vanesa, cars for Erik, and games for both of them.

Then I looked at her and said, "Mom, you need to go to your room. I have to wrap your gifts. I will call you when I am done."

She looked at me with a devilish look in her eyes and closed the door behind her. Mom was probably waiting by her door as she came back as soon as I said that I was done. Then she counted the presents and figured out which ones were for her. Watching her humming and laughing like a child made me extremely happy. I observed silently with a smile.

Christmas dinner was lavish in my mom's eyes. She admired the entire preparation with curiosity and amazement—the baking of the ham, the vegetable side dishes, and the pumpkin and apple pies. Christmas Eve was Vanesa's birthday, which added to the excitement of the festivities.

New Year came before I knew it, and I was ready for my first class after a long absence from school. On January 3, 1977, I kissed Mom and the kids goodbye. I did not feel the drive to Ann Arbor. Arriving extra early on campus, I hurried to find the room and got a seat in the front, waiting anxiously for the beginning of the class.

The first semester went fast. I was reading with great zeal the books every day as I planned, 150–200 pages. In the evenings, I caught up on assignments and wrote papers (there were no computers at that time, but I was very lucky to have a typewriter, which allowed me to go back a space and correct spelling and grammar). The kids did not notice the change as I still took time to prepare meals and eat dinner with them. I did not want to be away from them, so I adapted to study with the TV on and with Vanesa and Erik playing around me.

I finish the semester with all B's which for me at the time was a big deal considering that all my classes were classic literature, requiring a lot of written assignments, quite different from the way of writing papers in Bulgaria, not to mention that I also had seven years of school interruption. I calculated the credits I needed to major in Russian, and it appeared that I could add another foreign language to my program. I hesitated between German, which I could still speak well, and French, which I studied with my mother's aunt and in high school. I loved the sound of French, so French was the language of my choice. I picked up the curriculum for the French program and mapped out a two-year plan of the courses I needed to take to graduate with both majors in Russian and French languages. My targeted graduation date was the end of spring 1979.

As much as my life seemed to be in order, the relationship with my husband was not healthy. He had an explosive personality with outbursts of anger, and his behavior worsened since Mom's arrival. We went through marriage counseling, which was useless; he resumed his old ways shortly after such sessions. There were periods of calmness during the birth of the children, but that did not last long. I found a place for Mom close to my house, taking care of an elderly woman living with her son who was about Mom's age. That was ripping my heart, so in the summer of 1977, I contacted the university housing office. There was a town house available on North Campus in the family housing section, which I immediately took. I called Mom and told her that I was moving with the children and asked her if she would like to come.

"Of course, I will come, Nina," she said. "I know you will need help with the kids while studying."

"It's not that, Mom. There is free childcare at the university. I just miss you."

Moving was not difficult as I took basic necessities from the family house, the beds for the kids and us, a table, chairs, and one couch. I packed the car with clothes still on hangers and swung by

Mom to pick her up. The place was a two-story wooden townhouse with basement, living room, and kitchen on the first floor and three bedrooms and bathroom on the second floor. I liked that all buildings faced a courtyard with a playground for kids and that the parking spaces were in the back. There was regular bus transportation, free for students and their families, to the main campus. All my neighbors were students with small children, and we all got along fine as one big family. Vanesa and Erik were extremely happy making new friends, spending all day playing in the yard or visiting.

There were also funny episodes where one day, after classes, I found the entire walls in the living room decorated with nonerasable crayons, the only ones on the market at that time.

"Who was drawing on the wall? I asked the children.

"It wasn't me."

"Me either."

I tried to hide my smile as I explained that this was forbidden and that now we had to paint the living room. My children liked to draw, and the next thing I knew, Vanesa painted her brother all over his body. It took some time for the colors to fade away. Sliding down the stairs on the crib mattress was another game the kids invented in my absence. There wasn't a dull moment, and I fully enjoyed my new life. Vanesa learned how to ride a bike with me running behind her for a few days, and then one day, she took off by herself.

She started school in the fall of 1977 at the neighborhood public school, which turned out to be a problem. The kindergarten teacher was amiable, but something was not right—Vanesa was complaining about certain children being mean and picking on her. One day, I could see that there was a fight, as there were marks on her face. Vanesa was not learning in this class, which made me concerned. The teacher hinted that I should consider a special class at the University of Michigan to enroll Vanesa in first grade. I went to check out that program and was stunned observing the pale and serious-looking children in the face. I realized that there was something very wrong with this special program. Vanesa was shy and did not speak much, but she was a happy and lively child. My instinct told me to check out private schools, and after some research, I transferred her to start first grade in the fall of 1978 at St. Thomas Catholic School. Vanesa's first-grade teacher was a very dedicated and professional lady committed to teach and help the little ones. Vanesa seemed happy at the new school as she was smiling and bubbly when I picked her up. It wasn't long before she caught up on what she missed from kindergarten at the public school and was reading and writing quite well.

Final exam week was approaching, and my attention was fully focused on completing all assignments and preparing for the tests. This was when I received a surprise letter from the immigration office in Detroit for an interview for American citizenship. I waited so long for this moment, ever since I stepped on American soil in September 1970. But that meant adding to the preparation for final exams the subjects of the American history and government. On the date of the interview, I showed up at the immigration office with swollen red eyes from sleepless nights of studying. The immigration officer met me at the door of his office, introduced himself, and showed me to a seat. I felt relaxed as I sat down and exhaled deeply.

"Sir, I am extremely grateful for the opportunity to become a US citizen. This is a historic moment for me and my children to know that their mother is American. But you know it could have happened at a better time, like next month after my final exams," I added jokingly.

"You are a student. Congratulations. Tell me about your studies."

This was my favorite topic. I started to talk passionately, with sparkling eyes and vivid facial expressions, about my student life at the University of Michigan in Ann Arbor. I explained in detail not only my classes but I spoke with zeal and enthusiasm about my goals as well.

The man was listening with big interest, and when I finished, he said, "This is a fantastic success story, but let me ask a couple of questions in history and government. Antonina, briefly describe the American federal government." When I finished, the man thanked me and escorted me to the door. "Good luck with your finals, and congratulations, from today on, you are an American citizen. You will receive a letter inviting you to a ceremony and you will receive your citizenship document in the mail." I shook his hand heartily and hurried out to the parking lot. I was an American citizen. I was so happy; my heart felt being at the right place. It was an incredible sensation of achieving a lifetime wish.

The long-awaited day finally came; I graduated successfully with 3.4 GPA from the University of Michigan with a bachelor of arts degree having double majors in French and Russian languages and literature. And I had stayed on track with my plan, completing both programs in two and a half years from January 1977 to May 1979. We had a simple dinner that Mom prepared for us to celebrate, but it was one of the best dinners I had as I was sharing my success with the most important people in my life—my mother and my children. It was my first big scholastic achievement, and now it was time to get a job where I could realize myself.

I Graduated and Now What?

I was at the job placement office the next day. My advisor pulled available positions for someone with knowledge of French, and they were all for bilingual secretaries. There was nothing for a graduate with a Russian major. I was extremely disappointed, thinking about all the hard work of studying French and Russian classic literature. For what? To be a secretary? My first advisor proved to be wrong; I could not find employment in business with foreign language majors.

My other option was to teach, and this time, I did my own research. I already knew that teaching in high schools paid more than teaching in college as an instructor. I needed a teacher's certificate, which meant another year of studying at the university's Department of Education. I picked up the curriculum that same day and signed up for classes. The program required teacher observation of two hours per week for the first semester combined with a full set of classes and full-time student teaching for the second semester. I scanned quickly the high schools offering student education opportunities and noticed a Catholic high school adjacent to Vanesa's elementary school, where Erik was also starting kindergarten in the fall.

The school was on university campus, so I ran, arriving breathless and feeling anxious. Walking in the building, I found the principal's office. I approached the secretary's desk and requested a meeting with her. The principal was a nun. A short, stout woman with short blond hair and round face. She examined my credentials and then asked about my religious affiliation. I explained to her that my children were enrolled at the adjacent St. Thomas school and that the family was Eastern Orthodox. Ms. S listened carefully and then smiled and started to speak, "I like your enthusiasm and your accomplishments at the university. You will need to become a church member, and with that, there is a privilege—you will get the lower tuition rate for the children. You can meet with the French teacher and arrange your teaching schedule with her."

I shook Ms. S's hand firmly, thanking her for her time and the opportunity to teach at her school. This same day I met the French teacher, an attractive young woman with a son in preschool, whose husband was completing his doctoral work in chemistry. We talked at length and parted with the understanding that we would stay in touch and meet again before the beginning of my second semester to work on the details about my student teaching. She shared valuable teaching strategies, which served me for the rest of my life.

"Nina, when speaking, you need to observe the faces of the students, and if they are perplexed, explain the same sentence using other words or use another sentence. Teaching is like acting, and the way you speak and use body language is how you will keep their attention. Teaching French means teaching not only the language but also French culture. There are French bakeries and restaurants close by where you can take the students on field trips." That sounded fantastic as I loved French food and could share with the students facts about life in French speaking countries.

"Thank you, Linda. I am extremely grateful for your remarks. I can see their value, and I will definitely implement them." We scheduled our next meeting in the beginning of January 1980, and I went home feeling as if a burden was lifted off my chest. I felt that I was finally in control of my life, with a future in high school teaching.

Summer went by quickly. I enjoyed my time with the children outdoors at parks and swimming pools. Before we knew it, the leisure days of summer were gone. Vanesa started second grade after completing first grade with all As, and Erik was starting kindergarten. The first day of school was always special, being happy but also nervous in anticipation of starting the new school year. I kept my grandma's tradition of having the children always dressed in new clothes—Vanesa in a uniform of a dress or skirt with a blouse and Erik in a shirt and pants, both with shiny shoes and attractive haircuts. Walking in the building, I held their hands and walked them to their classrooms. After spending time talking to their teachers about the program, the requirements, and the rules, I walked with them around the building to ensure they knew how to get to their rooms, bathrooms, gym, and library. Then with a big sigh, I smiled at them, hugged them, and rushed to my first class at the college of education.

I settled into an everyday routine—driving the kids to school, attending classes, observing teaching of French classes at one of the Ann Arbor public high schools, and picking up the kids from school. I was not impressed with the teacher at the high school as she did not talk to the students in French. Mom always made snacks to hold us till dinnertime. After school, I checked the kids' backpacks for grades they received for the day (there was no internet with student portal in those days) and made sure they did their homework. Both Vanesa and Erik were doing great with excellent grades and learning a lot. Vanesa was reading and writing fluently, and Erik was catching up to her very fast. After dinner, I talked to Mom for a while and then locked myself in the room to study. Sometimes I studied in the living room with all the distractions and noise, which I learned to tune out.

Christmas holiday came and went, and here I was at Gabriel Richard Catholic High School, getting to know my students and colleagues and learning about the schedule and the French program requirements. Linda observed me teaching for a couple of weeks and then left me to teach on my own.

My students were mostly from affluent families and very per-sonable and kind. They were from grades 9 to 12 and were eager to learn French. Following the French teacher's recommendations, I established a very amicable and agreeable classroom setting with conversational exercises to practice new vocabulary and grammar. I taught French the way I learned English, with a lot of supplementary material and photos regarding French life and customs for differ-ent regions in France as well as other French-speaking countries. I took them from taking walks in Paris to the beaches of the French Riviera, the Basque Country, Provence, and Alsace and discovering amazing places like Mont-Saint-Michel. I awakened in them the love to experience French culture and to hear French people speak. Mondays were days to share how everybody spent the weekend using French language, and I was amazed to learn how close they were with doing things together, resembling my high school life in Bulgaria. I felt extremely happy as I could finally apply what I learned at the university. I made my students aware of the close ties between the French and American nations by talking about the Statue of Liberty, a gift from the French people, about France being the first ally of the United States, and about the French Revolution, inspired by the creation of the United States, and about French and American troops fighting side by side against the Nazis. I also felt blessed being close to my children. Every day around noon, one of my students sitting by the windows would let me know that Vanesa or Erik's class was having recess.

At the end of the school year, we had lunch with Linda, the French teacher, to celebrate the successful ending of my student teaching. We chose for the occasion a French restaurant, and as soon as we were seated, Linda started to speak, "Nina, you are a wonderful teacher. You not only took my advice about focusing on conversational exercises but also inspired students about learning French by including lessons of geography, history, literature, art, even business. I could see you care as I observed you helping students. They all accepted you from the very beginning, which is unusual when there is a change in instructors. Nina, I will be quitting. My husband will be interviewing for jobs in different states, and we will be moving. Will you be interested in teaching in my place? The students know you, and it will not be difficult for them to accept my departure. I already spoke to the principal, and she is in favor of you staying."

I squeezed Linda's hands in showing gratitude. "Linda, this is awesome. Of course I would love to teach here. You just made my day." I met with the principal the same day. Leaving her office, I jumped with joy. My first job after graduating college and at the school where my kids were, I was so lucky. The church was across from the school, and I went in to thank God and St. Mary for looking over us and granting me the job that I wanted so much. I sat in silence feeling a wave of calmness overcoming me and filling me with warmth and love. Crossing myself, I left the church and rushed to get the children.

I took a step back in my personal life and returned with the children to their father in an attempt to patch things up. Women are easily deceived with promises for changes, especially when there are children involved. Mom left for Bulgaria; relations between US and Bulgaria were not as strained, and she could travel on a United States permit as a resident. We moved to a house in Canton shortly after I finished my student teaching program and was awarded with a teacher's certificate. Life in the suburbs was different from that in the city. Our house was like others, built in a subdivision with a nice yard and not close to stores or movie theaters. Museums and cultural life existed in Ann Arbor, Michigan, about twenty miles west of Canton.

The new school year in 1980–1981 was very enjoyable as I was teaching a subject I enjoyed in a respectful high school in Ann Arbor, and my students shared my love for French language and culture. We visited French restaurants and bakeries on cultural days to celebrate the students' progress. My children were also doing wonderfully at school with teachers who made them feel comfortable studying and learning. My professional life was complete, but my personal life was not in a good shape. There were again outbursts of anger coming from nowhere to which I just frowned. My husband went back to his old tricks. It was already May of 1981 when one morning, he arrived tipsy and laughing. I felt so tired. Looking at him, I simply said, "This is the last time you and I are talking. I am going back home." A week after the last day of school, I packed all of my clothes, and my children's too, in three suitcases (we did not have that much of clothing by American standards), and we left for Bulgaria.

I was traveling with an American passport, and my last name was different, but I couldn't help but shiver arriving at Sofia Airport and while waiting in line at passport control. Nothing happened. Once clearing customs, we were outside, and I immediately spotted Mom with Ivan (a cousin), who had roses in his hands. Funny that the children shared later that they thought Ivan was a new man in my life. Seeing the suitcases, Mom exclaimed, "And these, why do you have so much luggage?"

"I left the house. I left everything, Mom. I am moving back in with you."

Things became very emotional as the children's father arrived in Bulgaria unexpectedly. He realized we were really gone when he opened the empty closets. I guess he did not take me seriously when I said I was leaving. There was a big scene with him begging my mother to let him stay and try fix our relationship. Mom's response was that of a very dignified woman. "Listen, you have done wrong by Nina. You have caused a lot of grief to the family, but you are my guest, and I will not send you away."

We all pretended that everything was fine and even took a trip to the Black Sea. We rented a flat in a house between Varna and Golden Sands, and my cousin Ivan drove us every day to the beach. My son Erik was glued to him, and Vanesa loved it when they all played in the sand. But I already had made up my mind not to go back and had no intention of following this man back to Canton, Michigan.

Returning to Sofia, I had the opportunity to talk with Mom. "I cannot live with this man, Mother. He is poisoning me." I described unwillingly with a head down some of the bad days. "I filed for divorce. Will you come back to the States? I need you. Otherwise, I will stay here and throw everything away."

"You cannot do that. You are a fighter. You have worked so hard, and your life is just beginning. But I am a mother, and it is difficult for me to see you unhappy. I can see that your personal life is in shambles if you are willing to throw away everything. But Bulgaria is still a Communist country, and the only reason you had no problems at the border was because you are married to a Yugoslavian. Life here will be very difficult not only for you but for the kids as well." She paused and, after a minute of thinking, continued, "Okay, I will come to see you through this, but I can't come until September." I took her hands and kissed them. I knew she was sacrificing herself for me, and I felt sad knowing how much she was giving up for me.

Adding to my confusion, I decided to try and visit my father, whom I had not seen since I was nine. I was not totally conscious of what I was doing when I walked up the stairs at the University of Sofia and knocked on his door. He responded, and I walked in his office.

"Can I help you?"

"Dad, it's me, Nina."

His face became pale, and his hands started to tremble. "Nina, is this you?"

"Yes, Dad, I just wanted to greet you and invite you to lunch if you are free." My voice was shaking, and I was avoiding to meet his eyes.

"That will be nice. It is almost lunchtime. We can go now."

We had lunch at a place close to the university. Our conversation was about my studies and work.

"I am very pleased to hear about you graduating with majors in Russian and French languages. But why don't you teach at the university? I can talk to the chairman of the Slavic department. By the way, I will be coming to Ann Arbor, Michigan, to attend the International Congress of Linguists next month."

"That's wonderful, Dad! Please call when you arrive. You will be staying with me."

"Nina, you know, when you went to America, I was interrogated by the police, but they let me go because I had no contact with you since you were little. I did not raise you, and I had no idea where you were."

"Dad, they fired Mom as an enemy to Communism for not raising me right. Luckily, they did not send her away."

"I am sorry. But she is all right now, and that's important. You know, your grandparents passed away," he continued. "I was in a hospital myself for a surgery of hernia when your grandfather fell and broke his leg. He developed pneumonia and died shortly thereafter. I took them to live with me. After your grandfather's death, your grandmother went to bed refusing to eat or drink and died soon after him. I feel so bad that I wasn't home to take care of them." We parted that evening without any bad feelings about the past.

A few days later, we all left Bulgaria. I walked in a daze behind my husband, holding the children's hands. He rented a car in Belgrade, and we traveled to Bosnia, where I met his entire family—two married sisters, his brother, and his mother. They were all very amicable, polite, and nice people, surrounding me and the children with a lot of attention, care, and love. His sisters shared that their father was very mean to my husband and not to the other children, which was probably the reason for his outbursts of anger.

We all returned to the States and continued to live as if everything was normal. One day, the doorbell rang, and a man served my husband the divorce papers. He took them quietly without saying a word and put them away. Days went by, until one day, I received a phone call from my father.

"Nina, I am in Ann Arbor staying with a professor from the University of Michigan. There is a gathering at his house tonight. I told him about you. Come if you are free."

I was excited and happy to hear that Dad was close by. I jotted down the address and drove to the professor's house, which was in Saline, Michigan. My father introduced me to all his colleagues, after which I asked him to get his luggage because I was taking him to my place. Dad did not object, and soon we were in Canton. I offered to help him unpack, and we both laughed viewing the contents of his suitcase. He had a loaf of bread, a Bulgarian yellow cheese, a pair of socks, underwear, and a couple of shirts.

"There was a strike at the airport in Italy, so I packed some food from home," he explained. Then he washed his socks, and soon we all turned in for the night. My husband did not act up in front of him, and life at the house was uneventful and peaceful. I believe he was in denial and, after being served the divorce papers, continued to live at the house as if nothing happened. Dad spent most of his free time typing. I cooked, we ate, and I drove him to lectures at the university and stayed to attend his lectures.

Dad arranged for a luncheon with the chairman of the Slavic department, who was thrilled to meet him. Halfway through lunch, Dad picked up the topic of me following in his footsteps. I could teach a class or two at the university, but the chairman mentioned the low pay for assistant teaching instructors, which ended the conversation. For the rest of the time at lunch, they both talked about linguistics and my father's books on Thracian language. I already spoke with Dad that with the way my personal life was, I needed an income to support myself and the children. I would have loved to teach French, Bulgarian, possibly Russian, and Serbian at the university, but that was not possible. While studying at the University of Michigan, I met a European lady in one of my French classes, and we became friends, as we had a lot in common based on our upbringing and views on life. Her husband was a doctor, and she found part-time teaching jobs in colleges in the area. Unfortunately, I did not have the luxury to work for my own satisfaction.

My husband knew how important my father was and behaved himself. All of us even took a trip to Chicago, visited the Sears Tower, and grabbed lunch at a restaurant nearby. Dad was amazed at the politeness of the servers, which I could understand, compared to the rude attitude of Bulgarian waiters at that time. In Communist Bulgaria, if you asked for something in a restaurant, you would receive a smart remark like "I have only two hands." The week went by fast. Dad left with the impression that my life was good. And everything seemed perfect on the surface. We lived in a new quad-level three-bedroom house, drove nice cars, and had more than enough food in the refrigerator.

It was the end of the summer of 1981, and this meant setting up schedules for the upcoming school year. My teaching certificate was probationary, and to make it permanent, I had to take a number of graduate classes, which made me think I might as well sign up in a master's degree program. The day after Dad left, I drove to Eastern Michigan University in Ypsilanti. I already knew what I wanted to study—international business and a foreign language. I was finally going to combine business and language classes, which was my dream from high school. The registration process was easy. I selected classes in economics and Spanish. Examining the curriculum, I marked the classes I needed to take each semester in order to graduate in May 1983. What made this program attractive was that it was offered only at a few universities in the country, and there was a placement opportunity to work overseas in a country speaking the language you chose.

Mom arrived in September 1981, as she promised, and I got us a two-bedroom university town house in Ypsilanti. Unexpectedly, my husband helped with the move, and soon we settled at the new place with me teaching during the day and studying in the evening.

My principal, the Catholic nun, was not pleased learning about my separation. She did not fire me but reduced my classes to bare minimum with nine thousand dollars annual salary. I could not survive on this pay, so Mom found a babysitting job, and I started teaching an evening class in Bulgarian at the University of Michigan.

Dad sent me textbooks and dictionaries for the students, and my class took off extremely well. I lectured with authentic stories of Bulgarian life with all cultural differences from north to south and from east to west. There were references to literature, art, architecture, music, dancing, and food throughout centuries of Bulgaria's rich history. While teaching Bulgarian language, I also introduced concepts of cultural trends and customs, and I touched on the evolution of the Bulgarian language with influences from France, Greece, and Turkey. The class became very popular and had the highest enrollment of classes in the Slavic department.

It was a tough schedule, and the only way I managed was by focusing on one day at the time. I had only a couple of hours with the children between teaching in high school and going to the university to take classes or teach. What was comforting was that the move from the house did not seem to affect the children. I was so proud of them being excellent students and behaving well in school. I reviewed their notebooks, books, and report cards every day, and their work was always perfect. Every evening, I thanked God for blessing me with kids who were responsible and doing so well in school. I was also happy to be back on university campus enjoying my evening language and business classes. Learning Spanish was easy because of similarities with French, and I liked my economics classes.

Thanksgiving that fall was skimpy, with baked turkey legs and sauerkraut. Mom made strudel for dessert. I had no time to breathe, but I was free and happy, living in peace. It was after the New Year in 1982 when I met G, a smooth-talker and very good writer in his thirties, saying all the things I wanted to hear, and showering me with weekly flower deliveries. Nonetheless, I attempted to reconcile with the kids' father, which was a huge mistake. There is a Bulgarian saying, "The wolf changes his skin, not his nature," which is very true. There was peace for a few days after my return to the family house, but not for long, I could never guess what mood my husband would be in after work. One afternoon was more than what I could take. He called from work with threats and accusations, which made me freeze with fear. I walked to Mom, who was cooking in the kitchen, and cried out, "Mom, pack all your clothes. I am packing mine and the children's. We are getting out of here." I didn't like seeing Mom nervous and stressed, but I had no choice. Mom hurried into her bedroom then grabbed the pot with the stew from the stove, and with a car packed to the top, I drove off not knowing where to go.

After driving for a while, I thought of calling the guy whom I met when I lived at the university housing in Ypsilanti. He sounded happy to have us. His house was close by in Plymouth, Michigan, and we arrived shortly, feeling safe for the night. It was close to the end of the school year, and the divorce was nearing. When it was finally over, my ex husband asked me if I felt bad. But I was completely numb; there was nothing left. A few days later, G proposed, and I accepted; it was a nice switch to be with somebody attentive to me, especially the children and Mom. We married at the courthouse in Plymouth. I hit the books that same day as it was final exam week at EMU. I was also getting ready for a trip to Mexico City for a summer scholarship program of Tulane University at Universidad Iberoamericana. This was a big honor as only a handful of students were participants in this program at one of the most prestigious Mexican universities based on high recommendations from their professors.

Discovering Mexico

I will always remember the date; it was June 26, 1982, when I departed for Mexico City. I was happy but also worried as I was leaving my mother with the children at G's house, whom I recently married. The kids were as cheerful as always, playing together and making new friends in the neighborhood. Mom assured me that she would watch over them, so off I went.

Getting on the plane, I felt a little apprehensive flying by myself to a different country with nobody meeting me. While looking around the cabin, I recognized an instructor from EMU sitting a few rows in front of me. I walked over to him, introduced myself, and asked him if he could help me with information about airport transfer and hotel in the city. He smiled and congratulated me for the scholarship that I was granted by Tulane University. We talked briefly, and he wrote down a name of a hotel he knew that was reasonable and safe.

"You don't need prior reservations," he said. "Just grab a cab from the airport and give them the address."

I returned to my window seat relieved. Now I could enjoy the view from the plane without worrying about my arrival and without being anxious. Below were the majestic Sierra mountains, a very imposing and beautiful sight of rigid cliffs and peaks. Soon we were flying over Mexico City, and as the plane circled in, observing its enormity, my heart started to beat fast. It was huge, bigger than New York City.

Upon landing, I did exactly what the man from EMU told me and found myself in the downtown area in front of a nice hotel. The room was small but clean and pleasant. I decided to take a walk as it was still daylight. I marched down the street curiously to explore the culture and the fashion, to hear people speaking Spanish, and to observe their behavior. All of a sudden, there was a man talking to me. I responded that I wanted to be alone, but he did not pay any attention to what I was saying. Then another one joined in talking to me, which quickly ended my walk. I ran up to my room and put the chair at the doorknob as I did a long time ago when first arriving in New York City.

Needless to say, the next day, I was first at the Universidad Iberoamericana, examining with interest the small buildings of classrooms and tropical flowers and vegetation in the yard. I felt at ease and smiled at students walking by. I could tell that the student population at the university was of affluent families as there were bodyguards accompanying some students. Later, I found out they were the president's children. I always felt at peace on university campuses. I took a deep breath, forgetting the size of Mexico City and focusing on the arrival of students and staff. I was curious to meet the other students and find out about the program. The information was very useful; it ranged from dress code to safety and food consumption. Since there were a lot of street food vendors especially at Taskenia metro station, the joke was that eating from them was like choosing your own decease. Then we were provided with a curriculum offering a variety of classes. I signed up for intermediary Spanish language and Mexican folk dancing since my thesis was on Mexican dancing and its significance in Mexican history and culture. The university also scheduled cultural trips on weekends. I picked up my class and weekend trip schedules and headed to my hostess's house, which was close by, a fifteen- to twenty-minute walk.

Doña Ana greeted me joyfully and showed me to my room. My roommate Julieta was in her early forties, very pleasant and talkative. We immediately clicked and shared stories of our past. Julieta was from Latin America, married with a grown-up daughter. We met the other two girls, Diane and Cindy, who were in the room next door. They were younger and single; Diane was engaged. Doña Ana had a boy and a girl attending the same university. They arrived around noon, and we all had lunch. Doña Ana explained the rules of the house: No visitors. Meals were served at 7:00 a.m. (breakfast),

1:30 p.m. (lunch, the big meal of the day, and if missed, no meal to replace it), and 7:00 p.m. (snacks, usually Mexican doughnuts, which I loved, and tea). I was staring at the woman's mouth trying to understand every word she was saying, and on the third day, I gained enough confidence to speak to her.

"Doña Ana, te puedo ayudar en la cocina?"

Doña Ana's face lit up. "No lo creo, hablas español."

From this moment, Doña Ana was my best Spanish instructor. My days were enjoyable with classes at the university. I loved my Spanish class, learning how to speak and write better and better. My folk dancing class was very pleasurable with the lively Mexican music and dynamic movements, plus it was a great exercise after sitting in classes all morning. Doña Ana cooked the most delicious Mexican meals for lunch, and in the afternoons, I usually joined other students to explore Mexico City, a magnificent place with old history and monuments of spectacular architecture. We loved to walk in Chapultepec Park and visit the castle. We discovered the National Museum of Anthropology and the Frida Kahlo Museum. We ventured in the historic district by Zócalo; visited the metropolitan cathedral, the Palacio de Bellas Artes, and the Palacio Nacional; and strolled down the pedestrian Calle Madero and the streets in Zona Rosa for its fashionable stores and gourmet restaurants.

We learned to avoid the evening rush hour at the metro as trains were packed to the point of police shouting, "Metese o matase!" There was a separate car for women, which we discovered later, since men on the train would pinch or feel women being so close to them. We found that out one evening returning home when Julieta screamed, "He pinched me!" at which the guys in our group surrounded her to avoid more problems. There were two crimes in Mexico City in the summer of 1982. The first one was a petty theft, which meant no loose jewelry as necklaces and keep wallets and purses in front of you. A guy from our group lost his camera one day as he had it over his shoulder. The second was attacks on women, not necessarily rape but groping them. And of course, I could not wear my sundresses in the city.

We made friends with Mexican students who invited us to glamorous parties with music, dancing, and fabulous treats usually held in courtyards with incredibly picturesque patios covered with lush, colorful tropical flowers and vegetation. One evening, we attended a Latin music concert, which was incredible, with bands changing every hour from different Latin American countries. The Mexican college guys reminded me of the ones I knew from Yugoslavia—good-looking, flirtatious, and very attentive. But I was married, and my going to parties was to enjoy the food, music, and dancing.

I called home every evening to check on the kids and Mom, and my new husband assured me that the kids were doing well playing with children in the neighborhood. On Saturdays, I woke up early to attend university-organized tour to miraculous sights such as the Pyramids of the Sun and the Moon in Teotihuaca (the place where gods were created) and we visited Tepotzotlán with its aqueduct and Jesuit church and the incredible sights of Cholula, Toluca, Tepoztlán, Tlaxcala, Puebla, and Taxco with their attractive cobblestone streets filled with silver jewelry shops. Saying goodbye to Mexico was hard as I fell in love with the people, the culture, and the history of this country.

New Beginnings

The fall of 1982 was extremely beautiful as I noticed again the golden and red colors of the leaves and relived the experience of visiting apple orchards for hot cider and doughnuts. I enjoyed life again, although there were problems with the high school principal, who, as a Catholic nun with a remarried teacher on staff, was openly hostile. She trimmed the French program to a minimum, but this did not affect the love I had for the students and for my subject.

The school year was going quickly with everyday work at the school and night classes at the university in Ypsilanti. The children adapted well to a new Lutheran school close to the house in Plymouth, Michigan. Vanesa became the star basketball player and was very protective of her younger brother. The classrooms were small with a couple of classes in one room, but this gave the kids more personalized attention. I was happy to see them bringing home papers and reports with excellent grades. Mom always had snacks for them after school, then they went playing in the small park by the house or by their friends. I was proud of them walking by themselves to school and occasionally stopping to visit G's mother. The elderly woman was paralyzed on the right side and lived alone in an apartment. She was always happy to see the kids and would treat them with cookies and candies. Her face always lit up seeing us on weekends and taking us out to dinner. I admired her positive attitude being in a wheelchair by herself and always smiling. I never asked why she lived alone; something like that should make you wonder. But I was young and accepted things the way they were.

It was spring again, and the big day came. I graduated from Eastern Michigan University with a master's degree in international economics and Spanish. I did not attend the ceremony as I was preg-

111

nant with Anabelle, and I didn't think I could stand up for too long. This time, there were job placement opportunities to work in businesses abroad. I could choose any Spanish-speaking country where I could work in advertising or business management. However, this was not an option for me, although it sounded very attractive. I always wanted to work in an international company, being able to use my business and language skills, but I could not do it with the family at that point of my life. So I returned to my work as a French teacher and organized for my students the trip to France and other countries in Europe, which I promised them the first year of my teaching. I was happy because I could take along Vanesa, who was eleven at the time. My mom took Erik with her to Bulgaria, where I knew the child was going to have fun with my cousin Ivan and his girlfriend. The kids finished great the school year with excellent grades, and that was very important for me to see them adjust so well. I saw off Mom and Erik to the airport and packed ourselves for the trip to France.

Arriving in Paris, I felt so happy observing how my students' eyes opened wide as we circled over Paris. At the airport, we were met by our bus driver who drove us through narrow Parisian streets to our hotel. Our program was packed with sightseeing tours and experiencing French culinary art as we raced through the country and other places in Europe.

"Madame C, this is incredible! Are we going up the Eiffel Tower?"

"Yes, guys, we are."

I could see my students' faces lighten up as we went up the tower, then we visited Louvre, running from painting to painting and taking pictures in front of *Mona Lisa*. We strolled down to Place de l'Étoile and Arc de Triomphe, said a French prayer in Notre-Dame de Paris, admired Paris from the steps of Sacré-Cœur in Montmartre, and absorbed the liveliness of the Latin Quarter. A separate visit to Palace of Versailles left my students speechless as this was the first palace they saw in their lives. It was such a good feeling to see them applying what I taught them in class by recognizing all the remarkable places of Paris and their place in history. The trip continued to the glorifying Loire Valley with its breathtaking castles of Chenonceau and Chambord, to name the most impressive ones with their rich history and splendid architecture. From there, we reached the lavender fields and the Pont du Gard aqueduct in Avignon, as well as the famous Pont Saint-Bénézet from the famous French song "Sur le pont d'Avignon" of Provence to the French Riviera. I knew we arrived at the French Riviera when all my students stood up shouting "Look!" pointing at the beaches—we were at Cannes, and the French women were without tops. And by evening, we reached our final destination in France—the city of Nice. The following days were mostly on the road—a lunch in Milano, dinner in Lucerne, breakfast in the Bavarian Alps. At the end of the trip, I sent my students home, escorted by a couple of parents.

Vanesa, my new husband, and I headed to Bonn, the capital of West Germany, to spend time with my father, who was a visiting professor and was lecturing at their university. Being with Dad after galloping through Europe was a delightful break. For the first time in my life, my father treated me by taking care of the hotel and restaurant bills. It wasn't just the money but the way he cared for me and Vanesa, making sure we had everything we needed. The hotel was centrally located, so he stopped and had breakfast, lunch, and dinner with us in between his lectures. The last day of our stay, he surprised me even more.

"Nina, here are tickets for you and Vanesa to fly to Sofia and spend time with your mother and Erik. I also left an envelope with money with your mother for you all to go for a few days to the Black Sea." I didn't know what to say, so he continued, "Don't be shy. I am enjoying all this. And you know, I don't like your new husband because he does not act like a man." Acting like a man meant paying the bills, and in European standards, a man should not be expecting somebody else to pay for them. G, when we met, was a maintenance supervisor, but his pay was not sufficient to take overseas trips.

Traveling to Bulgaria in 1983 was still risky, but I was hoping that there would be no problems since I already traveled there a couple of years ago. There were no questions at passport control. We were traveling on American passports, and our last names were American. G adopted both Vanesa and Erik to end the continuous law suits with the kids' father and his refusal to pay child support.

Mom met us at the airport, standing with Erik and my cousin Ivan by her side. Ivan picked up our luggage and jokingly said, "So this time, you are not bringing all your clothes." The next two weeks were splendid being with Mom, my aunt, my stepdad, Ivan, and his girlfriend. Sunny Beach at the Black Sea was as spectacular as ever with its sandy beaches, lined up with colorful umbrellas, hotels by the sea with open restaurant verandas serving the best of Bulgarian dishes of meat and vegetables with special spices baked in clay pots or barbecued meat on open pit. In the evenings, there was music and dancing, laughter and mingling with other tourists from all over Europe. It is times like this that remained in my heart forever, the closeness and warmth when surrounded and loved by family.

The new school year in the Fall of 1983 started with the well-known feeling of excitement for getting the kids settled in their classrooms and meeting the teachers. I was also happy to see my students and continue our journey in exploring French-speaking countries. On the day after Thanksgiving, we were getting ready to do Christmas tree shopping when my water broke. I was not due for another month. On November 27, 1983, Anabelle entered the world dramatically. I had an emergency Cesarian section surgery. There was no maternity leave offered by the Catholic high school, so I had to quit. Anabelle was not a quiet baby like her siblings; she was a screamer but was adorable with a red skin complexion, dark-brown hair, and sparkling dark eyes. The day after she was born, her father looked very perplexed.

"I should have told you, but there is American Indian blood in the family from my mother's side." I did not understand why it was such a big deal. Anabelle was so delightful.

"Well, we will have an Indian princess at home," I said jokingly.

Teaching in the Inner City of Detroit

Winter had settled in with the accumulation of snow and subzero temperatures. Spending six weeks with Anabelle and the children was a very happy time for me. There was a big hill in Plymouth, and I took Vanesa and Erik sledding on weekends. I can still see them running up the slope, pinky cheeks with radiant faces, and screaming with joy coming down. When I felt strong enough to be on my feet, I called all high schools in the area looking for a French teacher vacancy. The answer was the same: "Sorry, ma'am, we have a tenure teacher who will be with us for a long time." I researched and applied at numerous companies and organizations, but the responses were all negative. G also had a teacher's certificate for teaching social studies. Coming from work one day and seeing me with the list of schools I called, he said, "I can quit my job as a maintenance supervisor. It does not pay well anyways. And I'll go to Detroit to teach with you. The Detroit schools are always hiring new teachers."

It was a very cold January morning when we drove up to the Detroit Board of Education. Since it was the middle of the school year, the only available positions were for substitute teaching—for me, it was a middle school in the Latin part of town, and G was assigned to a different school. The next six months, I spent translating geography, science, and history lessons and teaching in Spanish so the kids could understand them. They were very polite and disciplined children and very appreciative of the extra work I did to help them comprehend their lessons. G, on the other hand, had issues. One day, picking me up, he looked very nervous and anxious. "There was an incident at the school. A kid went home and came back with a gun. I was teaching on the first floor, and he pointed the gun inside my classroom. Nobody got hurt, but I cannot go back to teach in Detroit. I quit." I did not know what to say. Everybody was silent at dinner, and the next day, I drove to Detroit by myself.

At the end of the school year, the HR officer at the Board of Education called me to his office.

"We have an opening for you to start teaching French at Kettering High School at the east side of Detroit. This will be a tenure position as you have taught for three years and you have a master's degree. Will you be interested?"

My eyes brightened up. "Of course I am."

"Then you need to meet the principal and the department head to get details about starting in the fall."

I'll never forget my first day teaching at Kettering High School. The school was by I-94 highway and Van Dyke Avenue, so it was easy to find it. I was greeted by police and security officers at the door who were checking the kids for guns and knives. Walking in the building was like going into a different world. This was an all-black community, and the kids were dressed properly, but it was obvious that they were poor. Lots of girls were wearing shower caps, and boys were with low-hanging jeans as the fashion at the time dictated. I could sense some curious looks my direction, to which I responded with a smile, and I kept walking to the second floor where the English and foreign language office was. Pausing in front of the door, I knocked and entered into a spacious room with tables and chairs. Behind a desk was a slim Caucasian lady with short silvery hair and a pleasant complexion in her late forties.

"My name is Nina, and I am the new French teacher."

The woman stood up and extended her hand. "Welcome, Nina. I am the department chair. French is the only foreign language we offer, and we are so happy to have you." She handed me a few booklets and paperwork, saying, "Here is the description of the French program requirements, which will be a guide for your lesson plans. This is your schedule for teaching freshman to senior year along with the list of students assigned to you and a booklet for the school regulations as mandated by the Board of Education, but I understand you have been in the system for six months, so you are well acquainted with them." She handed me the package and continued, "Let me introduce you to the principal, and then there will be a school assembly. The classes for today are short and mostly to get to know the students and explain to them what your program is about."

We walked to the principal's office. He was a tall African American man with a friendly face.

"Welcome to our school. My door is open for anything you need." And we all headed together to the gym, where students and teachers were waiting for the principal's speech at the beginning of the school year.

As I expected, the freshman class was like an unruly herd, loud and not paying attention to what I was saying. At that time, the football coach peeked in, and I saw everybody startled, staring at the door. The coach was of medium height, a very well-built African American man. He walked in the room, nodded at me, and addressed the students, "I came to tell you that if you disrespect your French teacher, you are disrespecting me, and I will see you and hold each one of you personally responsible for any disruptive behavior. Are we clear?" They responded "Yes, sir" in one voice, and he walked away.

I had five classes, and on the first day, after taking roll, I spoke about my life growing up in the oppressive Communist regime of Bulgaria, my escape, and my arrival in America with twenty dollars and a suitcase, never giving up my dream to return to college and finally becoming a French teacher. At first, they were all quiet, and then I heard their stories.

"Madame, we live in houses whose roofs leak, with no furniture, mattresses on the floor, chair, and table. Every morning coming to school is a challenge because we can be attacked and stabbed for no reason. We do not wear sneakers or sportswear of known names like Nike because we will be beaten and robbed in the street."

Looking at their faces, I felt like crying, but I remained composed. I knew there was sadness in my eyes when I started to talk. "I am here for you. I will help you get out of this neighborhood."

"But how, ma'am?" a girl asked.

"By educating you and showing you the way out of this community. You will be successful only if you study. Your knowledge and your diploma will be your ticket to a nice life."

That first day laid the foundation for our friendship, with mutual understanding of our responsibilities. In the next weeks, I understood that my approach to teaching in Detroit had to be much different than that at the Catholic school in Ann Arbor. Advance classes were on the same level as the freshman year. We had to use verbs, nouns, pronouns, prepositions, etc. to compose sentences in French, and the children did not know anything about grammar concepts. It was sad to see that ninth-grade students were conjugating the verb *to be* as *I be*, *you be*, and so on. I knew I had to teach the kids English and French grammar at the same time. We started to build simple sentences, adding adjectives, nouns, and prepositions. But I also taught them about the world and life in French-speaking countries. They were all eager to know how children their age lived abroad, how their houses and schools looked like, what they studied, what they liked, and about their families. I brought in pictures from my trip with the students from Ann Arbor, telling stories about each one of them. We had cultural days when I brought in crepes, and we listened to French music as well as songs and dances they liked. I wanted to take them badly on a trip, which, unfortunately, did not materialize because of unrest in Paris and a state department travel advisory to avoid travel to France.

During the school year, we had parent-teacher conferences, and the lines in front of my desk were the longest. They were mostly the children's mothers, and I could see excitement in their faces, observing them talk in low voices to one another while waiting. Each parent was listening very attentively to what I had to say about their child, taking notes of their grades and assignments. It made me extremely happy to see the interest they had in their kids' studies. French was an elective, and my students had to apply themselves to stay in my classes. But it wasn't the requirement that kept them motivated; it was the spark I gave them to learn about the world. I could see in the eyes of the parents the anguish about their children's progress. "How is she or he doing, ma'am?" was the first question they asked. They knew that education was the only salvation for their children. Their eyes lit up learning that their son or daughter were on top of their assignments with good to excellent grades. Each one of them offered me support for anything regarding their child or the school. They were sincere, simple people who wanted the best for their kids. Upon leaving, I shook each one of their hands, assuring them that all my students were already on the right path to become responsible and successful individuals. The end of the school year was emotional, saying goodbye for the summer and instructing the children to stay safe.

In the fall of 1985, we moved to Plymouth Township. Vanesa started her freshman year at Plymouth Canton High School, and Erik his first year in middle school. We all needed to adjust to a new routine. I was leaving the house early in the morning, and the kids had to get ready and go to school on their own, which was about a mile away for both of them. Erik was riding his bike, and Vanesa walked, which scared me, especially when it rained and snowed. Anabelle's father was changing jobs from painting to drafting. For some reason, he could not get along with people at work. His only responsibility was to drop off Anabelle in the morning at the day care.

My second year at Kettering High School started with a double enrollment, which I discovered as soon as I walked into my first class; there were not enough desks for everybody, so some students were sitting on the floor, leaving me a small path from the door to the desk in front of the room. I looked at the students' list—sixty names—and they were all quiet, waiting for me to start the class. All of a sudden, a male, drunk or high, walked in the room and said in a slurry speech, "I heard about you. I want to be in your class." I quietly explained to him that his name was not on my list and that we needed to go to the principal to straighten this out. He followed me, and I left him in the principal's office. Later, I found out that he wasn't even a student but snuck in the building. He was a young man but, sadly enough, was already on the wrong track. The principal called me to the office and showed concern that this could have ended in a very tragic way. Later, in the teachers' lounge, all teachers were discussing what happened, and I learned that some of them carry guns in their briefcases. Somehow, I did not feel threatened or in danger from this young man; I felt sad and bad because he obviously came for help, and I wasn't able to do much about it. The school hired a second French teacher, Bob, Caucasian and gay, who was very pleasant and adopted my style of teaching, saying laughingly, "I don't need to invent a style. Yours obviously works, so I will borrow it." This made the transfer of students to him much easier.

This year, I volunteered to be a chaperone for the sophomores' roller-skating event. I wasn't out of the car when a student yelled "Gun!" and pushed me to the ground. Nobody got hurt, but that ended out-of-school activities for these children. It was a stupid incident about a girl. My students did not show any disappointment; they were so much used to being denied things in their lives. School life continued as usual. I was happy to observe the students' progress and enjoyed seeing their happy faces every day.

Nonetheless, I did not give up my desire to use my knowledge in business, and I talked to the principal about teaching a business class. Unfortunately, my teacher's certificate specified teaching all subjects in middle school but only French language in high school, and I could not teach any of the high school business classes. I was curious to see what business careers were in demand outside education, so I started to look at help wanted ads in the Sunday paper—the internet was not in use in the year 1985. There were pages and pages of accounting positions, so an idea popped up in my head—I would go back to college and earn a business administration degree with accounting major. At the time, it made sense to go back and get a business degree in a field that I already worked as business manager in Austria and bookkeeper in Ann Arbor. After researching business schools in the area, I selected Cleary College, which was in Ypsilanti between my two former universities—University of Michigan in Ann Arbor and Eastern Michigan University. I scheduled a meeting with the dean the following day and enrolled in the business program starting January 1985. As with my prior degrees, I made a plan of the classes I needed to take each semester in order to graduate in May 1987.

I knew that the new 1986 year was going to bring changes in my life. I was happy going back to college and taking more business classes. I enjoyed my first desk job in the States as a bookkeeper and then at the photo studio in Ann Arbor (a summer job while in college), so majoring in accounting seemed to be a very smart choice. My days were long—teaching early in the morning, picking up Anabelle from day care, driving home for dinner, spending a couple of hours with Vanesa and Erik, and heading to Ypsilanti for my night classes at Cleary. There were times in the evening when I packed and took all the kids with me to the university. Vanesa was old enough to watch Anabelle, and Erik found his own ways to keep himself busy. Driving in the winter was what made it difficult and sometimes dangerous. It was especially scary in the fog when I could not see past the hood of the car. At times like this, I told myself, "God is with you. It will be all right. You know the road. Just go slowly."

On the home front, Vanesa and Erik were exceptional, not missing a day at school and keeping up their good grades. I was very proud of them and thanking God for keeping them safe and well while I was at work. School year 1985–1986 finished well for everybody. I shook hands with each one of my students and took my principal's advice to go and smell the roses. Heading to Anabelle's day care, I decided instead of going home to take her to Kensington Park, which had a lake with a sandy beach. Anabelle's eyes opened wide seeing the sand. "Mommy, what a big sandbox!" she shrieked. *Yes, this is what it meant to smell the roses,* I thought, *spend the summer with my children in nature.*

Back at the house, I planned a trip with all the children in Northern Michigan on Lake Huron. Packing up the van with sports and beach wear, toys, food, and drinks, we headed to the cottage that we rented for the week. There were other families with kids, and Vanesa and Erik played all day long with them in the water with water tubes. In the morning and evening, we enjoyed the beauty of the lake at sunrise and sunset. At the end of the week, I planned a little detour and traveled to Mackinac Island for the best fudge in the world. I took my time driving back, stopping at a deer park, having lunch at a restaurant by the water, and stopping to buy smoked fish and cheese from food stands along the road.

The rest of the summer, I buried myself in the books as I took a full load of summer classes—finance, banking, and fund accounting. It was a hot summer, and the house did not have air-conditioning. I still remember clutching my teeth and perspiring studying late at night. These were serious subjects taught in six instead of twelve weeks in the regular semesters, and the intensity made me want to scream, but I dealt with it in silence. I studied tenaciously with so much passion and zeal that I finished the summer semester with all As. So far, my GPA was straight 4.

The school year in the fall of 1986 started as usual. I had a couple of months to get the freshman year students adjust to high school. Coming from middle school, they looked like an unruly crowd, not sure what the difference was to be in high school. One case in particular bothered me, as a male student sitting in the front, not talking to anyone but refusing to work, became extremely surprised for failing my class. "But why are you failing me? I am not causing any trouble." I found out that the boy was illiterate; he was passed along because of good behavior. Working with his counselor, we had him placed in remedial classes to catch up with English and math.

My method of teaching continued to be the same. I taught about French-speaking countries in the world and the life people lived at those remote parts of the earth. Most of the kids did not know anything beyond their crime- and poverty-ridden neighborhoods. Opening the world to them made them realize that they had to study hard to be able to experience life at those enchanted places like the French Caribbean islands, Tahiti, the former African French colonies. My lessons taught them about the diversity of people from different parts in the universe. Being that young, they were interested in French music for teenagers, so I organized for them cultural days with experience of French food and music—I cooked crepes and played French songs.

One morning, as I was teaching, I heard sirens and knew something was very wrong. I rushed to the teachers' lounge at the end of the hallway. One of the male English Caucasian teachers was badly beaten by a student and taken to the hospital. *What happened?* was my first thought. This man was young and very easygoing and was getting along with students, so I could not figure out what triggered such violence. "He placed this kid on probation, and because there were so many prior detentions and other probations, the student would be expelled from all Detroit schools. He didn't know about it," a colleague said. Later, I found out that the man survived but had numerous face surgeries. The incident was shocking for all students and staff, but soon we resumed work as usual. Violence was a part of life in Detroit, and the children were used to it. My only goal was to see them graduate from high school and enroll in college.

I had students who were extremely intelligent like my teacher's aide Francesca. She was an exceptional girl, very smart, polite, punctual, and reliable. One winter, I noticed that she was a little chubby, but I thought it was because of lack of exercise. Everybody gains weight in Michigan when it gets cold. But that wasn't the case. Her sister confided in me that Francesca was pregnant, which made me sad. She knew that I would not approve and did not want to confide in me; she was right. I called her immediately.

"Francesca, why did you do such an irresponsible thing? How can you get pregnant at this stage in your life? What about your future? You promised to go to college. And what about the future of a child not knowing who the father is and growing with a mother on food stamps?"

Francesca shriveled as I was giving her the facts of life about raising kids. "I know I messed up, but I was accepted at Wayne State University, and I will study. It will be difficult, but I will not give up." I hugged her. Students were entering the classroom, the bell rang, and the class began. I was different from other teachers congratulating pregnant students. I could not congratulate them for destroying their lives and that of an unborn child.

I need to add that not all my students were well-behaved; I also had defiant students. Maurice, who was on the football team, ignored all my requests to work and not talk to students around him. Because of his failing grades, he was kicked out of the football team. He came to class crawling on his knees from the door to my desk, begging me to change his grades. That was tough as I knew he was young and not fully grown to realize that there were consequences for bad behavior. But at the same time, the rest of the students were watching, and I had to react. I asked him to stand up (he was taller than me) and to look me in the face.

"Listen, Maurice, there are things in life which can be corrected when done on time. Your request is not timely. I am a reasonable person, and I can't do that. Look at your classmates. It is not fair to them." He did not respond; he just turned away and left. There was absolute silence to the end of the hour, I decided that because of the strenuous situation, it was appropriate to do writing exercises. To my surprise, Maurice started to come see me at the end of each day telling me how his classes were. I listened carefully and encouraged him to never give up his dream about football.

There was another incident that totally blew my mind. One of my excellent female students stopped coming to school. Her counselor could not find her at any of the addresses on file. "There is no phone, and it is dangerous to drive around the neighborhood looking for this girl," he told me. And one day, she appeared and walked straight up to me. "I am sorry I was absent, but I had to run away from my house. My uncle was on crack and was chasing me. He wanted to hurt me. I was lucky to manage to sneak out and take a bus to the other end of town. I live with my aunt now, and I am safe." She was almost a 4.0 student with perfect attendance. Her counselor excused her absences, and I noticed that soon she started to relax and get back to her studies.

I enjoyed teaching at Kettering High School because I could see that I could make a difference in the kids' lives. And that was what they were—just tall kids in need of guidance and direction. They didn't mind when I took their earphones or I had them write ten times that they should not talk and bother their classmates. And I made sure that my classroom was safe. There was a school policy to keep the doors unlocked during class, but I always locked them. My classes with windows were on the upper floors, so there was a slim chance of bullets reaching the classrooms, but one of my classes was in a room without windows. One day, walking in this room, I almost got hit by a flying object. The lights were out, and the teacher, a white male of older age with all-white hair and somewhat overweight, was hiding behind the desk. Some of his students turned off the lights and started to throw books at him. "What's going on here?" I yelled out, holding the door open. The commotion immediately stopped with students sneaking out the door. Maintenance fixed the light switch, and I taught with no problems. But the image of this man with sweaty red face and puffy eyes wide open with fear would not leave my mind. I started to seriously think about the difficulties of teaching at old age with a generation gap between me and the students.

There was another time when I had to intervene with students in the room next door. They had a substitute, an elderly white female, and were completely wild. The noise from the room was tremendous as we could hear objects hitting the walls or desks. I walked over to see what was going on and found the teacher sitting quietly while students were throwing anything they could find around them, and a couple of them were smoking pot. The noise subsided when they saw me, but as soon as I left, it picked up again. *I have a very good relationship with my students,* I thought to myself, *because I am young and they can relate to me. What will happen when I get older? Will I have the same issues as these older teachers?*

I was finishing the last semester at Cleary with only one B in income tax preparation for individuals, corporations, and partnerships, which later I found very ironic. The professor jokingly said as I told him that this was my only B, "You need one B. It is not normal to have a four-point average for a degree in business with accounting major." Then he added, "Besides, I do not give As, so you have one of the best grades in the class." Because of my high grades, my name was listed in books like *Who's Who among Students in American Universities and Colleges*, which made my mother very proud. This was my third university degree, which I earned in two years. But this was the first time that I attended my graduation ceremony wearing a gown and a hat, waving at my children and my mother.

Cleary College held a job fair, and attending it determined the path of my career and my life. I stopped at all tables and met with representatives of businesses and government offices. The IRS representative was a man in his early forties, medium built, with glasses and small moustache. His presentation was everything that I ever wanted to hear. I was immediately intrigued hearing details about the revenue agent career. The man explained the mission and vision of the Service, emphasizing fairness, honesty, and integrity. He proceeded by describing all phases of the training program and job appointments in different areas nationwide and internationally. This presentation was extremely appealing as I did not feel confident in dealing with tax law application after taking a couple of classes at Cleary College. He also explained that there would be a background investigation and an employee tax audit, which I understood was a condition of being employed.

"Antonina, what are your particular interests as IRS offers tremendous opportunities in various areas such as computers, engineering, international tax law, education, as well as promotions? Hiring is at grade 7 with one year probation during which you need to complete successfully classroom and on-the-job training. There is advancement every year thereafter until you become grade 11. Following grades are competitive based on performance and successful presentation at interviews in answering correctly technical questions."

"Sir, I am extremely impressed with the training program, and my dream job has always been to work in the international business area. I am very much interested in the revenue agent position at the Internal Revenue Service."

"Tell me something about yourself, your current job, your studies," he asked.

My eyes lit up as I started to describe my job as a French teacher in the inner city of Detroit and working with young adults in need of help. "Sir, I love my job as a teacher, but I need to grow. I have a master's degree in international trade and Spanish and currently completed another bachelor degree in business administration with major in accounting. My GPA is 3.9 as I have one B. While working as a bookkeeper at a bookstore and a photo studio in Ann Arbor, as well as an office manager at a manufacturing facility in Vienna, Austria, I discovered that I like working with numbers."

"Fantastic!" His voice picked up, and he looked me straight in the eyes. "Here is the application package, which you could leave with me today."

My face must have been glittering with joy. I grabbed the package, moved to an empty table, and eagerly started to fill in all information. "Sir, thank you for the opportunity," I said with enthusiasm, shaking the man's hand and heading toward the hallway.

I was telling the students goodbye at the end of the school year in 1987 not knowing that this would be the last time seeing them. As usual, it was a very emotional day as I was more than a teacher to them. I was their support; I was their spokesperson. There was love and gratitude in their eyes as I wished them a safe summer, and safe in this neighborhood meant staying alive.

I spent the first week of summer vacation enjoying the children. Having breakfast with them was a privilege after a long year away from home from early in the morning and studying at night. Then I decided to check the job market and contacted a dozen of companies with entry-level accounting positions. The problem was that most places were requiring two to three years of experience even for entry-level accounting jobs. I had a couple of lengthy interviews and written exams at Little Caesars for an accounting position, which I was told was filled by a more experienced individual. I applied at government agencies, like the US Commodity Futures Trading Commission and the Food and Drug Administration, and I already left my application at the Internal Revenue Service. The position that I aspired for was the Revenue agent for the federal tax administration.

Correspondence in 1987 was primitive by modern standards— it was done through the mail. Toward the end of June, I received a letter from the US Commodity Futures Trading Commission, which was very promising. A gentleman from New York City was offering to interview me in Detroit. I accepted it and received a confirmation for the date, time, and location for the meeting. Arriving extra early, I was greeted by a man in his late forties with slightly gray hair, high cheekbones, with glasses, and of medium height.

"Hello, Antonina, thank you for accepting this interview. I read about your credentials, and I must say they are impressive. I am very pleased to meet you."

"Thank you, sir, for the opportunity," I answered timidly.

"Well, I am impressed with your achievements, which you pointed out in your résumé. You studied in Europe and now currently hold two bachelor degrees, one in business administration, and a master's degree in international business. You graduated with honors all three times, and your last GPA is 3.90 with only one B. Very impressive. My question is, why was there a period of seven years' gap before you resumed your studies?" I felt at ease and gave a brief description of my life when I arrived in America, followed by raising three children. When I finished, the man looked at me and said, "You are hired. Please show up at this address in New York City at nine a.m. next Monday." I felt so excited realizing that my hard work was recognized, and I was offered a very attractive position.

My mother accompanied me to New York City, and we stayed at the apartment of people she knew from Bulgaria. The place was bug infested and shabby, although at a good location. We arrived on Saturday, which gave me a chance to look at the Sunday newspaper's classified ads for rentals and homes for sale. Based on the entry-level government salary, I estimated I could afford to live at a distance of two to three hours outside the city, which meant a working day of fifteen hours away from home. Spending the weekend at the bug infested New York city apartment of my mother's friend and looking at the reality of an impossible commute to work, I started to get discouraged. I particularly did not like seeing kids chained to one another taking a walk in the streets of New York City after being used to the parks and open spaces where my children played in Michigan. Early Monday morning, I called and declined the position. The gentleman was disappointed, saying that they had an office prepared for me and that he had newspapers with housing information. We left New York, and I was actually happy to be back at our suburban Plymouth Township home. Looking back, who knows, maybe I could have settled well in New York City with the assistance of this very pleasant gentleman.

I renewed my search for accounting positions, and by mid-July, I came across an entry-level accounting position at a small CPA firm in West Bloomfield. The owner reviewed my résumé, and after a brief interview, he smiled and said, "You are hired. The starting salary is ten dollars per hour. I do not offer insurance." I accepted the position, and he took me on a tour. It was a house converted into business, with a waiting room, main office, kitchen, and bathroom facilities on the first floor. I met the other accountants—a guy and two women in offices on the second floor. I was provided with a desk in an office that I shared with one of the women. The staff appeared to be very pleasant and friendly from the secretary to my colleagues. The kitchen was supplied with snacks and drinks available to all employees (I haven't stopped noticing food since my days of hunger in Vienna).

My first day at the firm was very busy as well as challenging. The owner assigned me accounts of different entities—sole proprietorships, partnerships and their partners, corporations for their tax preparation. I spent the day reviewing files and taking notes of their current filing requirement. They all had extensions for their personal and business returns, which meant they all needed preparation of partnership, corporations, and individual tax returns. I had to think fast on how to approach the return preparation of my clients in the most efficient way possible. I decided to make a schedule and placed their names with contact numbers on a calendar based on the complexity of their last year's tax returns. Next, I jotted down questions about their business operations, record keeping, and needed documents, as well as specific accounts and items that I came across that needed clarification or seemed peculiar and whatever changes might have occurred during the taxable year. At the end of the day, I met with the owner and presented him with my plan. He smiled and nodded in approval. "Very well, Nina, excellent approach to handling new clients. Reviewing their files and learning about their businesses and, most importantly, their filing history is a great start." That evening, I returned home tired but in a very good mood, realizing that my boss was satisfied with my work. On the way home, I turned on the radio in the car to the first rock station and started to sing, "You are the champion."

I arrived early at the office on the next day, stopping for a minute to enjoy the view of the yard with blossoming flowers and chirping birds. I walked in the kitchen, made coffee, and headed to my desk. Being all alone, I had the chance to quickly review my notes from the previous day and gather enough courage to start making phone calls, introducing myself as the new accountant in charge of their tax returns and scheduling appointments. The day went by fast, getting to know people on the phone and setting meetings. I was extremely happy to find out that everybody was genuinely friendly, easy to talk to, very accommodating, and eager to provide necessary information and documents. I peeked in my boss's office on the way out. "I am all set. I have all meetings lined up starting tomorrow with a couple of appointments."

The summer of 1987 went by fast. I was the first one at the office preparing myself for a busy schedule ahead of me with appointments, record keeping, paperwork, tax law research, and return preparation. What really mattered was the relaxed work atmosphere and the cordial and supportive relationship with my colleagues and staff. They all worked as a team, and whenever there was a tax or accounting question, it was resolved in a group setting. A man in his early thirties was the go-to person as the senior CPA, and he was always glad to assist. I wasn't sure of tax law application in all situations. I did not feel that the couple of classes provided me with enough knowledge, and I lacked confidence when it came to partnership issues. I remember the first time I approached him.

"Mike, this is the first time I am doing a like-kind exchange. Can you check if my computations are correct?"

At which he put down his work, asked about the documents, threw a glance at my work paper, and responded with a smile, "You are doing great. No need to check with me."

There was a library, which I used for research, and I eagerly read the accounting magazines to be on top of current events. I remember wrestling with adjusting entries for accrual taxpayers (yes, wrestling, because I needed more information and review of past files to ensure that the entries were correct). Meeting with clients was enjoyable as I learned about their business operations and record keeping. The owner used to take each one of us for lunch to discuss our work rather than scheduling meetings in the office. This contact with the owner in a relaxed atmosphere was very effective as I shared the status of my work, my findings, and my opinion about efficiency in return preparation at ease. During these lunches, I learned a lot about my clients, the peculiarities and requirements of their businesses, and tax laws, especially for partnerships applicable to them, which seemed complicated.

I was content getting experience in subject matters that I enjoyed—accounting and tax law. But I missed the children and my mother. Being totally immersed in work, I had no time for walks in the park, swimming, or simply quietly enjoying their company. One day in August, I came home tired as usual. I knew there was something new as my mother was smiling, holding a letter in her hands. "Look, Nina, it's a letter from the Internal Revenue Service."

I grabbed it and started to read eagerly, skimming through the lines to get to the important part. "Mom, they are calling me for an interview. You know this is the dream job I wanted for so long."

That August morning was different. Driving to the CPA office, I felt uplifted, seized by an indescribable feeling of inner happiness. My interview was at 11:00 a.m., and I preferred to finish some work rather than wait in anticipation of the time to leave. Needless to say, I was running late, so I drove seventy-five miles per hour on Lodge Freeway in Detroit, where the speed limit was fifty-five. God was on my side. I arrived on time, dressed in my accounting outfit of dark-blue skirt, white blouse, and black shoes. The receptionist smiled at me and handed me a paper and a pen to take notes if needed. Two men greeted me as I walked into the interview room—one in his forties, of medium height and posture, with short brown hair and a serious but pleasant look and the other in his fifties, tall and big, with wide shoulders and slightly silver hair.

"Hello, Antonina, our names are Mr. C and Mr. T. We will ask you a few questions which are not tax or accounting related. You will get results from the interview in two weeks, and if no questions, let's start."

It seemed that they knew about my work and studies from my application package as the younger man asked the first question, "You are a policeman regulating traffic, and two cars are driving way over the speed limit—the one in the first lane is an old car driven by a woman with children and the other a new Porsche in the third lane driven by a young man. You cannot stop both cars. Which one will you stop?"

Funny they are asking this question as I broke the speed limit driving here, I thought to myself. "I will stop the woman as she is endangering the lives of the children, and being in the first lane with cars entering the ramp, she is running the risk of creating an accident."

"So you are not going to stop the rich guy in the Porsche? He is rich and can pay the fine easier."

"No, sir," I responded. "Being rich has nothing to do with the more hazardous driving on the road."

"Very well. Next question, there is a procedure which you need to follow, and your manager is not applying it correctly. Will you tell him/her that they are wrong?"

"No, sir," I responded, looking both men in the eyes. "I will not tell my manager directly, but I will ask to see him/her in their office or, even better, in the coffee room or lunchroom and provide him or her with written documentation of the details and facts regarding the procedure." The remaining questions were of the same nature, dealing with honesty, loyalty, and ways to communicate. One question was about Oliver North, whether I approved of his behavior. "He is a Marine, sir, and he will follow orders as told." The man smiled, and with this, my interview was completed. I left the McNamara Federal Building in great spirits and was just as happy as I was after my interview at the American embassy in Vienna. I was extremely impressed by the gentlemen from the IRS, as I felt at ease sharing my views of fairness and honesty. I could sense their approval of my understanding of law enforcement and justice. They also explained the revenue agent position and the different phases in training, which I already knew about from the recruiter at Cleary College.

I was walking in a daze for the next couple of weeks, completing all my tasks at the office, but not fully conscious of my surroundings. The senior CPA included me in a team for conducting an independent audit of a company and gave me the opportunity to apply what I knew about writing an auditor's opinion. I continued to be happy with my accounting position, until one day when I received the long-awaited and desired letter from the IRS. I was accepted for the revenue agent position grade 7 because of my high grades; otherwise, entry-level position started at grade 5. September 27 was the day I started work at the federal building. I was ecstatic, reading the letter multiple times, jumping with joy, and shouting with tears of joy. "I got it! I can't believe it, but it's true." My annual salary decreased by ten thousand dollars of what I was making as a teacher in Detroit, but it didn't matter. I was proud to join the internationally recognized government agency known for destroying crime from Al Capone times.

I had time to give notice at the CPA firm and to the principal of Kettering High School. The following day, I walked anxiously in my boss's office of the CPA firm and without any hesitation started to speak: "Good morning, sir, I would like to thank you for the opportunity you gave me to work as an accountant at your firm. I enjoyed a lot learning and improving my skills as my tax knowledge is just narrowed to taking a couple of college courses. You have created an office of an ideal working environment with a team of intelligent and pleasant colleagues who accepted me and made me welcome. I extremely value your professionalism, encouragement, and support that you provided me for preparing tax returns. I am saying all this because there is something I need to share with you. Prior to starting work here, I applied at the Internal Revenue Service. I had an interview a couple of weeks ago, and they offered me an entry-level revenue agent position."

At which time my boss responded, "Nina, you are a fast learner, and I really appreciate you working for me. I will match benefits such as health insurance and paid leave. I need you to stay."

I felt bad; I could not respond and just thanked him for his time and went to my desk. I was working for one of the most agreeable and accommodating people in the world, and it was extremely difficult to leave. The rest of the day, I muddled through my tasks for the first time, not being able to concentrate. The next day, I decisively stepped into my boss's office and started to speak distinctly in an even tone.

"Frank, this is one of the hardest things I need to do in my life, but I need to give you a two-week notice. I know you are providing me with everything an employee could ask for, but the IRS is offering an extensive training and opportunities which I can't pass up. The two tax preparation classes I had at college don't make me feel confident enough to be able to handle successfully an accounting position."

Frank raised his head. "This is something I can't offer you, Nina. I wish you good luck."

I sighed as I felt bad and uttered again words of gratitude. I parted with everybody in the office, thanking them for being the best people to work with, handed in the keys for the building to the secretary, and walked out. The air was fresh, and the wind gently caressed my face. I felt at peace, sat in my car, and drove home in silence. I did not feel like listening to music. I had a long and tired face when I walked in the kitchen. As always, Mom looked at me with concern when she saw me worn out.

"I did it, Mom. It took me two days to quit. I had a wonderful boss, and it wasn't easy to just leave."

"Don't take it so hard," Mom responded. "You need to follow your dreams. Don't be afraid to look forward to your future. The man will find a replacement for you." Mom knew how to comfort me with simple words, and somehow, everything seemed all right.

I had to do one more thing—give my resignation at the high school. The principal was not happy as the first thing he said was, "Why didn't you quit at the end of the last school year so we could find a replacement easier?"

"Sorry, sir, I was just offered the job. I had no idea this was going to happen back in June." I felt bad about leaving my students, but I hoped I made a difference in their lives and touched their hearts to have them continue with their education.

Being off for a couple of weeks before starting work at the IRS gave me a chance to relax and spend time with my family. I was thrilled to sit on the porch watching Anabelle ride her tricycle. She was only three and had these chubby red cheeks, wavy dark hair, and devilish brown eyes. I couldn't help but smile looking at her making noise going up and down the sidewalk with a little girl from across the street. Vanesa and Erik were already in school, and I was happy to see them off in the morning and be home when they got back.

One day, as I was having my morning coffee, enjoying the sun on the patio, the phone rang. It was the new French teacher at Kettering High School. "Ms. C, I wouldn't bother you at home, but I am desperate. The students don't want to have anything to do with me. They want you. I have been crying every day since school started. Could you please come and talk to them?"

I was quiet, feeling the pain in the woman's voice and having a heartache visualizing the kids' faces learning that I left. I felt very sad as I said in a low voice, "I don't think it's a good idea for me to come. That will disturb them more. Could you please tell them that my message to them is to study because education is the only ticket to success, and I want them to be successful doctors, lawyers, scientists. You sound like a very caring teacher. They will turn around. Give them some time."

This was one of the most difficult decisions in my life, but I knew that seeing them would be very emotional and would not help. The lady hung up, and I remained motionless for some time. I shared what happened with my mother. We all had a quiet dinner that night.

Realization of My Career Dream

The day I waited for so long finally came. On September 27, 1987, I got up extra early to start a new life as a revenue agent. A lot of emotions were going through me, but there was this distinct feeling making me anxious, nervous, apprehensive. I could feel that destiny was about to take me to the world of importance and high calling.

"Nina, wait!" Mom yelled, carrying a bucket of water and pouring it in front of the car for good luck. I waved and speeded to I-94 highway to beat the morning rush.

I could feel my heart beating as I showed to the security guard my appointment letter. The man smiled and pointed to the elevators. Stepping off the elevator, I joined a group of about eighty people to be sworn in as federal employees and directed to a training classroom. The swearing-in ceremony was solemn and emotional, pledging loyalty, devotion, and dedication to serve the public with respect and dignity. Walking into the training classroom, I quickly glanced at its setup. There were six tables with five seats at each one, and as usual, I chose to sit in the front. I looked around and noticed that most of the new agents were very young, recent graduates in their early twenties. I was thirty-seven, which made me feel old, but I spotted two other women who looked close to my age. Later, they became my best friends and support group at work. One was from Benton Harbor, and the other who was of German origin was from Brighton. Our instructors walked in, and I was pleasantly surprised to recognize two of them from my interview. Both of them nodded at me, and I smiled back, already feeling relieved.

"Good morning, Revenue Agents," the medium-height, brown-haired man addressed us. "My name is Mr. C, and I will be one of your instructors. Mr. L and Mr. T will also be your instructors. We are all group managers, and we will be taking turns in lecturing and conducting practical exercises. I would like to welcome you to the Internal Revenue Service. From now on, you will be providing one of the most important service to our country. Your duty will not only be to ensure that businesses pay their fair share of taxes but you will also be conducting investigations of tax crimes. This classroom training is for individuals and sole proprietorships. It will last three months with daily instructions and tests every Friday. You will need to score 75 percent and above at each of the tests as one of the probationary requirements for the position. I do not think there will be problems with test scores as you all have grade point averages above 3.5. We were very selective in picking your group.

"There will be simulated examinations as well as a week of tax research at the law school of the University of Michigan. Upon completing classroom training, you will go to your assigned exam groups and will be performing audits under the supervision and guidance of the on-the-job instructor, a senior agent with grade 12 or 13. Upon completing that practical training, you will be working on your own for six months. Your phase 2 training will be for C corporations with one month of classroom and two months of on-the-job training. Progressing from there, you will enter phase 3 training for subchapter S corporations and partnerships. Beyond this point, you will be fully trained revenue agents, and you will be able to pursue your personal goals. Auditing large corporations requires taking a test to be admitted to the program, followed by classroom training concentrating on tax issues such as reorganizations and audit procedures for examining large companies."

The next three months proceeded as described by Mr. C. The program was rigorous and intense with daily lectures of code provisions, regulations, and other tax law research with exercises from 8:00 a.m. to 4:30 p.m. There were simulation lessons with role-playing, preparing us for conducting interviews and identifying issues and different scenarios for dealing with problem taxpayers who could be belligerent or procrastinating. I would get up extra early each Friday to review and get ready for a three- to four-hour test. But we also celebrated every weekend, getting together usually at a hotel room of some of the agents from out of town, and we partied with pizza and beer—Michigan style. Training resembled college, and I was happy to have in-depth studying of tax law and its application. We all became very close for years to come, staying in touch and sharing stories of our audits.

Before I knew it, we were done with classroom training, and there I was, getting my first assignment of auditing Schedule C business tax returns. We were twelve agents in the group, and my manager gathered us for our first meeting. He was of medium height, with blond hair, glasses, and a pleasant complexion. As we all sat down around a conference table, the secretary distributed a plan of expectations, which outlined all our rules and responsibilities. Our manager stood at the end of the table, and as we settled down, he asked us to introduce ourselves. After an exchange of introductions, he proceeded, "I want to welcome you to my group. Congratulations on completing classroom training phase 1. Now you will be entering into on-the-job training, which will last a couple of months. There is a senior agent assigned to each one of you to observe you work, provide you technical and operational assistance, and accompany you to your audits. These on-the-job instructors will evaluate your performance, and at the end of two months, with successful accomplishment of performing in the field, you will be released from training to work on your own. You are field agents, and you will work at taxpayers' homes and businesses with minimum office work. The secretary will be assisting you whenever you need administrative help. You can't receive calls when in the field. In case of emergency, your families will need to contact the secretary, who will immediately get in touch with you." Then the secretary briefed us how to complete time reports, daily sheets, and travel vouchers.

The next morning, I met my on-the-job instructor. He was of Cuban descent, very dedicated and passionate about the job. "Antonina, take a few minutes to review five of the tax returns and fill in Form 4318, identifying the issues with corresponding tax law."

We reconvened in an hour. He was very pleased with my initial work. I looked at the time, and he nodded. I had to make my first call to a taxpayer truck driver who also had a Schedule C donkey show business. A lady answered the phone.

"Ma'am, I am a revenue agent from the Internal Revenue Service. Your tax return for year 1986 was selected for an audit. I am calling to schedule an appointment to start the audit in two weeks." There was silence on the other end, so I continued, "I will send you a letter confirming the appointment and a document request listing all the documents and receipts I will need to complete the audit. Do you have any questions?"

"No, ma'am," she answered with a quivering voice. I hung up, sighed with relief, and proceeded with my next call. It was an accountant with a CPA firm, also teaching at Eastern Michigan University. After doing the initial introduction with a suggested day and time for the first meeting, I received an answer of a difficult taxpayer, which we were taught about during classroom training.

"I am sorry, but I am busy this week. I cannot meet with you. And besides, it will take some time to dig out records from two years ago."

I took a deep breath and proceeded the way I was instructed in training, "Sir, I need to meet with you on the date I specified, which can be adjusted for a day or so no more. I will conduct an interview for which you do not need to be prepared, and if you cannot gather all records, I will schedule a follow-up appointment."

Two down and three more to go following the same script. By the end of the day, I mailed out the first five appointment confirmation letters with documents, requests, and pubs for taxpayers' rights and privacy notice. I felt good that I accomplished what I planned for the day. I was also very surprised and glad to find out that the phone conversations with taxpayers went as taught in the classroom's mock exercises, with some being cooperative and others not.

After a couple of weeks, I was getting ready to leave for my first audit appointment when the phone rang. There were no caller IDs in those times, so I answered not knowing who it was. It was the head of the English and French language department at Kettering High School. "Nina, I am calling to let you know that two men visited me from the federal government inspection office and asked questions about you. I praised you as a valuable colleague, always professional, very knowledgeable, a caring and giving individual who made a difference in a community in the inner city of Detroit. I gave them examples of the relationship you had with the students and the vital role you played in their lives. I was going to talk a lot, but they cut me short, saying that they want to leave before the bell rang. If your new position as an agent is somewhat dangerous, you will be able to handle any type of unusual situation after being such a successful teacher in Detroit. The men doing your background investigation can definitely vouch for that as they felt somewhat uncomfortable being at the high school."

"Thank you, Shirley. You know I miss the kids, but I needed to do this. I always wanted to learn more about the business world. I have the dream career I wished for since high school."

"You don't have to thank me, Nina. You contributed a lot to the school, and we all appreciate it. Good luck in your new job."

It was the day of my first audit. I hurried to my car and double-checked that I had everything I needed. My trunk was like an office. There were all possible forms, documents, and office supplies to work in the field for a month. My case file was already in the front in the passenger seat. I highlighted the trip on the map to the address of the audit and studied it prior to driving off. In 1988, there were no computers or mobile phones with Siri giving driving directions. As far as work, all was done by hand—accounting paper and mechanical pencils were used for work papers, hand numbered and indexed to Form 4318, which was again manually filled, summarizing administrative points and issues. We were provided with maps that we studied to figure out the locations of our appointments. And in case we needed to make a call, we were issued calling cards, which we could use at public phones usually found at gas stations.

It was a cold February day. The ground was covered with snow; the streets were cleared but somewhat icy. I arrived with no problem at my audit site, which was a personal residence with a barn in the yard for the donkey business. Shortly thereafter, my on-the-job instructor arrived, and we headed to the front door. I rang the bell with a little apprehension as this was my first case. A woman opened the door. She was crying and saying that she did not want to go to jail. "I talked to my friend last night." She was sobbing as she continued, "She told me that you are coming to arrest me." I knew I had to calm her down before I could do any work, so I asked her if we could come in and if she could please stop crying so I could explain the entire process. She nodded, wiped her tears, and invited us in. I started by explaining to her that I was not there to arrest her. I continued by explaining the course of the audit and the issues that I needed to resolve by examining her records and receipts. One of the field agent's requirements was to conduct on-site visit of the business, so I asked the lady to take me to the barn where she kept her for-show and for-breeding donkeys, a business reported on Schedule C. I was dressed professionally in a suit and high heels, not ready to walk in high snow to a barn, but I managed and discovered one donkey.

I made my way back to the house and proceeded with the interview, asking standard and issue-related questions all based on tax law. It was a simple case of a hobby versus business tax issue where all factors indicated that this was a hobby. I explained to the lady that she could not claim the activity with the donkey on their joint tax return. Since her husband as a truck driver had only wages, his presence was not required for the interview.

"Here is a report with adjustments to your taxable income disallowing expenses related to the donkey, as they have the character of a hobby and not a business activity. The report specifies each disallowed amount, the corrected taxable income, and taxes which you owe. There is also a penalty and interest. I will need your signature, and the copy that I am leaving is for your husband to sign. Please mail it in this envelope. I need to receive it back in a week. Do you have any questions?"

"No, ma'am, and thank you for being so professional and explaining clearly the mistakes we made." Her eyes were still teary, but she was smiling as we were leaving. My coach was pleased and impressed with my performance of resolving the case in one day and the way I was able to calm the lady. The first evaluation of my job performance was excellent, and I drove back home very satisfied of the way I completed my first audit.

My next case was with a tax attorney who had his accounting firm for more than thirty years. I must admit I was a little apprehensive because I thought that he was far more knowledgeable because of his experience. My coach accompanied me to every audit, and I was very relieved to see him at the parking lot.

"Good morning," I greeted him. This man had been in this business for a long time, and I was a little anxious being new at this job.

"Don't worry. You picked up the issues to examine. You know the tax law. You will be fine."

A man in his sixties greeted us with a pleasant smile and took us to the conference room. The interview was short as the issues were not complex. I reviewed the documents and could not believe that the attorney made an error on a simple issue as points on a mortgage. When I explained my findings, the man smiled, apologized for the mistake, and asked for the report. I still remember how my concern of being a new revenue agent disappeared. This audit gave me confidence that the training I received was so good that I would have no problems with dealing with any tax law issues. By the end of three months, I was released from the on-the-job training feeling sure of my skills in tax law interpretation, application, and research.

My first case on my own was a beauty salon, a sole proprietor Schedule C return in Inkster, Michigan, which was not a nice neighborhood. I backed up the car, facing the road, and kept the engine running until the lady showed up. She seemed to be pleasant, a heavyset woman with a big smile. After opening the door, she led me to the table where she had her receipts. I asked the interview questions, which I prepared in the office, dealing with the business history and operations. Just from the answers and glancing at the receipts, I knew that there would be issues. Drafting a quick sources and application worksheet, I quickly realized that there was unreported income. In those days, the instruction was not to discuss issues of unreported income with the taxpayer but to refer the case to Criminal Investigation Division. I knew that this particular case was not going to be accepted, so I called on a special agent I knew from training to expedite the review of the case. The civil fraud penalties were still applicable. Once I received the case back from CID, I scheduled a final meeting with the woman. Sitting next to her, I explained the report line by line with references to my workpapers.

"I have so many expenses. I can't believe that I owe that much money," she uttered.

"Ma'am, you have paid all your expenses, and there is not enough reported income on your tax return or any other source of income to show how you paid them."

Her eyes widened as she saw the bottom number of the report. "I can't pay this amount. I don't have the money!" she raised her voice and looked with desperate eyes. I knew she had no money from examining her bank records.

"Ma'am, I only examine tax returns. I do not collect taxes. When you get the bill, please make sure you contact the person on the notice immediately to resolve your case about collectability."

She calmed down and asked in a dry tone, "Where do I sign?" I turned in the case in the morning.

Later in the day, my manager called me, "Nina, you handled this case very well. It is your first referral to CID, and by being proactive, you had the case resolved in an efficient manner. You also had a good rapport with the taxpayer by being up front and clear about her omission of taxable income. Good job."

"Thank you, sir." My thoughts were already on future cases and newly scheduled appointments.

Soon I realized that my life was organized around starting and finishing cases for weeks ahead of time. I loved that I could plan my own schedule and that I was at different locations all the time. I hardly went to the office except for turning in closed cases, my time report, and group meetings. I loved that I was working with different people every day and that the training I received had provided me with excellent knowledge of tax law for individual business tax returns. I was amazed that most CPAs did not know elementary issues like limitation amounts for business gifts. Interviewing was the part I loved the most as I learned about people's success stories in building their businesses as well as their accumulation of capital necessary to be properous.

As tax returns became more complex with high-dollar amounts of income, I did not have any more contacts with individual taxpayers. I remember being assigned my first case with over million dollars taxable income. I was so intrigued to meet the owner of the company that I asked the CPA to arrange a meeting with him as I have never met a millionaire in my life. The taxpayer was in his forties. His office was very personalized, decorated with trophies and paintings. Apart from his business, he owned apartment complexes. His accountant told him about my request, and he appeared very friendly and thrilled to tell his life story.

"I was raised in a very poor family, and I promised myself that when I grow up, I will never be poor," he started. "I studied engineering and opened my first business of designing parts for airplane companies in my garage. I patented a lot of the projects, and before I knew it, the business grew so much that we had to move to a spacious building to accommodate the design and manufacturing of parts."

I listened carefully, impressed by the determination of this person to build a successful life and by his accomplishments. Subsequently, my questions steered toward current operations, accounting, financing, banking, and selected audit issues. This was not a difficult case. It was the high-dollar amounts that were intimidating some agents, but for me, it was no problem. I learned a trick in these early days of auditing to drop the last three digits of amounts on the tax return and perform the exam as any other. The man looked at my report and, without a word, signed it. The adjustments could not be disputed as depreciation of apartment buildings should have accounted for the value of land.

And then there was the case of a man deducting his extramarital expenses on his Schedule C business return.

"Sir, what was the business purpose of the high-dollar hotel expenses in the city you live?"

"Just take them off the return and please don't tell my wife about them," he grumbled. I never met his wife as he hired a CPA to finish the case with me.

I came across a lot of irregularities in income reporting, which sometimes surprised my manager.

"What do you mean these two men operated a window installation business together, comingled all funds between their bank accounts, and reported the activity on Schedule C of the one?" My manager was looking with a face expressing disbelief of seeing the case in front of him.

"Yes, sir, that's what happened. This business is actually a partnership, which they never formed."

"So how do you propose to finish the case?"

"I do not intend to form a partnership for them. I will audit both of their personal returns," I responded quickly. And I proceeded as I found to be most reasonable. There were two audit reports for issues of income, personal use of trucks, and meals.

I was an absent parent most of the time as I stopped going out with the kids or taking them anywhere. I was still overseeing their schoolwork, making sure they did well in school. I would go shopping with Mom and have dinners with them. But I was so absorbed in my work that I had no time to spend with my family and enjoy the children. There were new cases every day, and I loved the challenges of solving them, applying my investigative skills and knowledge of accounting, auditing, and tax law. Looking back at that time, I was wrapped up in a never-ending case resolution of audits one after the other. Mom used to tell me how the kids' days were in the evening. My youngest daughter was playing with children across the street, and my son and older daughter were hanging out with classmates from their schools.

Time flew fast, and before I knew, it was the fall of 1988. My youngest daughter was starting kindergarten, and after I took her to school, she snuck out and returned home. At least the school was in the subdivision and there was no traffic later in the morning. Mom took her back to school, and there were no more issues after that. My son was starting high school, and that was a big adjustment for him coming from a much smaller school. Plymouth Canton High School was the size of a college with classes between two buildings. I always worried at the beginning of every school year, especially the first couple of weeks, until the children got settled in a routine at school.

I was scheduled to attend corporate training. I reconnected with people from our first training. It was very pleasant, just like a class reunion, but this time, we had a lot of stories to share from our audits.

"You know I did one audit in the bathroom on the toilet seat," a female agent said laughingly. "They said they had no room to accommodate me, so I said that this was no problem."

Classroom training was only for three weeks, and I was again doing on-the-job training for corporate audits with an on-the-job instructor. My probationary one year period ended, and I was promoted to grade 9.

"Don't get lost in the woods," my manager said as he handed me my cases. "Stick to the issues and follow the audit plan."

Soon I discovered that a lot of CPAs were glorified bookkeepers. At one of my first audits, I was questioning a depreciation expense, and the accountant's response was, "There are no records for this depreciation expense. I had to balance the books."

The other common mistake was to comingle corporate and personal funds. For one case, the lady taxpayer was an accountant doing the books and tax returns of her husband's corporation. There were numerous payments of personal expenses paid from the corporate bank account, which I reclassified as dividends.

"I have power of attorney and will sign for the corporate tax return report," she said. "My husband does not have to know about this." There was nothing I could say. I knew she was very diligent, but she did not know about separation of corporate and business bank accounts and assets.

Loans to shareholders account was totally misinterpreted by accountants. I had an interesting case of auditing a modeling agency where in the travel and entertainment account, I saw names and pictures of prominent Michigan businessmen. Two eccentric women owned the agency and preferred not to have representation.

"Please do not disclose in your report these individuals. Just adjust our taxes," the lady with the short blond hair asked. The loans to shareholders was a common account with no records and no intent for repayment. On the final day of the exam, I had a meeting with the ladies to provide them with the audit report.

I moved on to my next case of auditing a yacht storage and repair business. According to the records, there should have been a Jacuzzi and swimming pool at the location, which of course was not the case. A villa up north and snow mobiles in the shareholder's name were expensed by the corporation. As I was getting the audit report ready, the shareholder barged into the conference room where I was working and yelled out to his accountant, "You are fired!" I understood the frustrations of taxpayers relying on accountants and not knowing tax law. I did not apply any negligence penalties in those cases, but I had a hard time with people looking you in the eye and lying.

In another case of design and architecture business operating from a residence, the owner claimed that the van was used strictly for business. Arriving early in the morning, I ran into his wife and kids leaving for school in the same van.

Another year flew by when I was completely immersed in my work, but I still kept an eye on the kids' schoolwork and grades and their needs for school supplies and clothing. I also did grocery shopping with my mother. I shopped for Christmas gifts, arranged kids' birthday parties, and cooked Thanksgiving and Christmas dinners. But I was too tired to talk and spend time with them. I relied totally on my mother to be around the kids while I was at work, sometimes till late evenings.

In the fall of 1989, I became grade 11 and entered phase 3— partnership training. Partnership tax law was the most complex compared to individual and corporate tax law. Soon I discovered that accountants had no idea what I was talking about asking for owners' equity interest, inside and outside basis, or taxable events in distributions of cash and assets. They were treating partnerships as Schedule C's sole proprietorships. The common issue was taking losses without records of basis in the partnership.

"What do you mean asking for records from fifteen years ago?" an accountant was asking in a taut voice.

"Sir, taking losses in the current year needs to be documented with records of basis regardless of how long ago the partnership was formed." I even accompanied the man to taxpayer's service in attempt to recover tax returns, which the service did not keep that long. It was a striking reality that most accountants were not competent or appeared not to be in filing partnership tax returns for their clients.

My life rotated around starting and closing cases by focusing on big, unusual, and questionable items on their tax returns. There was a doctor whose assistant embezzled money, so he closed the business and bought a yacht to provide cruises on the Detroit River and a teacher with a side business of construction not realizing that discharge of income was taxable income.

It was a cold February morning in 1990 when my manager called me in his office.

"Nina, you have been doing an excellent job. Your performance is outstanding in all areas of auditing, starting with interviewing, investigating, tax law, dealing with taxpayers and accountants." I wasn't sure where this conversation was going, so I remained quiet, just listening and not budging. The man continued, "There is a new group in the process of being formed called revenue initiative group. Agents selected for this group are with superb auditing skills. This is a pilot program with only two groups in the country. Audits in this group will be on medium-sized companies and half of the month on large companies from the NYSE. Nina, you are selected for this group. I will be very sorry to let you go, but this is upper management decision. It is a very honorable position for a new agent like you. Being in this group, you will be promoted to grade 12 without competing for it."

"Thank you, sir. When do I start in the new group?"

"The first of next month, and if you have questions, I will always be available. You will be dealing with tax returns of high-dollar amounts. All you need to do is to drop in your mind the last three or six digits. The audits will be more complicated as these companies will have related entities, which you will need to look at and very probably audit." I liked my manager. He was in his forties, of medium height, with dark blond hair, always available and very supportive.

My involvement with my family continued to be limited and reduced to being the provider and supervisor, making sure that everything ran well. Moving to the new group meant even less time at home with more travel.

The day came when I joined the revenue initiative group and met my new manager, the secretary, and my fellow revenue agents. After a brief group meeting, we all set down to work. The cases solely of corporations and partnerships were much thicker tax returns with high-dollar amounts, as my prior manager said. The contacts were chief accounting officers and heads of tax departments, which facilitated scheduling appointments. There were no more stories of being busy and attempting to procrastinate. The emotions were taken out of the meetings, which I immediately recognized and appreciated. Shareholders' and partners' individual 1040 returns were also subject to reviews and frequently audited, but they all had representatives. Most of the audits required referrals to engineering, international examiners, and computer-specialized groups. There was also a senior agent assigned to the group whose job was to assist in the field or look up tax issues for us. At that time, our computers were like glorified typewriters with only programs of Word and Excel. There were floppy disks for generating audit reports and time sheets. I remember how great it was when we were issued a computer and printer and how proud I felt carrying them with me. It's hard to believe that the bulky Zenith computer and the slow-working printer existed not that long ago. For the tax research beyond the code and regulations, I frequently visited the tax law library at the McNamara Federal Building.

I embraced with enthusiasm my new assignment, which provided opportunities for learning complex tax issues and communicating with agents working in specialty areas. There was one last advanced audit training for revenue agents that I signed up for. After passing the entry exam for this advanced corporate and partnership training, I entered the last stage of training for revenue agents feeling proud and blessed for all my accomplishments so far. There were no tests at this level, but the training by itself was very involved and complex, dealing primarily with issues like reorganizations, liquidation, etc.

One Friday evening in May 1990, Mom met me with a sparkle in her eyes. I knew it was good news.

"Your aunt and your cousin Ivan with his wife were granted visas and will visit us for the summer. Here, I just received a telegram from Ivan." These were times with difficult means of communication. Calling overseas was through a Bulgarian operator, and telegrams were used for quick announcements of events. I hugged her, and we celebrated with a meal she prepared for the occasion—Mom made the best *musaka* in the world. The kids were also happy; they loved their uncle Ivan who played with them in Bulgaria and taught Erik how to swim. With the fall of the Berlin Wall, all Eastern European countries followed the same path by abolishing their Communist regimes and forming new democratic governments. The borders were open for travel, and finally, Bulgarians could see the world forbidden for them until now.

The long-awaited day arrived. We were at the airport with flowers, impatiently staring at the arrival gate. And there they were, my aunt with a broad smile followed by laughter of joy, hugs, and kisses and Ivan and Buba, his wife, laughing and not believing to be in America. My aunt, the woman who read me the Andersen's stories and inspired me to start reading, the woman who took me to the Black Sea in the summer after my long sickness when I was in second grade. She taught me how to swim and instilled in me the love for the sea, she used to stop by and see my grandma after work and occasionally brought me an orange. I held her in my arms, feeling tears going down her cheeks. "My child, I am so happy to be with you" was all she could say.

Luckily, it was a weekend, so we could catch up on stories about our lives and go grocery and clothes shopping. Their eyes were wide open at the abundance and variety of food. Shopping in big carts and filling them with food was an incredible sight for them. I knew that the shelves in the grocery stores in Bulgaria were empty; I saw them when I visited in 1983, and obviously, things got worse since then. Communism in Eastern Europe collapsed with broken economy systems, and people were impoverished and starved. After decades of dictatorship and persecution, freedom became a reality. Watching the news, I could feel the exuberance of joy in people breaking the bloody Berlin Wall, men, women, and children were swinging hammers and chipping it away stone by stone.

Back to my visiting relatives, they were amazed at things that we were taking for granted, like the size of the appliances—the refrigerator, washer, dryer (by the way, there were no dryers in Bulgaria at that time). Filling the refrigerator with food was a holiday. My cousin loved to cook, so he immediately set to prepare Bulgarian dishes like baked *guvetch* (a lot of vegetables with some beef and spices), and my favorite dessert, crème caramel.

My relatives arrived just at the time when we had to sell our house in Plymouth and move to the cottage in Lexington, Michigan, which we bought the previous summer as a fixer-upper. Anabelle's father was not a person who could hold a job for a long time, and bills were piling up fast. A son of a colonel from the Corps of Engineers, he wanted to go in the footsteps of his father as a draftsman and then his grandfather as a builder, but he could not succeed in either career for long. We could not afford renting a U-Haul truck, so the move was done in a pickup, making numerous trips. Soon after the move, I was in debt again, not as bad as before but the house needed new windows, floors, painting, doors, and bathroom. Ivan helped G while I was gone working during the week.

I was assigned to a large case audit where I stayed for weeks at the time, and for my other midsize company audits, I stayed at Mom's small house in Canton. The prior summer, I spotted an ad in the newspaper for its sale—a seven-hundred-square-foot house in need of repairs on a one-acre property. The owners were an elderly couple wishing to get it off their hands, and I negotiated with them a land contract sale. My daughter Vanesa and I spent all summer putting wallpaper and painting (the walls were not even, so we learned how to plaster them). Mom was not happy seeing me working hard while G was unemployed most of the time, so this little house was a gift for her to escape and have peace. It turned out as a very smart move since Lexington was one hundred miles away from my office and most of the audits were in the Detroit area.

Looking back at that time, I couldn't figure out how we all fitted in the Lexington cottage. It had three small bedrooms, a dining and living rooms, and a utility room. The living room had a pullout couch, and we all, the eight of us, fitted in this house. Oh, and we had Sammy, a red-haired dog. I loved Friday evenings when I drove home, did the grocery shopping (IGA was at the back of the house), and spent the evening with the entire family eating delicious meals and desserts. Ivan knew I loved crème caramel, so I found it in the kitchen every time I came back home. My aunt always ran out of the house to meet me. "How was your week? Did you have a lot of work?" Mom would be right behind her giving me a report for the week. The kids were bronze from being in the sun and were happy.

Saturday mornings were especially delightful. Mom would make tons of crepes, and after a couple of cups of coffee, I would yell out, "Everybody put on bathing suits! We are going to the beach!" The house was a block away from the harbor and the public beach, and living there was like being on vacation. Kids would be out the door ahead of us, and we would all head to the lake, talking cheerfully and laughing. My mother and aunt loved sitting on benches by the harbor and watching the crowds of people arriving for the weekend. Lexington had five hundred residents, but that number increased by the thousands in the summer.

Weekends went by fast, and on Mondays, I had to head back to work in the Detroit area or Northern Michigan for my large case audit. On Sunday evenings, I would load the car with clothes and basic necessities for the week and leave the house super early on Monday morning. The trip in either direction was two hours.

Having so many people to drive around, I started to think about trading in my car for a van. I thought of the way I acquired my Mustang. Last winter, I was driving a Ford Escort when its head gasket blew up on New Year's Eve, and the day after I drove it from service, the ignition went out. After jump-starting it, I managed to get to work, but in the afternoon, I peeked in my manager's office and asked, "Can I leave an hour early? I need to buy a car."

He looked at me, surprised. "You will buy a car by yourself?"

"I work, and I pay for my car, so I don't see why I can't trade it in by myself."

The truth was that I was responsible for all bills and taking care of my kids and my mother. G was supposed to at least pay for his pickup and gas and buy his cigarettes. Not a good situation, but that was how it was. So I went to the nearest Ford dealer in Royal Oak and started to bargain for the replacement of my Ford Escort. After two hours of negotiating a price, my eyes stopped at a silver Ford Mustang. The salesman was exasperated, and by that time, it was also getting late. He looked at me with a gloomy expression.

"We do not make money after New Year, and you are my first client. I will give you the Mustang for the price of the Escort."

I had a big grin on my face. "Let's wrap it up. I have kids to go home to."

When I pulled in the driveway, everybody ran out of the house to see the new car. I was ecstatic, laughing and telling the story of how I managed to get my dream car. But now that I had my relatives at home, I had to make two trips everywhere we went. I had no choice but look up a dealership in Croswell, a village by Lexington. The salesman offered me a van, a Ford Aerostar. We agreed on a price and the date he was going to deliver the car to the house. That was another amazing event for my aunt, my cousin, and his wife. They were all watching out the window as the man stopped in front of the house with the new van and walked up to the front door. I was waiting for him with all the necessary documents for the Mustang. We went to examine both cars and finished the paperwork in the house. The man drove away in the Mustang, and we all loaded in the van to take a drive up the coast to the next village. My aunt was shaking her head in disbelief that I could buy a car without leaving the house, and once settled in the back seat, she asked, "Isn't it difficult to drive this big van?"

"No, Aunt, it has a special steering wheel which makes it easy to turn and drive. The brakes are also special. They are called four-wheel brakes, which makes it very stable for the winter months." My aunt seemed relieved hearing that.

We stopped in Port Sanilac, walked by the water, and ate ice cream. On the way back home, Ivan shouted out, "I am not going back to Bulgaria! I don't care what kind of work I do since I don't even speak English. I am not going back!"

I glanced at him in the rearview mirror, and with a smile, I responded, "Okay, we will go to the immigration in Detroit, and I will sponsor you all to stay."

The following weekend, Mom told me that Buba, my cousin's wife, was crying because she missed her parents and sister. "They were staying up late in the night talking rather than watching movies as usual."

Ivan met me at the car looking tired and exhausted, and his face was pale. "We are going back to Bulgaria as originally planned in September. My wife is homesick, and we can't stay."

I hugged him. "It's okay. Bulgaria is a democratic country now, and you can always return."

That weekend, for the first time, the house was quiet. On Friday and Saturday night, we had dinner in silence and turned in to bed early.

Another week passed at work in the Detroit area. On Friday afternoon, as I was getting ready for my trip to Lexington, people in the office started to talk about a tornado sighted in West Bloomfield, twenty miles north of Detroit. I packed quickly, ran to the parking lot, jumped in my car, and raced to I-94. Once on the highway, I kept looking in the rearview mirror at the black sky, listening to the whistling wind. Some drivers already stopped and sought shelter under the overpasses. I was driving at a high speed. My heart was pounding, and my body was shivering. Past images of being caught in tornedo storms sprang up in my mind.

It happened in the spring of 1973. Vanesa was only one year old. I was visiting a Serbian lady friend in Ypsilanti. Vanesa played with her boy who was the same age as her. We drank Turkish coffee, having the usual women's talk, exchanging recipes, shopping, etc. Suddenly, the wind picked up, it started to rain, and the sky turned dark. I grabbed Vanesa and hurried to leave before it got worse.

"Where are you going? This looks like a tornado!" my friend yelled.

"It's only a storm. I have been in storms in Europe. We will be fine." I buckled Vanesa next to me (usually I had her in the back seat, but now I wanted to have her close to me) and took off. I didn't get too far when the sky became totally black and the wind started to blow fiercely, sounding like an approaching train. Tree branches were falling all around. I stopped the car, unbuckled Vanesa fast, put her on my lap, and covered her with my body. "God, please, God, help us. Don't let my baby get hurt." I kept praying and chanting until everything started to calm down. The wind began to let up, the branches stopped flying, and it got brighter. I looked up and saw a fallen tree on the road not far from the car. I placed Vanesa back in her seat and drove around the tree, amazed at the destruction from the storm. There were uprooted trees and broken branches all over. Arriving home, Vanesa's father met us in front of the apartment building.

"Where have you been? You know, a tornado hit a couple of miles from here."

"I know it hit. We were close to it." I spent the rest of the day praying and thanking God for being merciful and saving us.

I continued driving madly toward Port Huron, glancing at the black sky behind. By the time I arrived in Port Huron, the rain has stopped, but I could tell that there was a big storm in there too as there were uprooted trees and bushes and damages on houses. As soon as I parked in front of the house in Lexington, my aunt flew out, yelling, "Are you okay? It was horrible here. Everything was shaking. Your mom said this was a tornado." Then she walked around the car and said with a calm voice said, "Okay, I see you made it home safely. Thank God."

It was sad to say goodbye to my aunt and cousin, but now the borders were open, and I knew that we could visit freely. The next few months were exciting and extremely busy. I was learning a lot at my large case audit site, but I was extremely curious about international taxation. Audits for large companies were ongoing with most issues continuously appealed in cycles. We were given one of the floors where the regular and the international auditors worked. There were also visits from specialized groups such as computer assistance and engineering. Since we all worked together and had lunch at the same time, I had an opportunity to talk to the international examiners, asking them about tax issues that they were raising, which fascinated me. On one of these days, an international examiner looked at me and said, "Nina, we are hiring. There is a job announcement for our department if you would like to apply." This was a song to my ears, and I applied for the position on that same day. It wasn't long after that when the manager of the international division called me and informed me that I was selected to be in his group. This was not a promotional position and did not require an official interview and testing. I scheduled an appointment for the following day to meet with him at his office in Detroit for a briefing of the on-the-job requirements. I was extremely eager to hear details about the program. I drove to Detroit that same evening and got up extra early to beat the morning rush. The manager smiled as I walked in, asked me to sit, and started to talk.

"I know about your track record from your previous exam managers. You have proven to be an excellent technician, and I am glad to have you in our international examiners group. I am sure you are curious about the program. There will be an intense classroom training for six weeks in Cincinnati. You will come home for a month working under the guidance of one of my senior examiners and return to Cincinnati for another month of classroom training. Do you think you will be able to do this?"

I knew he was thinking about my family. I was sure that he probably spoke with my exam manager and knew that I had kids at home. "My mother lives with me," I responded. "The kids will be okay. When does training start?"

"Next month. You will be notified at work." I thanked the man and left his office with a big smile on my face.

I took the rest of the day off as I wanted to spend time with Mom and see the kids after school. I know I had a preoccupied look on my face as Mom lifted her eyebrows and asked, "What's wrong?"

"Nothing at work. Actually, I am provided with a great opportunity to work in the area that I am extremely interested in—international taxation. But the job comes with initial training out of town, and I won't be coming home on weekends for six weeks. Mom, do you think you can manage the kids for six weeks? Training is in Cincinnati, a four-hour drive from here, and if necessary, I will come back."

Mom was listening intensely, and as soon as I finished talking, she took my hands and said, "Nina, I know how much this means to you. Ever since high school, you wanted to work in the international business arena, and now you have a chance to do it. Don't worry about the kids and me. We will manage." The kids were used to me being gone every week, so they did not ask much of what I was going to do.

Training in Cincinnati was every weekday from 8:00 a.m. to 4:30 p.m. I was happy to see that a couple of agents whom I knew from Detroit were also in this training. The three of us stayed at Residence Inn north of the city and took turns driving to the training site. International tax law was the most challenging of all as there was no clear answer to an issue in one of the tax code sections; there was always a reference to subsections and regulations to find the final response. There was no testing, but the instructions required undivided attention and participation to understand the material. Anabelle's father brought the girls for a couple of weekends, which made me very happy. We had a great time laughing and joking, and one of the days, I drove them to Lexington, Kentucky, where we had the biggest chocolate dessert. My son was doing great in the new high school in Lexington, which was another happy news and a relief because I was worried about him changing high schools.

Back in Detroit, I started to audit midsize foreign-controlled corporations accompanied in the field by one of the best international examiners. Transfer pricing was one of the major issues, but there were also other manipulations with finances hidden in balance sheets recordings. One case stood out as for the first time in my auditing career in the IRS, I came across a highly professional and knowledgeable accountant from Price Waterhouse. What I remember from this audit was that the issue was complex with a domestic company doing business abroad. The man provided me at the scheduled appointment his research supporting the transaction. I was impressed and asked him about his background. He was young and shared that he was a carpenter when he signed up in college and supported himself throughout the program. I am mentioning him because he was the only representative until this moment who was versatile in tax law, considering that international tax law was extremely complicated.

My next four weeks in training were noneventful, except for learning a lot more about international taxation and getting to know more of the agents from my training group. We had dinners together, sharing stories from places we lived in and from our audits. Some of them were funny. My story was from an audit where the accountant of a medium accounting firm got frustrated and told me that I should go harass businesses overseas where I came from.

It was the last day of classroom training, and we were packing our materials and books to ship to our offices when one of the instructors walked up to me with a piece of paper in his hand. "Nina, I had a call from Washington, DC. They are expecting your call." I took the note, quite surprised, as I did not expect anything from the capital and headed to the first phone having the slightest idea what this was about.

There was a pleasant voice on the other end of the receiver. "Hello, Antonina. I am the director of TAAS. This is an IRS unit in the international division providing tax assistance to foreign governments. The Bulgarian tax administration is in urgent need of an advisory assistance. We reviewed your credentials and shared them with a tax official from Bulgaria. We all agreed that you are the perfect candidate to take part in the first phase of this task, which lasts three weeks. You will travel to Bulgaria with one of my employees, and the two of you will analyze their tax system and will provide recommendations for a long-term in-country assistance. Will you be interested? You will need to travel on Monday, first to the office here, where we will meet, and I will brief you on the assignment. The flight for Bulgaria is on the following day."

I did not believe what I was hearing—going on an assignment to Bulgaria to represent the American government after escaping the country in 1969. That was not easy to process. I felt hot, and I knew that my face was probably bright red. "Sir, it will be an honor for me to participate in this task. Of course, I am interested."

"Okay, we have faxed to Cincinnati the travel orders. You can pick up your ticket at the airport in Detroit on Monday. Thank you for joining our team. See you Tuesday." With that, he hung up and left me with an open mouth.

I drove back home to Lexington, Michigan, deep in thought about what just perspired, trying to imagine my life for the next few weeks. What was I supposed to do? How was I going to analyze a country's tax system? And of course, I was feeling bad for having to travel again, this time overseas after being gone for such a long time. My son came out as soon as I pulled and parked in front of the house. *He has grown big in my absence,* was my first thought. We hugged, and he helped bring in my luggage.

"I couldn't recognize you, son. You are so big."

"You should stay home more" was his answer, which made my heart sink.

"I am sorry. It's work," I mumbled.

I brought the news to everybody that night, and of course, it was shocking to hear that I hardly unpacked to pack and leave again. At the end of my evening, Mom came by me and smiled. "Nina, I am so proud of you. This is a big honor to be called upon for such an assignment. I know you are smart to be picked out to participate in such an important mission, especially in Bulgaria, your homeland."

"I will call once a week, and if you need to reach me for anything, these are numbers of my office in Detroit and Washington, DC."

It was Monday, and my plane was later in the day. I had time to see Anabelle during her lunch recess. I walked hastily toward her school, checked myself in at the office, and headed for the school-yard. "Anabelle." I waved at her as I saw her. "I am leaving today, and I came to watch you play before I go." Anabelle ran over and pointed at a bench. We sat down, and she snuggled next to me. "Aren't you going to play?" At that time, her friends came over. Anabelle did not want to go with them, so they ran off, cheerfully laughing and chasing one another.

"Mommy, why are you leaving? Do you have to go?"

I felt pain in my heart. It became dark in front of my eyes as I hugged her closely. "I love you, Anabelle, and I'll be back before you know it."

Her break ended, and I watched her tiny body disappear as she slowly walked back to the building. A couple of tears came down my cheek. I started walking as in a dream. Back at the house, I loaded the trunk of the car with my computer, the tax code, a couple of my advance tax law textbooks, and a suitcase with clothes. Mom was standing by the door. She blessed me and poured water in front of the car (a Bulgarian custom wishing everything to run smoothly as water).

I arrived in DC early in the evening, checked in at the specified hotel from my travel order, and looked outside my window—there was an incredibly beautiful sight of the city all lit up in the spring night. I ordered room service, unpacked clothes only for the next day, jotted down questions that I had, and made sure I had a notepad and pens in my briefcase.

The TAAS office was nearby the hotel on L'Enfant Street. I was eager to meet the director but, at the same time, had mixed feelings not knowing exactly what my duties would be. I was walking fast, feeling exhilarated but also anxious of the unknown. I knocked timidly on the door.

"Come in." A man in his forties, of medium height, with slim figure, stood up from behind his desk and walked toward me with a broad smile. "Glad you could make it. Did you have a nice flight?"

"Yes, sir, everything is fine."

"Okay, our meeting will be short. The most important thing you need to know is that the government officials who you will meet are all former Communists. It will take a couple of generations to change this, but for the time being, you should not be in a shock or refuse to communicate with them. You are traveling today with one of my male employees, and he will give you details about the assignment once you arrive in Sofia. He is in the office today. We will stop by his desk on the way out." And this was all I heard from my briefing with the director. I truly expected a long explanation of exactly what I would be doing during this visit, but I preferred not to ask more.

"Antonina, there is time for your flight. Grab a bite in the cafeteria with us."

The cafeteria had a better food selection than the one in Detroit, and after a very tasty breakfast, I thanked the director and turned to my future companion. "Nice meeting you. I am truly looking forward to working with you. I already checked out from the hotel, so I am leaving straight for the airport." The man was also in his forties, with a round face and receding hair, had a pleasant composure, and was easy to talk to.

"Fantastic, I will see you at the gate."

Returning to My Homeland—from Escapee to Government Advisor

The flight was uneventful, watching a movie, having meals. Most people were napping, but I could not close an eye. Glancing at my colleague, I timidly asked in a low voice, "This is my first overseas assignment. Can you please tell me exactly what is expected of me?"

The man looked at me with smiling eyes. "Relax, you come with high marks from your office and of your achievements with the IRS, which means you have the necessary knowledge of the organization and expertise in the exam program to handle this project. You are well equipped with tools which you will use in analyzing the current state of the tax offices and existing programs of the Bulgarian tax administration. We will meet with the assistant minister of Finance for taxation, equivalent to our commissioner, regional tax Directors, and managers of local tax offices in Sofia, Plovdiv, and Varna. During these meetings, we will gather information about their operations, we will respond to questions they have about our assistance, and we will take notes of their concerns and requests for aid. Upon returning home, we will formulate a report with proposal for assistance outlining our actions. My understanding is that one of our IRS people from TAAS will be assigned to spend a couple of years in Bulgaria to provide hands-on assistance to their initiatives. Our involvement is strictly technical, and whoever is selected for this position will be able to use resources from the States for different areas outside of their specialty, such as collection, criminal investigation, etc. I will definitely submit a request to be considered for the position as Bulgaria is in Europe and will be easy for my family to adapt. But now rest. We will have a long day when we arrive."

I nodded and closed my eyes. This was my dream assignment, returning to Bulgaria to help the country where I was born and grew up in build a new tax system after the fall of Communism.

It was not a direct flight; we had to transfer in Frankfurt, and after twelve hours, we arrived in Sofia early in the afternoon. My colleague recognized a face and waved at a man in his thirties, with dark hair and well-built. The man smiled and headed toward us with another man, same height and age, slightly overweight, with light-brown hair and oval face.

"Hello, sir. This must be Antonina. Hi, Antonina. I am the general director from the Ministry of Finance, and this man is the head of customs. Welcome to Bulgaria. How was your flight?" Without waiting for an answer, he walked with us to the baggage area and had a person take care of the luggage. Bypassing lines of passengers, we followed our host to a car where a man with silvery hair introduced himself as the driver from the Ministry of Finance.

Soon we arrived at Sheraton Hotel. I am mentioning its name because this place in the past was known as Balkantourist and was one of the prestigious hotels located in the city center on a square called Baba Nedelya. I secretly glanced at the magnificent St. Nedelya Church dating from the tenth century and hurried to the hotel. Walking in, we were greeted by the concierge.

"I will leave you now to settle in and rest," our Bulgarian host said. "Tomorrow I will come at eight a.m., and we will walk to the Ministry of Finance. It's very close. I have scheduled meetings for you with the minister of Finance and the commissioner of the tax administration. Again, welcome to Bulgaria."

I was tired, but I had to see my aunt. I called her and soon heard her deep voice and laughter on the other end of the receiver. "My child, I am so happy for you. Maria called and said you were coming on a business trip for a couple of weeks. I know you are tired, so I'll come to you." I was standing on the steps in front of the hotel feeling my heart beating anxiously in anticipation of seeing my aunt. And there she was. I spotted her from a distance crossing the square in her worn-out red skirt.

"Auntie!" I cried, running toward her. She hugged me, and I felt like a little girl again. She came up to my room and, walking past the closet, she stopped for a minute. She looked at my clothes in amazement, touched some of them (mostly suits for work), and exclaimed, "Why do you need so many outfits?"

"Oh, Auntie, it's my job. I will have meetings every day and need to change, but I understand what you are saying."

We spoke of simple things and how she lived and had a friend who was visiting her every day. I told her about the kids, their school, and I showed her pictures. After her visit, I checked with my colleague if everything was okay and soon fell in a deep sleep.

In the morning, I jumped out of bed at the sound of the telephone. It was a wake-up call. I never took long to get ready, so in about half an hour, I was dressed in one of my favorite suits. With a portfolio folder in my hand, I headed to the breakfast area where my colleague was already expecting me. Our Bulgarian host appeared shortly thereafter and, with a broad smile, walked over, shaking our hands. "Are you ready? We have a short walk, but let's leave, so we don't have to rush and get sweaty."

It took us about fifteen minutes to arrive at the Ministry of Finance. After walking past the security guard, we took the elevator to the third floor. Lidia, the commissioner's secretary, met us with a cheerful voice. "Welcome, Antonina and sir. We have been expecting you." She walked immediately to her desk, picked up the phone, and announced our arrival. I was surprised at myself as I did not feel nervous or anxious entering the Bulgarian commissioner's office.

A man in his forties, tall and dark-haired, stood up from behind his desk and walked over to meet us with a smile. "Welcome, we are very grateful that you are here to extend us assistance." Then he looked over at his secretary and asked, "Lidia, could you please bring us coffees." I remembered Bulgaria's hospitality; treating guests was a part of life. The man, still smiling, continued, "Did you have a nice flight? We are going to use one of the conference rooms so we don't get interrupted. Please follow me." With that, he led us to a room with attractive antique furniture, and we started by getting information about the Bulgarian tax administration—its structure, lawmaking, operations.

I was speaking Bulgarian and translating to my colleague. After all the training received at the IRS, I was curious about the Bulgarian tax administration, their organizational structure, methods of operation for exam, collection, and taxpayer services. "We are here to analyze the condition of the existing tax administration and write a proposal for improvement in each phase of your operations. TAAS is an IRS unit with a function to provide necessary tax advisory assistance worldwide, which is the purpose of our visit. We will appreciate your input, and we would also like to meet with senior tax officials in the major cities of Sofia, Plovdiv, and Burgas, as well as managers of local tax offices."

"You will have a direct access to all tax offices and tax officials to conduct the necessary interviews and collect the information you need," the man responded. "Here is a chart of our organizational structure."

We looked closely at the chart and noticed that the country was divided in Regions headed by Regional Directors. Each region had tax offices with managers supervising groups of inspectors; each tax office had customer service counters with clerical staff. At the ministry, there were legal and excise tax divisions for alcohol, tobacco, and gambling. I asked for the basic responsibilities of the regional and tax offices.

"The regional tax directors report to me about the state of their tax offices. The local counter offices' function is tax registration and collection of taxes. Each tax office has a tax manager who supervises the clerks and heads a group of inspectors who conduct audits and collect the assessed taxes. It's a simple system." The commissioner waited for me to translate and then continued, "Our tax policies and administration are obsolete as they were created to serve a state economy and are not functional in a free market economy. Our existing laws for state-owned enterprises cannot be applied for sole proprietors, corporations, and partnerships."

"Thank you, sir," I responded. "We will need to interview regional directors of the biggest regions, those of Sofia, Plovdiv, and Burgas, as well as a tax office in Sofia."

"I will ask my secretary to schedule appointments, so please stop at her desk to give her details of your requests. I will also arrange for your transportation. You already met our driver."

I thanked him and looked him in the eyes. "We will inform you, sir, of our analysis and will provide you with a rough draft of our proposal for assistance prior to our departure." This was a good start. We stopped by the secretary and gave her dates for the appointments she needed to make and arrange for a car.

Back at the hotel, we planned our activities for the next couple of weeks with specific agenda. Later in the afternoon, we met with the general secretary, and he confirmed our travel days and appointments already scheduled by the ministry secretary.

It was early morning when we headed to Sofia's regional office. It was about half an hour walk from the hotel, but it was a beautiful day, and it gave us an opportunity to do a little sightseeing. We turned right toward Ruski Boulevard, and I started pointing the more important buildings and sights. We were facing the ministry council's building, formerly the seat of the Bulgarian Communist Party. There were tulips blossoming in the middle, a very pleasant sight, which filled me immediately with joy. And here we were at the famous Ruski Street with its golden cobblestones; the street looked majestic as ever. Soon we approached the palace, which was an art museum now, and across it was a park where I used to play as a child. There were outdoor cafés in the park with blasting American music and people sipping coffee—something new I noticed. The mausoleum was gone. I explained to my colleague that it was for Georgi Dimitrov, a communist leader and the president after the Second World War, who was in favor of creating a Balkan Federation with Tito. Rumors had it that his mysterious death after a visit to Moscow was because of his friendly relations with Yugoslavia. We passed the Russian church with golden domes and then came upon the impressive Alexander Nevsky Cathedral, built in memory of Russian soldiers who died in the war with the Ottoman Empire for the liberation of Bulgaria. Considered one of the largest Eastern Orthodox cathedrals in the world, the cathedral is an imposing sight with its domes and design of a basilica in the middle of a big square. Continuing down the boulevard, we passed the parliament to the left and the Monument of the Tsar Liberator to the right—the Russian tsar in reference again to the war with Turkey. We turned right at the university and again right in a small street called Aksakov. We reached our destination and entered the building of the regional tax office.

Once inside, we were met by the director's secretary, who immediately led us to his office.

"Welcome, Americans." A man in his early thirties sprang to his feet, smiled, and extended his hand. He was expecting us, the secretary served us coffee, and we started our interview.

"Sir, how many tax offices are in your region, and can you please describe them? We are particularly interested in the exam program, which is the work of your inspectors."

The director provided us with a chart of the city's tax offices and their locations. I noticed that there were three offices in the center of the city. Then he started to explain the setup and functions of the tax offices. "As you enter the tax office buildings, there are counters served by clerks to register businesses and accept tax declarations and payments. A tax manager supervises the clerks and the inspectors who perform audits and collect taxes. The inspectors are all college graduates with degrees in accounting and economics. Our exam and collection is not successful because the old approach to auditing does not work anymore. Inspectors usually ask for records and documents which they compare with the amounts from the tax declarations [later, I found out that these were tax returns]. There is a word on the street that businesses purchase invoices when audited and asked for receipts of expenses. In reality, there is no much collection going on after audits."

"Sir, could you please arrange for us to visit one of your tax offices and meet with their tax manager?"

"Of course, I will recommend that you visit the Lozenets office, which is close to the National Palace of Culture."

We shared information about the organizational structure of the Internal Revenue Service, the seriousness of tax evasion (which is a criminal offense), and the indirect methods used to assess taxes for businesses and individuals when big discrepancies were observed in lifestyle and income tax reporting.

"This is exactly what we need." The man's eyes lit up. "We all know about Al Capone, and right now, Bulgaria is exactly in this period of criminal activities and tax evasion as in America at the turn of the century."

"Sir, we are here for three weeks during which we need to gather enough information and write a report with recommendation for assistance from the Internal Revenue Service. How soon can we interview the tax manager at the Lozenets office?"

"As soon as tomorrow." He picked up the phone and arranged the meeting.

We left feeling good as we were accomplishing a lot in a very short time. There was no need for a translator; I was asking my own questions, adding some of my colleague's, and translating. Back at the hotel, we put our notes together and headed for dinner.

The next day after breakfast, we decided to walk to the Lozenets tax office. It was a longer walk, but for me, this was a special and emotional experience as we were going to pass by the part of town where I grew up. For my colleague, it was an opportunity to get to know the city. We crossed St. Nedelya Square and walked by the St. Nedelya Church with its beautiful domes. The square was lively with people rushing to work, some selling *gevreci* (similar to bagels) and others selling newspapers or flowers. We walked toward Sofia's well-known commercial and pedestrian boulevard, Vitosha. This was the neighborhood where I grew up. My street was coming up, and I felt my heart beating faster. Childhood memories came to life as I could see myself playing ball in the street or in the schoolyard across my apartment building, shopping for my grandma, and later, as teenager, getting together with friends from school and listening to music and dancing. I looked around. The boulevard had changed. There were outdoor restaurants, cafés, and pastry shops. The displays on the shop windows were with fashionable clothing, shoes, jewelries, and souvenirs. As we passed my street, Parchevich, I noticed new, remodeled restaurants on the corner. There was no trace of the old, shabby, and empty stores with few things to offer. And the abundance of food and goods was definitely something new. I was absorbing it all with a smile, glancing at the man next to me, as we walked by pastry shops, inhaling the smell of delicious baked treats.

"These people live well. I didn't expect anything modern and definitely not the variety of goods. Looking around, I see everybody dressed well. The cafés are full with people. I really like this city. Everything seems to be very modern," he said.

"This is all new to me," I responded. "All changes happened so fast I can't recognize my own neighborhood. You can't imagine the pleasure it gives me to see a new image of my hometown. Now across is the park of the National Palace of Culture. There were army barracks here in the past. This new, beautiful building holds cultural events, hence its name. Soon we will be at the Lozenets tax office."

We walked into the building, and the porter directed us to the tax manager's office.

"Welcome and please sit down." The tax manager was a tall, well-built man in his early thirties. We shook hands and, after exchanging words of formality, moved to specific questions relative to their work. "We work in a very difficult environment," he started. "Similar to yours at Al Capone times with mafia and crime. We all know how your tax officials put behind bars Al Capone. My inspectors are educated and very professional, but they are intimidated at businesses with armed bodyguards, especially the women. We are eager to hear about your methods of work, your tax policies." The man confirmed what we already knew; the inspectors were accepting invoices for business deductions without any questions. The usual scenario was that deductions exceeded income. Fake invoices were sold in the street, but there was no law allowing the inspectors to raise any questions about the validity of the documents. I proceeded by giving the man a brief synopsis of the IRS Exam and Criminal Investigation Division's work.

The tax manager introduced us to some of his inspectors who were in the office that day and the clerical staff at the counters.

They provided us with blank forms of tax documents—registration for businesses, tax receipts, correspondence, and declarations (tax returns). The manager explained line by line the forms and added, "Tax season is crazy here as the lines are long and people spend a day in order to file their declarations."

"There is no mail system?"

"No," he responded. "Filing is done in person."

We left the tax office, taking the same route back, amazed of the crowds of people out in the street, in restaurants, and in cafés—it was lunchtime. We couldn't help but notice expensive Mercedes, Audi, or BMW vehicles. Later, I found out that car theft of foreign cars in Bulgaria was prevalent, hence the abundance of luxury cars in the streets.

The following Monday, we visited the second big city in Bulgaria—Plovdiv, an ancient city built on seven hills with the river Maritsa providing relief in the hot summer months. It's believed to be the oldest city in Europe. Since we arrived on a Sunday, we used the day to walk around and explore. We were ready for our upcoming meetings having worked hard at the hotel the previous two days. We headed toward the old town. I was also curious as this was my first time in Plovdiv. I was taking it all with eyes wide open, the scenery of street vendors offering beautiful paintings with landscapes of Bulgarian villages and the Black sea or portraits and icons of saints. Handmade embroidered tablecloths, napkins, pillowcases, and handkerchiefs of colorful designs reminded me of Grandma's woven rugs, making me sad and happy at the same time. We were both astounded at the sight of the outdoor Roman theater, an amazing structure of ancient civilization, built in a semicircle facing the mountain with seats surrounding the stage. I took a deep breath and sat on one of the benches, just absorbing in bliss the scenery. Our driver left us for a while and returned a little tipsy. That was not like him as I was told that he did not drink.

He pulled me to the side, sighed, dropped his head down, and said, "You know that the officials at the Ministry are former Communists."

I lifted his head and responded, "I know," to which he was dumbfounded.

"Nina, I had to drink to get the courage to tell you this."

"I appreciate your desire to help and your honesty, but we know that a lot of the government officials can be linked to the past. My mission here is to help the country with my knowledge and skills in taxation," I responded.

"Oh, okay, so long as you know. I just wanted to be of help." He seemed relieved, and his face lightened up.

We continued our walk past the Kapana area with trendy shops (a sign of the new life in the city), outdoor restaurants, and cafés. Fashionable clothes and handmade jewelries of semiprecious stones were all displayed in the windows of the shops. Heading toward the old town, we walked down cobblestone streets lined with historic houses from the Ottoman Empire, some of which we visited, and we peeked into the antique shops. We could see on one of the hills the monument of Alyosha, a Russian soldier who died during the occupation of Bulgaria in 1944. There was a controversy with this monument as some people wanted it torn down.

The next day, meetings at the Plovdiv regional tax office were very productive. The regional director and his assistant gave us a tour of the building, specifying the functions of each of the administrative staff. The methods of work at the Plovdiv tax office were similar to those in Sofia. Inspectors were operating under the old rules for auditing state offices by matching receipts and company records with reported income and deductions. Mafia was on the rise, governing the lives of small businesses with extortion. Major sources of revenues for the tax regional office were payroll taxes on wages.

Next stop was Burgas, a city on the Black Sea. My colleague was enjoying the countryside of the Balkan mountain with tucked in villages and seeing unusual sights, he would ask the driver to stop for pictures. Meetings with the tax officials were not any different from our previous ones. We received similar information about the tax inspectors' ways of work. The local tax office we visited was not in a good condition as I recall old offices with worn-out desks and chairs, and there was a need for computers. Back at the hotel, we walked by a very lively casino with loud English music. Once in my room, I propped a chair against the door, as I did a long time before in New York City and Mexico City, and collapsed in my bed from exhaustion. In the morning, we headed back to Sofia, a drive of five hundred kilometers, crossing the beautiful Rose Valley at the bottom of the Balkan mountain.

My colleague and I were very content with the gathered information from the regions and the tax offices. Having visited three major cities, we were confident that our findings were a reflection of the entire country's tax law operations. Tax offices were structured the same way in every region with a regional office and a director in charge of local tax offices. We were greeted everywhere with smiles and eagerness to provide us with all necessary information. There was a genuine interest to learn and work in the same way as their American counterparts. Tax officials everywhere extended their warm welcome, showing gratitude for our visits and enthusiasm to learn about the Internal Revenue Service. Because of time restriction, we both agreed on providing a condensed one-day workshop about application of indirect methods in auditing for all regional directors in Sofia. We had a week to wrap up our work with final meetings with top tax officials. My colleague was counting on me to put together the report for TAAS with proposals for a long-term tax assistance to the country.

We were back in Sofia on Saturday, April 17, 1992. This was a day to remember as at the hotel's reception desk, they said that in the evening, there would be Easter services for the first time at the churches in the city and the whole country, with a midnight procession where everybody follows the priest around the church, holding lit candles. I definitely wanted to attend the service at St. Nedelya Church by the hotel as this was a historical event—attending services was unthinkable under Communism; actually, it was forbidden. Bulgarians remained Christians and preserved their Eastern Orthodox faith during five centuries of Ottoman Empire rule—a rule that failed to convert the people to Muslims—and later during a Communist regime of forty-six years from 1944 to 1990, when practicing religion was forbidden and punishable. Memories of my mother sneaking me as a child to light a candle and say a prayer in another church, St. Petka, popped in my head. This church was close to the hotel, but it was on a side street and not so visible.

I worked all day preparing for the workshop. My colleague provided me with a big flowchart paper, which I used to outline my discussion. The sources and applications' indirect method was the most comprehensive to teach, so for my audience to grasp it, I created teaching materials on this topic in Bulgarian language. I recalled hearing that there was no accrual method of accounting, which simplified the presentation. To reinforce the concept of gathering information and using investigative skills, I developed a scenario involving the participation of the listeners.

Before dinner, I met with my colleague, and I showed him all the materials I prepared for the course in Bulgarian with English translation for him to understand.

"This is amazing, Nina. Teaching in Bulgarian language will save us time. You did a great job of putting the course together based on our IRS model."

We grabbed a bite at the hotel for dinner and called it a night. I decided to take a little nap before going to church, as it was Good Friday. Soon I was dozing off in a deep sleep, hearing in the distance the loud noise of people chanting. I did not wake up until next morning, which was a big disappointment. I looked out the window and saw the entire square covered with wax from the candles. Running down to the reception, the girl looked at me all excited.

"It was a big party last night. The entire city was out. The square in front of us was packed with people holding candles, and restaurants and cafés were open all night. This was the first big Easter celebration since the fall of Communism."

"Wow, I slept through it all. I can just imagine the joy and happiness of people being free to pray and celebrate Christ's resurrection. I could visualize people crowding to hear the service, saying prayers out loud and later filling up the restaurants, laughing, singing, being genuinely happy." Churches in Bulgaria do not close, so I ran over to St. Nedelya and lit candles for the health of my children, mother, relatives, and friends and candles for my deceased grandma and grandpa and my uncles. My colleague and I spent Easter morning going over our schedule for the rest of the week—meetings with the minister of Finance, the assistant minister (commissioner), and Sofia's regional director; holding the workshop; and doing a roundtable discussion with government officials and economic specialists in a TV emission (there was an invitation left for us at the hotel with the time and place for it). We wrapped up our work talks and discussions, and I hurried to spend the rest of the day with my aunt.

For the first time in Bulgaria, I could worship, pray, and celebrate freely with family. My aunt was as jovial as I have known her; she always had a big smile and laughter showing how happy she was to see me.

"Come on in, child. I have red eggs, the color for the blood of Christ. Take one and tap it on mine. See which one remains unbroken." That is a Bulgarian custom for children and adults alike. We had the usual Easter dessert, *kozunak* (sweet bread with raisins), and I listened to my aunt talk, feeling like a child again. "Yes, Nina, times changed very fast. We are free to talk, to listen to music and news from all over the world, to go to church. The stores are full of goods."

I nodded in agreement and started telling my aunt about my impressions from traveling. "Auntie, we could hear American and English music everywhere in the restaurants, cafés, parks. The streets were so lively—vendors selling art, people dressed in fashionable clothes, especially women. Well, some of them dressing too skimpy, with transparent blouses and very short skirts and dresses and all on high heels. There's American advertising everywhere for American products. I really can't recognize the country."

Soon I bid my aunt goodbye and stepped out in the busiest pedestrian street in the city, Vitosha Boulevard. I took a deep breath of the fresh spring air and felt an overcoming sensation of happiness, something extraordinary, which I remember feeling when arriving in New York for the first time. It was freedom that I could taste, hear, smell, see, and touch in my homeland.

I woke up with a buzzing sound in my ear. Looking at the bathroom's mirror, I saw my cheek swollen and red. Leaving the window open to feel the fresh spring breeze at night let darn mosquitoes in the room (I did not pay attention that there were no screens). I don't wear makeup, but this morning, I was glad to hide the redness and puffiness of my face. It actually soothed my skin. I looked over my notes for teaching the workshop on indirect audit techniques. The session was starting at 8:00 a.m., and I had time to gather my thoughts and envision the entire sequence of teaching the lessons and holding discussions. The phone ring made me startle. "Hello?"

"Hi, Nina. Are you ready? We need to leave in half an hour." My companion was already in the restaurant when I went down for breakfast. We did not talk much. I guess we were both concentrated on the tight schedule of events for the week.

We arrived at Sofia's regional tax office early, and headed to the designated conference room. Walking in, we noticed that the place was already packed full of people having lively discussions with fiery eyes and gestures. I saw familiar faces, which put me at ease. Those were the regional tax directors of Sofia, Plovdiv, and Burgas, as well as tax managers of regional offices. I went over to greet them all and shook hands with others around them. I felt immediately at ease and relaxed. It was the friendly atmosphere setting the tone of my speech, giving me confidence and reassurance. I walked back to the podium setting up the flowchart, then I took out my notes, arranged them in order, and looked at my watch. It was time. My colleague nodded at me, and I started.

"Good morning. I want to thank you all for taking time from your busy schedules to come and spend the day with me. My name is Antonina. I am a representative from the Internal Revenue Service. My area of specialty is exam. I am a native Bulgarian. I graduated from the English language high school in Sofia in 1968. I have lived in the United States since 1970. The purpose of my visit is to analyze the current state of the Bulgarian tax administration and provide recommendations for changes suitable for a system with free market economy. I had the honor of visiting the Sofia, Plovdiv, and Burgas tax departments, meeting very dedicated, enthusiastic, and competent tax officials. Their directors are among us, and I thank them for providing me with necessary information to accomplish my task. Today I am going to present you with materials used to track tax evasion since Al Capone time." There was a giggle among people, and I continued with enthusiasm my presentation of indirect methods use, concentrating mostly on sources and applications.

By noon, I covered the essentials of conducting an effective interview for setting the audit (something not known in the Bulgarian audit practice of document matching). We had a working lunch during which I was bombarded with questions for specific cases. Returning to the conference room, I noticed a photographer and a middle-aged, tall, and somewhat heavyset gentleman. I recognized him immediately; it was the Bulgarian prime minister. Our eyes met, and I headed toward him.

"Hello, sir, it's a pleasure meeting you."

"Hi, Antonina. I heard about you and the workshop you are teaching. Thank you for coming to help."

"Sir, it is a tremendous pleasure for me to be able to share my knowledge and expertise. Thank you for offering me this opportunity. It means a lot to me as Bulgaria is my homeland. And this is my colleague from Washington, DC."

After shaking hands, the prime minister looked around the room. "Well, this is an occasion to be remembered. Let's all take positions for a photograph."

I did not notice how time went by in the afternoon. The problem I presented was from my own cases, which caught everybody's attention. To my surprise, my audience comprehended the concept immediately.

"Antonina," the regional director from Kardzhali said as he stood up, "this is wonderful, and thank you for providing us this information, especially with a real-life case scenario. All the cases we have qualify for use of indirect methods you just talked about. However, the issue is that we do not have tax laws allowing us to apply this method."

"Sir, you have an appeals court. You can take the cases to court, and the court's decision will set a precedence." There were no more questions; silence meant that they were thinking about it, but it also meant that they needed time to internalize this process. I looked around staring at their faces. "I am very hopeful that my lecture today will be of help to all of you. This is a very simplified presentation given the short time I had to talk to you. But it is the basis for auditing and I encourage you to introduce it in your regions. What you are experiencing now is what happened in America at the turn of the century. Mobsters were reigning the country and terrorizing small businesses. It was the Internal Revenue Service which brought them to justice. You all know Al Capone." All of a sudden, there was a movement, and I could hear words of approval exchanged among the directors.

My colleague and I said goodbye to each one of them, meeting them at the door and shaking their hands as they were leaving. My colleague looked at me. "What did you say to liven up the audience? I heard you mention Al Capone."

"Oh, I just compared Bulgaria to America at the turn of the century when IRS was the only government organization successful at dealing with the mobsters."

"How clever, Nina. This is a very good assessment."

The roundtable discussion on national television was early in the morning. I dressed in the suit I liked most, navy skirt and light-pink blazer. I sat together with my colleague surrounded by top Bulgarian tax officials and economists. The topic of the discussion was the transition from state to free market economy and its impact on tax policy and administration and was, of course, in Bulgarian language. The TV facilitator opened the discussion by introducing each of the participants. He was intrigued by the purpose of our visit and role in Bulgarian taxation, so he directed the first questions to us. He started to speak looking at us.

"I'd like to welcome to our program visitors from the American tax administration." Then he addressed us, "Your presence is much appreciated as our viewers will be interested about your visit. Can you describe your impression of the current status of the tax administration here?"

"I am sure it's everybody's guess that the current practices are not just outdated, they are ineffective," I spoke slowly, observing the faces of all present and looking at the facilitator's eyes. "Privately owned businesses operate completely different than the state-owned enterprises of the past. Therefore, introducing new tax policies and effective exam and collection programs are crucial for Bulgaria's successful development. Bulgaria's infrastructure depending on tax revenues is experiencing difficult times sustaining programs such as education, health, and transportation, to name a few." I took a moment to translate for my companion as the second question came in.

"What is your involvement in this process?"

I caught my breath and continued, "Our goal as representatives of the American tax administration was to evaluate the current operations of the tax offices and provide recommendations for changes." I again whispered the translation to my colleague, and he nodded in approval. I was energized, speaking with passion, feeling my eyes being wide open, which I was sure were sparkling from the excitement of delivering a speech about necessary changes in Bulgaria, the country where I grew up, the country I left twenty-some years ago, and the country where I came back to assist.

That evening, my aunt and my father called, both thrilled to see me on TV. My aunt's voice was shaking, as if she was crying. "I saw you, Nina. You were so pretty, and you talked so well. I could feel the emotions you were going through. My child, I am so proud of you."

Dad was more reserved, but I could sense that he was also affected by watching me on TV. "Nina, I want to congratulate you. I am very happy for you. Stop by for dinner tomorrow."

Another day full of emotions was ahead of me. The minister of Finance, equivalent to secretary of Treasury, requested to meet us. His secretary announced us and led us to the minister's office. As we walked in, he stood up and greeted us with a wide smile; he was a young man in his late thirties, of medium height. "Hello, Nina. I heard about your work and how much you accomplished in such a short time. I wanted to thank you and your colleague in person."

I translated for my companion and turned back to the minister. "Sir, this visit has a great significance for me. I came back to help my homeland. Thank you for this opportunity."

At which the man looked at me and said jokingly, "Why don't you stay? We can make you a minister." I smiled in return.

We wrapped up our trip by holding final meetings with the commissioner, the general secretary, and Sofia's regional director. We provided them all with a brief outline of our findings with recommendations for changes and improvements. Before leaving, I informed them of what would take place next. I thanked them for providing us with the opportunity to evaluate the current status of the Bulgarian administration, which we would use to write a report. I explained that based on this report, I would formulate a plan for providing advisory services, and upon approval and invitation from the Bulgarian government, a long-term assistance would be offered with an IRS official stationed in Sofia.

Saying goodbye to my aunt was sad. She had a female friend visiting her every day, and that made me feel better, but still leaving her was heartbreaking. She was like a mother to me. I left the apartment with tears in my eyes. I kept my promise to stop by my father's. My stepmother Budinka was friendly, very different from the cold lady I met when I was eighteen and looking for my father to say goodbye. That was when I was fixing to leave for Belgrade after being admitted to study economics there. It was shortly after I graduated from high school. I haven't seen my father since I was nine, the time when he took me to a restaurant and asked me if I wanted to live with him and a woman he was planning to marry. He disappeared from my life after that day, but nonetheless, I wanted to say goodbye before I left for Yugoslavia. The memory came back to me, anxiously going up the stairs where I knew Dad lived on Rakovski Street. A tiny dark-haired woman opened the door, and at her feet was a little boy, with light hair and bright eyes, looking curiously at me.

"I am Nina. Is my father, Professor Duridanov, at home? I want to tell him goodbye before leaving to study in Belgrade."

"Your father is not home. He will not be home any time soon. Wait here." She went to the phone and came back shaking her head. "Just talked to him. He is not coming home today." The tone of her voice was cold and dry, and her face was stern. I turned and walked away. After all these years, he still did not want to see me.

But here I was twenty-some years later at my father's apartment.

"Come on in, Nina. We are so happy to have you come. I am glad you found time to have dinner with us." Budinka's voice brought me back from my memories, and I smiled. She was talking away, leading me into the living room. "I hope you like my cooking. It's chicken and vegetables with Bulgarian spices."

"Thank you for inviting me." I looked at my father. He was more reserved but animated with a sparkle in his eyes.

"Nina, I am very happy for your achievements. I know you succeeded on your own, and I cannot take credit for it. But you are my daughter, and you make me proud."

Back home in Lexington, Michigan, Mom and the kids were very excited to see me. I missed them so much. The older ones had big smiles on their faces as I hugged them, but Anabelle was jumping and dancing around me. I dropped the suitcase and hugged my mom, taking her to the living room. I did not want to eat or drink; I just wanted to talk.

"Everything is different in Bulgaria, Mom. People are nice and friendly. The passport control and customs officials were very polite, and I did not feel scared for the first time in my life crossing that border. You know, the other two times I came to Bulgaria in 1981 and 1983, I was very apprehensive crossing the border, and they were so serious and stern. And the stores are full of goods and food. Everybody is dressed well. You could hear American music blasting from the cafés in the park and outside in the streets. There are commercial ads about American products everywhere you look and go. There are more luxurious cars—Mercedes, Audi, BMW—in the streets of Sofia than here in the States. One day, in the elevator at Sheraton, a man laughed and said, 'I don't know what we are doing here with our assistance programs. These people are doing fine.'" I must have babbled for a couple of hours, showing pictures of what I saw.

That evening, I crashed from exhaustion, overwhelmed with feelings beyond imagination. The images of new Bulgaria were so vivid in my mind; the dramatic changes were powerful and unbelievable to conceive. My contact with the government officials in

Washington and Bulgaria and realizing the importance and impact of my visit occupied my thoughts.

Back at the IRS international exam group in Detroit, my manager was very intrigued to learn about my assignment, and I recaptured for him all important parts of my stay and work in Bulgaria. I brought for the group small souvenirs, including Bulgarian grappa, which was consumed after work and was remembered for a long time.

I do not recall much of the summer in 1992, except rewriting my report for TAAS a few times. Until one day, in September, the TAAS director called to inform me that the Treasury director in charge of the assistance programs to countries in Eastern Europe had included me in a follow-up visit to Bulgaria, this time for six weeks. The assignment was scheduled to start at the beginning of October.

"I hope I am not travelling alone," I whispered.

"Of course not, Antonina. Another one of my employees will accompany you. His specialty is collection, and you will be working as a team as you did in the first visit."

"Thank you." I sighed with a relief. "When will I get the details for the travel?"

"My secretary is working on that, and you will get them in a week or so. You did a great job the first time, and we feel you will accomplish a lot the next time. I will be contacting your manager today to arrange for your leave."

"Thank you, sir. I am glad that you found my work in April successful, and thank you for your confidence in me."

I met my new colleague at Dulles Airport in DC. This time, I did not have a briefing, and my flight was straight to Bulgaria. I recognized the man by the description he gave me on the phone prior to my departure. He was about my height (five foot five), slim, with light-brown hair. He was different from my first companion. In a short time, I learned about each of the TAAS employees—their professional careers and personal lives, if they were single or divorced, and who they were seeing. We had to switch planes in Frankfurt, and in about twenty-five hours, with all the delays in transfers, we arrived in Sofia.

"Hello, Nina." I turned and recognized the customs official from the Ministry of Finance. I was pleased to see him and immediately introduced him to my colleague. The man from customs did not speak English, so I translated the next few sentences of the conversation. Bulgarian customs officials arranged for our luggage to be picked up and walked us through passport and customs control. The same driver was waiting outside the airport and drove us to Sheraton Hotel, where all the staff, from the concierge to the receptionist, welcomed me back. After unpacking and resting for a couple of hours, I met my colleague for dinner. We stayed in as we were both suffering from jet lag and were not in a mood to go out.

"I have the contact information for all tax officials whom we need to meet, starting with the commissioner and the regional director for the city of Sofia," I started to speak as we were seated at the table.

"That's fantastic. Let's sit together tomorrow morning and organize our schedule and activities. We can call at this time and arrange meetings. We need to be flexible as they might present us with requests and tasks which we can assist with on policy and administration questions. I am beat, and I am sure you are too. Let's call it a night. See you tomorrow morning."

This mission flew by as fast as the first even though it was twice as long. I briefed my new colleague on all contacts of Bulgarian government officials in the capital and the provinces. We scheduled meetings, some in private with the commissioner and tax directors and others with tax officials nationwide, with weeklong lectures on auditing and collection activities. I was excited to see familiar faces again, and before I started my speech, I saw a raised hand in the public. It was the Kardzhali tax director (this is an area close to the Turkish border). I nodded, and the man stood up with a radiant face.

"Ms. Nina, we did it. We applied the indirect method of sources and application from your lecture, and we won the case in Supreme Court." At that moment, everybody started to clap. I was ecstatic. This was working, and my efforts were already showing results. The man described the case with the business history and operations of the company, the issues being the typical enormous losses common in the entire country. He talked about the auditor's work using the techniques and formulas that I provided, the appeal process, and the final outcome. I heartily shook his hand, thanking him for the great work and congratulating him for the successful outcome of the audit in his region, setting precedence for tax offices nationwide to apply the same auditing procedures.

My new lectures were more detailed with information on specific interview questions, request of pertinent records, third-party information, and collaboration between tax offices, all based on US tax codes. I was examining faces while speaking and immediately reacted to individuals with expressions of disbelief or frustration. Was it going to work for all businesses? This being a mini audit workshop, I explained that in the IRS, we had audit technique guidelines for specific businesses such as restaurants, gas stations, or trucking and that I will look into supplying this information.

The five-day workshops each on exam and collection (my colleague had a collection background) with regional directors and tax managers nationwide, were held in Sofia, Plovdiv, and Varna. I added to my discussion the already won Supreme Court tax case in Bulgaria, which picked up the curiosity and the interest of all attendees. I taught in Bulgarian and my colleague in English, which I translated in Bulgarian. I had my lectures translated in English for my colleague to follow, so I did not do simultaneous translation for the exam portion of my teaching. My colleague gave examples of executing a levy and seizure of property with citation of US tax laws, which also stirred up interest with people exclaiming wow. We could tell that our teaching was successful from the reaction of our audience. Men and women were nodding in agreement, smiling, and eagerly taking notes.

We were at the end of the program, having a late dinner after a long day of teaching in Varna, when Sofia's regional tax director called. "Nina, I need you back in Sofia immediately. We need to present arguments for doing tax criminal investigations before the parliament in the morning. There will be a plane waiting for you and your colleague at the airport in Varna in one hour."

Arriving after midnight at the hotel in Sofia, I worked till dawn translating internal revenue code provisions and specific federal criminal code and rules citations used by the Criminal Investigation Division in the States in investigating and convicting individuals committing tax crimes. We met Sofia's tax director in the early hours of the morning. He glanced at my papers and nodded his head. "You are terrific. This is what we need. But why are you saying secretary of Treasury? You probably meant minister."

"Yes, I meant minister. In the States, these positions are called secretaries."

He started to laugh. "And how do you call the secretary of your secretary of Finance?"

"Good question." I was tired from teaching for three weeks straight and staying up most of the night. This question made me laugh. I guess we all needed a little humor.

My colleague left before me. The night prior to his departure, we met at the hotel's nightclub to summarize notes from the three weeks' work. As we were talking, he exclaimed, "She is completely naked!"

I turned around and saw a naked female dancer on the stage, to which I shrugged my shoulders and responded, "So what?" We managed to finish our discussion, but before leaving, the man said that the big boss, the Treasury director in charge of all tax assistance programs to Eastern European countries, was arriving the following day to meet with me. I had to prepare a briefing of our activities, findings, and a rough sketch for future assistance.

The director arrived late in the afternoon from Paris. We met briefly in the lobby to concur on what was perspiring the next day. He was a man in his late forties with piercing blue eyes and cold complexion, showing no emotion. "We need an appointment with the Bulgarian commissioner. During our meeting with him, you will provide a report of your work, your accomplishments, and your opinion of necessary future involvement based on your observations. You speak Bulgarian, so you will be speaking in Bulgarian and trans- lating for me. I will prefer a meeting not later than ten a.m. Get a good night's rest." With that, he turned around and left, which gave me an opportunity to prepare for my presentation the following day.

I arranged the meeting and reviewed my notes, which I prepared the night before, of a speech regarding the status of the current Bulgarian tax administration, deficiencies in the system, and necessary changes. The Bulgarian commissioner greeted us very cordially, thanking us for the visit, and after the usual exchange of handshakes and introductions, he led us to the familiar conference room. I immediately started to speak, outlining my topics and describing in detail how we toured the country to gather information of current tax administration practices. I was speaking directly to the tax commissioner in Bulgarian, with simultaneous translation to the Treasury director.

"Mr. Commissioner, the current work of auditors is futile as they simply compare invoices to reported numbers on tax returns. I heard that businesses purchase invoices on the street or just falsify blank invoices. Cheating is common and present in all visited tax offices of the major cities starting with the capital, then Plovdiv, Burgas, and Varna. I conducted workshops outlining authority for US revenue agents to conduct effective examinations. My lectures outlined specific stages of a tax exam necessary to reach a correct conclusion for the real tax liability of the audited entity or individual. The sequence of executing these steps is of great significance for a successful audit, and they are conducting interviews, touring businesses, requesting records, contacting third parties, and collaborating with other tax offices nationwide as well as government agencies, for example, customs. Tax officials nationwide confirmed that all businesses report huge losses [luckily, you do not have a provision for net operating losses carryback and carryforward], so highly profitable businesses do not pay income tax. I feel that my courses on auditing are already showing positive results. After our first visit in April 1992, the Kardzhali tax director had his auditors apply indirect methods, which I taught in a brief workshop. The case was appealed and decided in favor of the government. The Bulgarian tax authorities already have a precedence to use successfully indirect methods."

As I made this statement, both the Bulgarian tax commissioner and the Treasury director exclaimed, "Unbelievable! Wonderful!"

"Nina, go on, what are your recommendations?"

"My colleague and I discussed our observations, and we both determined that the exam program as well as collection need manuals to unify the efforts of all tax officials in the field. The best approach to accomplish this is to use a pilot tax office, centrally located as the one in Lozenets. Our assistance will consist of daily work with auditors to gain insight of current conditions—accounting methods, cutoff periods, business practices in different sectors such as trucking, manufacturing, etc. This will be the basis for creating an audit manual similar to the one used in America but adapted to capture peculiar Bulgarian conditions. Auditors will be introduced to interviewing, touring of businesses, and conducting audits on site rather than in the tax office."

I continued talking for a couple of hours, hardly catching my breath, emphasizing every point I made and looking both gentlemen in the eyes, studying their reaction. My speech was passionate. I relived all the time I spent with Bulgarian inspectors and managers, describing their feelings of helplessness and desire to learn real auditing used in a free market economy. And then I was done. Looking intensely at the Bulgarian and American tax officials, I said in conclusion, "That's it for now. What I am proposing is a long-term work for the creation and application of an income tax exam manual. This will also involve a lot of training not just in lecturing but also in the field." Both men seemed very pleased with my presentation, smiling and congratulating me for a work well done.

Back at the hotel, I had a chance to gather my thoughts and relax. I was satisfied with the accomplishments and results of my assignment. And suddenly, I felt the urge to go home and be with my children. I missed them so much. I had a model airplane for Anabelle, which I bought on the way to Bulgaria. I painfully remembered how sad she was when I traveled the first time. And Erik was a freshman in college. I was so proud of him getting a high GPA to be accepted at Hope College. Leaving him at the dormitory was difficult; I kept thinking of all kind of things to buy so I could spend more time with him. "You need a microwave to warm snacks." So I made one last run to Meijer before heading back to Lexington, Michigan. I also missed Vanesa. Her best friend's mom passed away, and I needed to hug her and comfort her.

I was finally on the plane. Taking a big breath, I took my seat and closed my eyes.

"Ma'am, I am taking your suitcase down because it is above my seat," shrieked a middle-aged German guy, so he did that. But another German man behind me stood up, took my suitcase, and placed it back on the rack. That went on for a while until a stewardess came and resolved the argument. The man who took my suitcase down was from former East Germany and believed that the luggage rack above his seat was his; the man from behind was from former West Germany and expressed indignation for all these people from the east shaming the German nation. I am mentioning this incident because it was an experience to compare behavior of people from the same country coming from different social systems.

After fifteen hours of flying, we landed at Detroit airport. I was watching the Fasten Seat Belt sign, eager to get up and run. I could hardly wait to get off the plane and see the children and my mother. Spending time with my family was the most precious time that I remember of those days. I would just sit and watch everything around me—Mom cooking, Anabelle running in and out the house, Vanesa studying—and of course, I had to go see how Richard was doing.

Back home, I continued to audit foreign corporations and spent weeks at the time on the road. It was in March of 1993 when my manager called me to his office, and smiling, he asked me to take a seat.

"I have news for you, which I know will make you happy. The TAAS director called me and said that you are selected to represent the Internal Revenue Service in Bulgaria for one year. This is a big honor and a testimony of your hard work and dedication to the Service in promoting United States values. He faxed me the departure notification and details for your assignment. You will be leaving in April." My manager did not even ask if I agreed. He stood up and shook my hand.

My head was spinning as I left the office. Such assignments were given to tax officials of higher grades and ranks in senior management. There were no computers with internet at the time, and I knew I had to pack the tax code with all tax regulations, classroom books with all possible materials, textbooks, and information from managers of specialized groups, CID being the most important.

Destiny or Hard Work

I had a month and a half to prepare. First, I packed all my training books for revenue agents and international examiners, the Internal Revenue Code, all the regulations, the audit manual, and the audit techniques materials for auditing gas stations, restaurants, gambling casinos, and other specialized businesses. I contacted a manager of a revenue agent group in Vegas who provided me with an audit manual for casinos, asked an excise tax manager for audit techniques for excise tax, and interviewed a CID manager to obtain information for proceedings in criminal investigation leading to indictment and conviction. I knew about the collaboration between revenue agents and special agents, and that was a start. My government computer Zenith had only Word and Excel, so I took along saved hard copies of some of my most important cases, which I knew would come in handy. I also packed blank tax forms and documents used for auditing.

I received authorization to take along my girls and Anabelle's father. My mother had already left for Bulgaria to take care of my aunt, but shortly before that, she became an American citizen, which made her extremely proud. We had a private celebration at home starting with a prayer to thank God for providing Mom with an opportunity to be a part of this beautiful, free, and heroic nation. She showed her certificate to all neighbors, telling everybody how hard she studied to pass the citizenship test. I admired Mom for her courage and determination to become a United States citizen. I was concerned about leaving my son behind as he decided to stay and study at Hope College in Holland, Michigan. But I talked with his roommate's parents who agreed to keep him for the summer in their Chicago home, which made me feel better knowing that he would not be alone and would be safe.

It was May 1993 and here we were at Frankfurt Airport surrounded by our luggage of thirty boxes and twenty duffel bags. It was an extreme effort to hire a cart and have them transferred to the plane for Sofia, not to talk about the extra fee. If this was today, all I would need would be my computer, maybe a few books. At Sofia Airport, we were met by familiar faces from the Ministry of Finance customs department. "I can't believe the luggage you brought," said our host.

"I know, but the boxes are all for my work. Do you think we can take them directly to the Ministry of Finance?"

"This is a great idea," he responded. "They have already assigned you an office there, and that will be the best solution." It was evening when we finally settled in at my aunt's apartment, where we were going to live for the next year.

The next day, I arrived earlier than other employees, feeling good that I had the key to my office and that I could get to work right away. But the security guard had a different idea, and since I had no Bulgarian ID for the ministry, he was very reluctant to let me in. "Listen, here is a key to my office. I arrived yesterday, and I will be working in this building for the next year. You could call the commissioner's secretary if you want to confirm. Otherwise, I will go back to my apartment and call my boss to tell him that you did not let me in and I am not working today."

He looked at me with a grimace on his face. "Okay, go in." I knew he had seen me before from my last visits, but he just wanted to be difficult. This did not occur again.

My office was very small; the furniture consisted of two desks with enough space to walk in front of them and a bookcase. It was facing south, looking into an enclosed courtyard with a view of other offices in the building, and of course, no air-conditioning but a window, which I could open. Apart from my Zenith laptop, I brought a humungous desk computer from DC with the same word processing and Excel spreadsheets capacity. The Ministry of Finance provided me with another desktop computer having Cyrillic alphabet, which I requested, so I could prepare training materials, tax administration and tax law documents, and correspondence in Bulgarian language.

The desk computers were huge, occupying most of the space on the desks. I appreciated the bookcase for being able to arrange my books.

I immediately got to work. First, I called the commissioner's secretary to inform her that I arrived, then I walked over to the office of the Treasury advisor (I forgot to mention that Treasury also assigned an individual with statistics background to be an advisor to the Bulgarian Finance Ministry at the same time, whose job was to assist with computer programs monitoring tax revenue. He was a tall, slim man from the East Coast with state government experience. He met me at the door, smiling. "Hi, Nina. I heard of you. Didn't think you will be in today, probably suffering badly from jet lag."

"Hi," I responded. "I heard of you too, and I wanted to meet you. I know our specialties are different, but if there is anything I could help you with, let me know. I grew up in this city, and speaking Bulgarian helps."

"Thanks, Nina. I want to show you something very neat. It's called e-mail, and I can keep in touch with my wife all the time."

"I like that, but none of my computers have internet," I responded.

"Well, then if something comes up, I am here to offer you my computer."

On my way back to my office, I was thinking about the e-mail service. I knew that I did not need it since none of my bosses, my son, or my friends in the States had one. I was supposed to provide TAAS a weekly report and Treasury a monthly report using a fax machine. I got to work unpacking and arranging the materials and textbooks on the bookshelves and in the desk drawers by topics. It was noon when there was a knock on the door. It was a short and stout young man who extended his hand as soon as I opened the door.

"Hello, ma'am, I am assigned from the Ministry of Finance to be your assistant. Let's go to lunch."

I suggested we go to the cafeteria as I had so much to do. The food at the cafeteria was very good with a menu of typical Bulgarian dishes.

"I can schedule your appointments," the man started.

"Well, I appreciate that, but I already have all phone numbers of the people I need to see, and since I know the individuals whom I need to contact, I prefer to schedule my own appointments. I will need a hand with straightening out the office to begin with."

He looked at me in astonishment. "There is a cleaning personnel and other workers who can do that."

"I understand, but I need to organize all the books in a way that I can find them easily."

"Well, I can't help you with that because I can't lift anything, so I'll come tomorrow same time for lunch."

Strange, I thought to myself but did not say anything.

The next day, I scheduled all appointments—one with the commissioner, then with the regional tax director of the city of Sofia, and finally with the tax manager of Lozenets tax office, which I selected for a pilot program. I also called the tax manager of Vazov office in Sofia, a lady whom I felt close to, and was going to share with her materials from my work at the Lozenets office. My assistant showed up for lunch as he promised. During lunch, I found out that he did not type, he did not take notes, and his English was not that good, which made me wonder how he was supposed to assist me.

"I thought that my job as assistant is to only arrange for your meetings." He added, "By the way, do you have a car? I can find you a new Audi for five thousand dollars, but you cannot drive it out of the country."

I knew exactly what that meant; he was dealing with stolen vehicles. "Thank you, but I don't need a car. I use taxis, and for trips outside the capital, I can rent a car." He shrugged his shoulders and left.

I had everything arranged in my office by the end of the day. The following day, I met with the commissioner who welcomed me back. I thanked him for the accommodations at the Ministry of Finance and informed him of my plans for the week. After meeting in the afternoon with Sofia's regional tax director and getting his approval to start my pilot program at the Lozenets tax office, I was ready for my first day working on the project. My plan was to gather as much information as possible and then provide hands-on experience, which I was going to use for creating an income tax manual based on IRS model. I already knew the tax manager at the Lozenets office, who was aware of my work and was proud to provide his place for launching a new exam program for the Bulgarian tax administration. He arranged for me to observe a revenue inspector performing an audit. It was a sole proprietorship with the usual at the time tax return losses. I am saying *usual* as I was told that none of the privately owned businesses reported profits from their activities. I observed a boring and useless process of comparing amounts from invoices to corresponding deductions taken on the tax return. It was no surprise that the audit resulted in no change. Bulgarian companies at the time were operating only with cash, which meant that extensive use of indirect methods had to be applied in all cases.

The next few months I spent developing an audit process in Bulgarian language, starting with interviews, tours of businesses, third-party contacts, and establishing a network of collaboration between tax offices in the country. The Bulgarian tax inspectors were very intelligent and fast to grasp the necessity and purpose for applying various audit steps in a certain order. My bosses in Washington were pleased with my work, praising the accomplishment I had in such a short time in response to my reports. My TAAS manager fully supported all my proposals and written work outlining the future Bulgarian exam program. I knew that I had to test my writings in the field. The Lozenets tax manager arranged for me to be present and assist a team of his inspectors in auditing a deli store with tax losses ever since they opened a few years ago. I accompanied the agents assigned to the case and observed the owner arriving in a Mercedes, dressed in stylish clothes, and wearing big gold necklaces, bracelets, and rings, which I pointed out to the inspectors. The businessman joined us at the entrance and led us to a conference room. I watched the inspectors following my script for asking questions about the business history, operations, cash on hand, and cash hoarding and taking notes while touring the store of merchandise prices, employees, and inventory. The owner was very cooperative and provided answers to all questions as well as furnishing records—the latter being useless as we all knew they were not authentic. I was extremely pleased seeing that my hard work was giving results. The inspectors were already calculating the daily profits of the store, extending the amount to the entire year, numbers way in excess of what the tax returns showed. I could see them being proud of getting audit results based on their investigative work.

"Sir, in your opinion, do you think you have a successful business?" I asked the owner.

"Of course I do. This year, I bought the Mercedes."

"Well, are you aware that the filed tax returns since the opening of your business show big losses? Maybe your tax preparer made a mistake in transposing the numbers for revenues and expenditures."

"Let me see. I don't believe that." The audit ended with agreed report by the end of the day with sizable adjustments.

I briefed my manager in Washington, and he was extremely excited about the tremendous progress I made so far. He approved my approach of assisting at the inspector's level for testing my written audit materials. Back at the Ministry of Finance, I replaced my assistant with a lady who was eager to learn and truly assist with every aspect of the project. Her background was Bulgarian language, so she did a great job with taking notes at meetings and writing reports and training materials, as I started to travel extensively in the country sharing the work from the pilot tax office. My Washington bosses, both from IRS and Treasury, were interested in measuring the results of my work, so I met with my colleague, the Treasury Advisor, who confirmed that he was already noticing increases in tax revenue. I knew that this initial success was due to my working with tax managers and inspectors in the field. Interviewing and talking to tax personnel in the field made me aware of the tax policy and administrative areas that needed to be addressed, created, or changed. In the first months, I already drafted parts of an income tax audit manual outlining initial audit procedures.

Upon the request of the Ministry of Finance, I visited tax offices in the country starting with Blagoevgrad, a city south of Sofia, then Pleven, Tryavna, Gabrovo (located north of the Balkan Mountains), Kardzhali by the Turkish border, Stara Zagora in the Rose Valley, and Varna, a port at the Black Sea. Tax officials everywhere welcomed me with open arms, expressing their gratitude for my on-site visits and training. Talking to inspectors, I provided specific audit guidelines based on the geographic location and business peculiarities in the region, as well as technical support for individual cases. There were times when I created my meeting notes and training materials in the car on my way to a place requesting immediate assistance. At one of those meetings, a tiny female inspector raised her hand.

"Ma'am, the proposed audit techniques are wonderful, but we feel threatened in the field when we are met by companies' body-guards carrying weapons. That's why we audit in the tax offices."

I looked her in the eyes and responded, "Were there laws protecting government employees doing their job in the past?"

"Yes, but these laws are not valid, and there are no new laws replacing them," she responded.

"I am not familiar with the Bulgarian criminal code and rules, but I am going to look into it as soon as I return to the capital. I assure you that if the old laws were not revoked, they are still in effect." I realized that there were so many legal aspects that had to be clarified, amended, and created, and they were not all related to tax policy. My work at the tax offices turned out to be most beneficial and useful as I heard the concerns and issues of people in the field, the ones who were contributing to the government's budget.

Back at the Ministry of Finance, I requested and studied a copy of the Bulgarian Federal Criminal Code, and sure enough, there was a clause for the protection of government employees, which was still effective. With confirmation and approval from senior tax officials, I distributed the information to all Bulgarian regional tax offices alongside with my preliminary materials for conducting an audit. The responses were overwhelming as all tax regions requested training. Due to the immensity of such undertaking, I proposed to the ministry to authorize training at the Sofia facility in a suburb city of Bankya, a place known for its mineral water. My audience consisted of tax directors, tax managers, and senior inspectors from each of the nation's regions. My new assistant did a great job of drafting the income tax audit training materials based on my preliminary studies and writings. My task was to also translate them for my reports to Washington, weekly to the Service and monthly to the Treasury, a work I did on weekends. My bosses in Washington continued to be extremely pleased with my achievements. "The international commissioner speaks of you as 'the only country with a single tax advisor,'" my TAAS manager told me at one of our following phone conversations.

The training facility at Bankya was also a hotel with cafeteria, which facilitated the contact with all attending officials and employees during lunch and dinner. My training extended in the late hours of the evening, answering questions for specific cases. It was a tiring but exhilarating experience, which I will never forget. I still remember the facial expressions of amazement, enthusiasm, eagerness, and gratefulness in the eyes of these people. I was not just teaching and sharing knowledge; I was actually back to my homeland assisting during one of the most important and critical times in history after the fall of Communism. The feeling was tremendous as I felt such closeness to the people I taught who were striving to make a difference. They were fast to absorb the material and eager to go home to apply what they learned. Back at the Ministry of Finance, I shared with the commissioner all concerns and requests from the field, my findings of tax issues, and necessary changes to tax law. Alongside with the development of the income tax manual, I spent weeks where I drafted tax policy proposals on complex corporate and international issues. The ministry's chief council was a young woman in her thirties, very ambitious and knowledgeable of state tax law. I gave her access to all my materials, and we spent hours discussing the creation of a new tax administration in Bulgaria.

"Nina, can you provide us with US tax code provisions for business reorganizations?"

"That was something I enjoyed auditing while in a large case exam group in Detroit. We need to know all the steps companies take in this process, but I'll provide you with different scenarios."

"This is exactly what we need," she responded. "By the way, I am working on a tax treaty document with the States. Do you mind taking a look at it?" I readily took the draft and translated for her parts of treaties with similar country conditions in the area as Bulgaria.

Christmas was around the corner without even noticing how time went by since our arrival in May. I went to get my son from the airport and could not recognize him from behind. He was taller since I last saw him, with a hairdo for young people at the time. I smiled, and he hugged me. Soon we were on our way to the apartment. The next day, I worked, so he had the task of getting a Christmas tree. Well, the tree was more of a branch; they did not have real Christmas trees at the market. That made me laugh.

"Don't you listen to music?" was his question as we did not have a stereo or even a radio.

"Well, son, I work late in the evening, and I travel a lot. Your sisters are also busy. Your sister Vanesa is enrolled in medical school, and her schedule is taking every waking minute of her life. Anabelle attends the Anglo-American school during the day and has homework in the evening. We usually eat out or at your grandma's."

"Everybody needs to listen to music Mom" was his response.

We celebrated Christmas with family. My cousin Ivan and his wife, Buba, prepared the traditional Christmas Eve meal with all Bulgarian vegetarian dishes—such as stuffed cabbage, stuffed grape leaves, beans, *banitsa* (cheese strudel), pumpkin strudel—homemade bread with the lucky quarter inside for whoever gets it to be lucky during the year, and homemade wine that they produced at vineyards they rented. A few days before New Year, there was a knock at my office door. It was a ministry courier who handed me an invitation to a New Year's celebration for my family to attend in the mountains. The kids were excited, and that was what mattered. For me, it was a working vacation. A van from the ministry picked us up and took us to a mountain lodge where the invitees were all from the Ministry of Finance. New Year's Eve was very festive celebrated in a huge room with a round decorated-for-the-occasion table. We were seated by the general secretary's family, and all children took off exploring the place. There was dancing and laughing and joking, but there were also talks about the Bulgarian economy and my role in assisting its development. The next few days, the girls were skiing on a small slope, and my son decided to stay at the lodge as the first day of skiing was almost fatal. He was with a young Bulgarian couple but was not aware that the slopes in Bulgaria were not always marked well, and almost flew into a forest. Back in Sofia, we all set into our routines, and I saw Erik off to the airport going back to college.

I completed the audit manual by February 1994, and while working on it, I maintained close contact with all tax offices in the country, assisting with technical issues they came across while applying auditing methods from my classes. Occasionally, I traveled to cities requesting assistance with information gathering while touring businesses such as a factory for wallpaper or a factory for weapons. I came across situations where plants were using bartering with companies from other countries such as Ukraine. In the Varna district tax office, officials had no idea how to deal with a pyramid scheme set up by a Serbian national married to a Bulgarian woman in order to gain the trust of the local people. Upon request from the Ministry I accompanied agents to assist in auditing a casino in Blagoevgrad. We stayed and observed the casino operations until closing after midnight, and then under my guidance, the agents got to work using techniques for casino auditing from Vegas. I was exhausted but extremely satisfied with the inspectors' ability to grasp all auditing concepts and move forward with applying them in the field. The casino in Blagoevgrad was owned by Multigroup, one of the well-known at the time Bulgarian newly formed big companies. One of the owners was present and was very polite and cooperative during the entire time. We finally wrapped up around 4:00 a.m.

I was looking forward to a hot shower and relaxing morning before we head back to Sofia. I wasn't in my room ten minutes, just sitting for a minute in the living area and recollecting all the details of the evening, when I heard a knock on the door. It was one of the agents. "What is it? Is something wrong?"

He seemed confused. "I am sorry. I thought..." He did not finish but left. I was also confused but pretended that nothing happened.

When in Sofia, I often stopped on the way home at tax offices and discussed tax policy and administrative issues with the tax managers. One day, as I was at the city of Sofia's tax office going over some of the manual chapters with the manager, the door flung wide open, and a man in his early forties, of medium height and weight, stormed in, pulled a gun, pointed it to his head, and shouted, "I can't live anymore! I cannot pay all the taxes I owe. I am going to shoot myself!"

The tax manager turned pale and did not move. I looked at the man and said softly, "You don't want to die. I can help you resolve your problem, but first, slowly put the gun down." He put the gun down. I continued to look him in the eyes and slowly moved toward him to take the gun. The man did not object; he was just staring at me. Once the threat of the gun was removed, I turned to the manager and asked her if she could get one of her inspectors to help the taxpayer. I sat at the meeting until the case was resolved with the man agreeing to paying his debt in installments. I left the office relieved that I helped prevent a tragedy. I guess I learned as a teacher in the inner city of Detroit how to handle critical situations involving weapons. My dear students, I hoped they made it out of there.

The historic day of publishing the audit manual came, and my assistant accompanied me to the publishing house where we ordered two hundred manuals in Bulgarian and five in English language for my bosses at IRS and Treasury. With the note from the government, the order was expedited and completed in a week. Armed with a few copies, I met with the Bulgarian commissioner.

"Nina, this is a tremendous job, and we are all very grateful for this material of uniform audit procedures for all offices in the country. Such an effort needs to be compensated."

"Sir, it is a great honor for me to create this universal manual assisting with auditing. My compensation will be to see it implemented nationwide in the field, producing audit results and contributing to the budget. I would like to ask if you could support me in this effort. What I need is to present it at a meeting to district and tax managers by providing an insight of its use. With the school summer vacation approaching, I would like to schedule it in the next ten days."

"That's not an issue, Nina." He picked up the phone and asked the general secretary to organize the meeting and arrange for the use of the training facility the ministry had in Bankya. Then he turned to me and said, "My secretary will get back with you and let you know the details for your trip and stay in Bankya." I thanked him; I was sure that he saw the excitement on my face as he smiled and said, "Thank you for your contribution to the creation of our tax system at such a critical moment. I know it makes a difference when this is your homeland, and you have your heart in assisting with all the knowledge and tools you have. Just want you to know that your work, your efforts are much appreciated."

We shook hands, and I headed to another meeting with visitors from the Treasury Department. They all claimed to be my bosses, which confused me, and I shared this when I talked on the phone with my IRS manager at TAAS.

"That's easy, Nina, just look at your annual evaluation. Who signed it?"

"You, sir."

"Well, then now you know who is your manager, but you still need to accommodate all other officials from Treasury and provide them all information that they request."

The gentleman from Treasury was curious to see a copy of the manual as none of the tax advisors in any country had created such a handbook by incorporating the country's condition and regional and structural peculiarities. The meeting lasted a few hours as we briefly discussed the different chapters and my plan for implementation in the field. Upon leaving, he congratulated me and wished me luck in completing my assignment.

"Nina, the driver is waiting! We have all the books loaded in the car," my assistant yelled out as I was double-checking if I had all my notes in my briefcase for the upcoming meeting with all regional and major tax offices' tax managers as well as their senior inspectors. The drive from Sofia to Bankya was short, about half an hour, and soon I recognized the training center with people in the yard. We stopped in front of the main entrance, and the driver helped with carrying the books to the training classroom. As I stepped out of the car, I noticed that people were not as cheerful as usual at my presentations. Most of them just nodded to my greeting. My assistant summonsed every- body inside the building, and we started as scheduled at 8:00 a.m. I had a copy of the manual for everybody at their seats. I glanced at the participants' faces; they were all serious and thoughtful.

"Good morning, everybody!" I started with a raised voice of enthusiasm. "Today is an important day as it marks the introduction of an audit manual, which I created with your help at various tax offices. The manual is based on my observations and direct work in the field with inspectors at Sofia's Lozenets tax office. The manual reflects universal audit techniques as well as peculiarities of your current accounting and tax reporting." Before I could continue, the assistant commissioner raised his hand.

"Tax laws are changing continuously. How could this manual be applied forever, and isn't it a waste of time as it will become obsolete?" I could see that there was a reservation toward the effectiveness of a manual use. The man was an influential figure, and by the looks of it, the audience was agreeing with his opinion.

"The manual that I created is for all times, regardless of policy changes. You definitely need tax laws empowering tax officials to conduct audits, to request documents, to visit business premises, and to summon materials and individuals to be interviewed. You already have these rights. Your commissioner has reviewed and approved the use of this manual. What this manual will teach is effective auditing and not matching of documents. I will discuss the entire process chapter by chapter, and you could add your comments as we go along. This is an interactive meeting where your participation is encouraged and your feedback will be considered. I would like to stress that the manual is the basis for universal audit techniques to be applied in Bulgaria. Any changes in tax policy affecting administration will be amended and added to the original version."

The three days of discussing and explaining in detail each point of the audit process drained me as I met opposition based on the assistant commissioner's attitude of resisting changes. The atmosphere finally lightened up on the fourth day set aside for interaction, as I invited and encouraged participation, reminding tax officials of previous conversations we had when I visited their offices regarding issues in need of change and their prior approval of new auditing methods. We all parted on good terms as I could see from the expression of their faces determination to make the manual work. Saying goodbye to each one, I offered to visit and help them in their regions to implement the manual provisions.

Shortly thereafter my boss and the TAAS director arrived in Bulgaria to discuss the progress of the program. They both had radiant faces as they got off the plane. Later that day, after they settled at the hotel, we met for dinner.

"Nina, we are here to let you know that we are extremely pleased with your work," my manager started.

"Your accomplishments for such short time are tremendous. We would like to meet the commissioner tomorrow if possible," the director nodded. Then he continued, "We are extending your assignment for two more years, which will be sufficient time for you to fulfill the planned objectives."

The next day, I arranged for an early meeting in the morning. Upon entering the commissioner's office, the man sprang on his feet and, with a large smile, extended his hand to greet my bosses. "Welcome, gentlemen. I am very pleased to meet you and share with you how grateful we are to have Nina as tax advisor. He called his secretary and asked her to bring us coffee and cola. Then he continued to talk, still smiling, "Nina's work was extraordinary. Her work methodology is extremely effective and innovative as she devised a plan to gather information before writing a manual. Nina visited our major tax regions, conducted workshops, and provided hands-on experience to agents conducting audits. She not only taught but she also gave tax managers and inspectors confidence to change their old ways of thinking and use new effective audit methods. I received extremely positive feedback from all regional managers, who, for the first time since the collapse of Communism, record audit results and tax collection from private businesses. We are also receiving assistance from Treasury in creating computer programs, enabling us to better track audit results and gross national income."

Oh yes, I thought to myself, *I have been so busy that I did not have a chance to talk to the other advisor. He is probably getting ahead with his programs and noticing increases in the country's budget.*

I blushed as I was translating for my bosses, at which the commissioner reacted, "Nina this is not a compliment but a very realistic and true description of your services. You deserve recognition for your tremendous accomplishments."

"We are extremely pleased to hear that Nina represented the US government so well in providing you the best of tax assistance," the director responded. "We are not going to take much of your time, but we would like to know if we could do anything more for the Bulgarian tax administration. We extended Nina's assignment for additional two years, and she will communicate to us if there is a need for any additional services that we could provide."

I noticed that my manual was on the commissioner's desk. He picked it up and looked at the TAAS director in the eyes. "This book is extremely precious and useful. The work ahead of us is to implement it nationwide and launch a tax reform to effectively deal with noncompliance and increase tax yield." At that, the three gentlemen shook hands, and soon I was taking my bosses back to the hotel.

I spent the following day with them outlining a plan for my future two-year work. It is not possible to explain all the emotions I felt those days receiving recognition from the Bulgarian commissioner for succeeding to provide the necessary tax assistance. It was a sensation of extreme happiness and inner satisfaction.

Upon my bosses departure I received a call from a gentleman working for the international Monetary fund.

"Nina, my colleague and I are from the International Monetary Fund, and we would like to invite you tonight to dinner at Sheraton Hotel. We need to discuss tax issues with you. Will seven p.m. be okay with you?"

The two men were of middle age, one taller with short dark hair. Both were dressed in casual slacks and shirts. They both stood up as I walked in the restaurant, extending their hands for a handshake and smiling.

"Thank you, Nina, for agreeing to meet on such a short notice. You are our guest, and we would like to treat you to anything you choose from the menu," the taller man said after I settled into my chair. I knew that there was something going on and was extremely curious to find out the real reason for this invitation. The waiter was already by my side, ready to take my order.

"I'll have T-Bone steak, salad, and ice water." Then I turned to my companions. "I am extremely pleased to meet you, but as an accountant, I like to come straight down to the point. What is the purpose of this business dinner?"

"Nina, all in its time. Let me start by saying that the European Union is committed to provide aid to Bulgaria in implementing a value-added tax. There was a gentleman from Brussels who was in Sofia whose job was to work with the Bulgarian tax officials at the Ministry of Finance in drafting the necessary policy and create the corresponding manuals for administering the tax dealing with registration, tax filing, and auditing. Unfortunately, it did not work out. During his one year stay in the country, the man did not even contact the ministry. We were informed of your accomplishments in creating an income tax manual and your close work with all tax offices. Bulgaria's budget is already improving due to your work. The VAT is crucial for Bulgaria since the country's goal is to enter the European Union and be economically competitive. Based on your track record, we would like to ask you to assume the role of an advisor in assisting the Bulgarian tax administration reach that goal."

"Sir, with all due respect, you know there is no value-added tax in the United States, and I don't know anything about it."

"We will arrange for you to get trained, if this is your concern."

"Okay, and what about my bosses in Washington? My contract is to provide technical assistance primarily with income tax."

"We already cleared this with Treasury and Internal Revenue Service in Washington. The Treasury director for Eastern European tax assistance programs and your supervisors at TAAS are on board and agreed to loan you to work on this mission," the other gentleman responded.

There wasn't much for me to say or decide except to follow through with the plan for my new assignment. The T-bone steak was hard to cut, and I started to laugh. "Never order steaks in Bulgaria.

I will need to wait till next summer when I take my R & R in the States to have a good steak. So how do I get training for this tax?"

"There is a one-week value-added tax class at Bankya training center starting on Monday for the Bulgarian tax administration conducted by German tax instructors. The class will teach everything you need to know about value-added tax, its mechanism, how it works. It's a theoretical study and will have numerous examples of its application. You are welcome to attend the class."

"Shall I assume that this also has been cleared up with my bosses in Washington?"

"Yes, Nina. We talked to your manager from TAAS. You can attend this training. Here are our business cards if you need anything. We will stay in touch."

In the next couple of days, I contacted all the ministry tax officials involved in initiating the new tax. The Treasury director assured me that it was only a sales tax, nothing to be concerned about. But I knew that VAT was different and more involved than a simple sales tax.

Another week at Bankya, this time not as a lecturer but as a participant, together with familiar Bulgarian faces from tax regions from all over the country. The instructors were three men from the German tax administration. They were very pleasant, easy to understand, and accommodated anyone with questions, including me. We all stayed at the training center, and that made it possible to extend conversations and take classroom training to the lunch and dinner tables. The guys also liked to joke.

"Nina, Bulgarian women are very attractive, but can you ask the one without a bra with a see-through blouse to wear something else tomorrow? I could hardly teach today." One of the guys laughed.

While learning about the nature of value-added tax, I was already putting down ideas about an audit manual, which I shared with my German colleagues.

"You are so right," they reassured me. "Since value-added tax forms are filed every month, audit control needs to be more proactive. And the audit techniques for obvious abuse cases with losses are not that different from those of income tax."

My audit tax guide was in a rough draft by the end of the week, with exam techniques for auditing sales and purchases, similar to the ones from my income tax manual. It took me a while to explain to the Treasury director the way value-added tax works and the reason for a more involved audit of value-added tax instead of just verifying purchase invoices. In countries with value-added tax, businesses file monthly tax returns, seeking reimbursement for made purchases. Auditing the validity of those claims required the same measures as those for income-tax verification. Bulgarian inspectors had to raise questions about cash hoard, sources of income, validity of invoices, and in most cases, cross-referencing with corresponding reported sales of vendors.

Returning to Sofia, I was introduced to a gentleman from the Danish tax administration whose task was to assist with value-added tax policy. He was a tall, blond, handsome man with a very pleasant composure. "Very pleased to meet you, Nina." He extended his hand, and we set up time to work together for the following two weeks. During that time, I added to my initial audit manual provisions based on value-added tax policy proposed by the Danish tax administration and approved by the commissioner. Exports being exempt from taxation needed more scrutiny, and I drafted audit steps for their audit. The deadline for passing the value-added tax into law was approaching, and I was very pleased to see how the Bulgarian tax officials from the ministry were working around the clock and on weekends to get all the necessary paperwork done and to provide all regions with the necessary information and documentation on policy and filing forms.

"Did you get the work bug from me?" I was joking with them. I sat down with them to complete the registration manual, which facilitated the process by eliminating waiting in line to register. The future filing of monthly tax returns was also simplified to reduce taxpayer's burden. My working day continued to be from dawn till late hours at night, drafting documents, creating tax forms, discussing every step of the process with the gentleman from Denmark and the Bulgarians assigned to the project.

The day came when all work was completed, and it was time to plan putting things into action. Walking into the Ministry of Finance, I could feel the morning being different. Entering the VAT office, I could see everybody with lifted spirits, content of what was accomplished. We were ready for training.

"Nina, can you manage to teach all policy and administration documents by yourself?" My colleague from Denmark was smiling at me.

"I don't see why not. I am very comfortable with the materials. My assistant will contact all regions and extend invitations for their participation. She will also ensure that we have enough copies for all attendees."

"I read the manual you created for income tax audit, and based on the progress you had with its adoption, I am confident that you will have great results from teaching value-added tax. I wish you good luck, and we will stay in touch. Contact me if you need anything during and after training."

I could feel the whole country anxious as I walked down the streets or in stores, hearing people talking loudly about this new tax about to be enacted. On the day of training, I packed what I needed for a couple of weeks. My assistant had all materials ready with copies for all participants, and we were off to the Bankya training center. As we arrived, I could feel the excitement of all Bulgarian tax officials scheduled for training, having animated discussions and gesturing in heated discussions. They all greeted me with enthusiasm and smiles on their faces. We started our first session at the scheduled time. My assistant distributed the materials, and I asked them all to take half an hour in reviewing them. The first lesson plan dealt with the substance of value-added tax, which I supported by examples and classroom exercises. Going over policy provisions, the registration process from the manual, and the tax forms and filing requirements took the rest of the week. What everybody was waiting for was to hear the audit part of the lectures as people were familiar with my way of teaching and were gearing themselves to see how I was going to approach the subject relative to the new tax.

The second week was dedicated to auditing, and I got right down to the indirect methods applicable to value-added tax. Walking in the room, I looked around and asked for everybody to pull out the policy and the tax forms and jot down basic auditing ideas.

"How can we figure out auditing on a new tax law?" a guy asked. "I know you created a manual, but reading and working are different things."

I walked up to the man and said, "Looking at the tax return, what is the issue that you are going to audit? Think about the income tax audit manual section for auditing purchases in relation to income, because the value-added tax has the two most important items that you need to look at—income and purchases. The monthly income and purchases from the value-added tax returns will be reflected on the annual income tax return, is that correct?"

"Now we see where you are heading," responded a lady from the back of the room.

"So what is the worst abuse with reporting purchases?" I asked.

"Fake invoices," responded the same lady.

"So what are you going to do when suspecting fake invoices?" I asked.

"That will be tough since the invoices are from different cities and regions. We have no way of checking them."

"Of course you do" was my response. "You have colleagues in those cities and regions. You need to reach out to them any time there is an issue in their area affecting your cases." I could see people looking around as if to confirm that what I just said was possible. "We have talked about this when I presented to you topics on auditing income tax. This is not different. Most of you here are managers and regional directors. With your direction and approval, tax offices will start to exchange information and assist one another in their audits."

I moved on to presenting how structuring the value audit tax audit as income tax audit has consecutive stages, each one depending on the previous, stressing the importance of interviews and tour of businesses. Somehow, because the material was referenced to a new tax law, I did not get much opposition as to the teaching of auditing income tax. While in class, I heard that on April 1, 1994, the day of the enactment of the Value Added Tax into law, the value of the dollar doubled to sixty-plus dollars a lev, and a lot of Americans and other foreigners benefited from the situation. But my Bulgarian colleagues were concerned that further devaluation of their currency would devastate the economy and would affect their families. I had read into the history of VAT adopted in other countries that the same occurrence happened, and everything was regulated after the tax came into law. I had already created an atmosphere of fired-up individuals to do their job; however, any slight disturbance in events set them back feeling insecure and concerned. I brought in class literature describing the struggle of other countries overhauling systems and creating new ways of life. I truly understood where they come from, and gaining their trust was my primary objective.

Shortly thereafter, my boss from TAAS arrived and was surprised of how skinny I was. His first remark seeing me was, "You are taking a vacation, and this is not a request. It's an order." The purpose of his visit was to evaluate my work on site, to review all the materials that I wrote, and to provide me with my annual appraisal after receiving the written feedback from the commissioner. I was exceeding all expectations for my performance, but in writing, he gave me "meets" for all aspects, which I did not even question. My attitude toward my superiors was to never question their actions, and in this particular case, I was recognized for my accomplishments by all US officials starting with the ambassador. And that was sufficient. The piece of paper did not have any significance.

Upon his departure, I headed straight home to plan a vacation with my younger daughter. My son was in the States, and my older daughter was attending classes in medical school, so it was going to be I and Anabelle taking a trip. Mom knew a travel agent who booked a weeklong vacation for the two of us in Tunisia. It was April, and this was the closest available warm spot. My daughter was thrilled at the thought of traveling with me. She kept chirping around me as we got on the plane and landed in Tunisia. But I was on edge entering an Arab country and traveling on US government passport. There was a tense moment when the Arab passport official took my passport and walked away with it, telling me to wait. Anabelle was watching me closely, not saying a word. Soon the man returned, gave me back the passport, and nodded at us to proceed. That was a relief. I called a cab, and soon we were at our hotel across from the Mediterranean Sea.

Seeing it, my daughter shrieked with joy. "Are we going to swim, Mom?"

"As soon as we unpack, I will get information at the desk about the area, and we will take a walk on the beach."

My daughter was dancing with joy around me as I carried the luggage to our room and straightened our things. First thing at the reception, I wanted to know if it was safe for me to walk with a girl outside the hotel and then, of course, things to do in the area.

"It is extremely safe," the man at the reception said. "In our country assaulting a woman is a crime punishable with death without trial. In case of a theft, the punishment is cutting off the hands of the thief. We do not have thieves."

Our week was filled with fun, starting with a camel ride, where my daughter shouted, "Mom!" I did not have time to respond as my camel shot up straight into the air. I was glad that we both were holding on tightly. We visited the nearby market where, for the first time, I felt the need for a camcorder to create videos capturing the sounds of the place. It looked very festive with the colors of merchandise in the shops, and the landscape was tropical. There was Arab and French music, and the people taking walks were all having a good time, laughing and chatting, especially the young ones. I was surprised to see girls in miniskirts, but there were also women covered up. Taking a taxi, the opposite direction alongside the coast took us to a town fortress where walking within the walls felt like being in medieval ages.

Anabelle planned another activity, mini golfing, which turned out to be real golfing, and we ended up losing all the balls in the small pond with obstacles created around the golf course. Our fun was spoiled by worrisome news from the States—an attack on the federal building in Oklahoma. Among the victims were children from the day-care center. What made it worse was that the president appeared on the TV, claiming that the Arab terrorists committing this crime would be caught and would pay dearly. Anabelle, in bed at the time, pulled the sheet over her head. She was only eleven, but she knew that this was serious for us being in an Arab country.

"Anabelle, we are not leaving the hotel, and we are speaking Bulgarian. No English, understood?"

"Yes, Mom," she responded in a faint voice.

I tried calling first Bulgaria at home and work and then Washington with no success. They had stopped any communication outside the country after the US president's announcement on TV. Luckily, in a couple of days, everything was back to normal, and we were on our way back to Sofia with no problems.

The next few months were like a roller coaster as I lived out of a suitcase crossing the country from west to east, from north to south, working in the field with managers and inspectors. A particular case comes to mind, which we all found amusing. It dealt with tax-free exports of big quantities of duck liver. The ducks were imported then transferred through multiple farms in different parts of the country for raising, slaughtering, and duck liver production. Supposedly, the cans of duck liver were exported, but the inspectors under my supervision tracked the entire shipment to local sales by communicating with all tax offices involved in this operation. Numerous fake invoices were discovered with simple phone calls and cooperation between inspectors verifying and confirming the use of phantom companies. My role in all this was to support and provide confidence to managers and inspectors in conducting their audits independently as this was a very well-educated, and intelligent group of people grasping and applying swiftly new tax law provisions. During my visit to a town in the south, I encouraged tax officials to do a tour of business as it was physically impossible for the company to store the claimed purchases on a value-added tax form.

My boss in Washington was extremely pleased with the results of my fieldwork, which was immediately reflected in the country's budget figures being stable, a phenomenon different from other countries with new VAT where the initial increase of revenues declined sharply shortly thereafter. He encouraged me to get help from colleagues in the States and Europe for additional classroom training, which I welcomed very much. A colleague arrived from Washington,

DC, with exam background as me, and we both provided indirect methods training in the city of Burgas. By that time, I inherited the Treasury advisor's two secretaries and added an additional man to the team, a recent business graduate from the American University in Blagoevgrad. The new secretaries remained on Treasury payroll reassigned to me. I gladly included them in my project with tasks of translating materials and reports, which freed up my weekends.

The Treasury advisor got caught in a love affair scandal and left the project. All I can say is that any American man arriving in Eastern Europe at the time was a game as women wanted a ticket out. One of the new girls on my team, very beautiful and smart, told me, "Nina, I don't care how old or how handicap the man is. I need an American to take me away from here." I found this very sad as these girls had no idea that life in America is not like in the movies.

My colleague from the Danish tax administration also revisited, and we scheduled to hold a meeting at the Ministry of Finance, which we believed was with high-level officials. To our surprise, when we walked in the designated conference room, we had an audience of at least one hundred people, so we had to quickly adjust our speech for a large group of people instead of a few individuals. Our speeches were different. His was mostly on policy, inquiring about implementation and comprehension of the law, while mine was about its enforcement and cases resolved in the field. I could tell the Danish tax official was pleased from the meeting with the Bulgarians.

Back at my office, we discussed the current status of the VAT groups in the country and future assistance that might be needed.

"Nina, from what I could tell by interacting with the Bulgarian VAT managers, value-added tax is working extremely well. The law is comprehended and upheld perfectly, and I am extremely satisfied with the way things are progressing. You have been doing something incredible by providing assistance where it matters to the people in the field. In most, or should I say all, cases that I know of, advisors work only with high-level officials and write reports, which does not have any effect on the actual implementation of the law."

"Thank you for your comments," I responded. "But I do not see another effective way of accomplishing such a task. I still write reports for my bosses at Treasury and IRS." I chuckled.

The man laughed then looked me in the eyes and said, "You are doing such a wonderful job here that I would like you to teach tax officials of other countries at the OECD center in Vienna. The class is in a couple of weeks. I will contact your supervisors to obtain their permission."

My eyes lit up. Going back to Vienna, this time as a government official and not escaping the chains of the communist regime in Bulgaria, was something I did not expect. In a couple of weeks, my Danish colleague met me at Vienna airport and took me to the training center, which was the Austrian customs building. He showed me to my room (as in Bankya, the place was a hotel with a cafeteria just for customs personnel, training staff, and participants; there were classrooms on a separate floor). That evening, I had dinner with him and the New Zealand commissioner, who was also a speaker for the upcoming weeklong VAT class. We discussed the schedule, the topics, the materials, and the arrangements for handouts.

The weeklong classes were very successful. My lectures were accepted with great interest since the trainees were high-level officials of Eastern European countries with same issues of noncompliance and challenges of creating a new tax administration system as Bulgaria. Of particular interest to my audience was sharing value-added tax field audits involving application of strategies outlined in an audit manual. Each individual was provided with a copy of my manual in English, accompanied with examples and problems targeting the importance of every aspect of the audit, starting with the preaudit stage of identifying the issues and formulating an audit plan. I was intrigued talking to the representatives from Albania, remembering the story of an advisor assigned to the country and screaming to be called back after a week because of bad sanitary conditions in the capital, Tirana. What I learned about Albania was that with EU and American assistance, the country improved considerably and had beautiful sea resorts.

We also did some sightseeing to places familiar to me, bringing back memories of times when I had no idea where life was going to take me but, at the same time, feeling safe and free. Strange that Mariahilfer Strasse, where I loved to window-shop and visit the music store, seemed much smaller of what I remembered.

Back in Sofia, I was briefed by my assistants of the tasks they accomplished, and work resumed as usual. Soon I had a call from my Treasury boss assuming that he wanted details about my teaching in Vienna.

"Hello, Nina. I hear that the value-added tax implementation is a tremendous success in Bulgaria thanks to your efforts and that you provided an excellent training in Vienna. The reason I am calling is because the International Monetary Fund has requested your assistance in Russia for six weeks. You still will be on our payroll." I was quiet, waiting to hear all the details. "Your assignment starts in February. Take with you the income and all value-added tax manuals that you created, alongside with the tax code and other materials you use in classroom training. Travel authorization has been approved, and there will be an advance for your travel. You may call me or your manager at the IRS if you need anything."

When he finished, all I could say was, "Thank you, sir. I feel honored to be a part of such an assignment. I will have my assistants make arrangements for my travel." After which, he wished me a successful trip and hung up.

The news was not accepted well at home as I hadn't seen the girls that much ever since my involvement with value-added tax. I traveled a lot before, but now it seemed that I was constantly on the road. I promised to have Anabelle's father bring her for a weekend to Moscow. Going to bed, I said a long prayer asking God to be with me on this important journey.

On the family front I had to prepare for a very important event in my older daughter's life. She met a Bulgarian young man who also attended medical school who proposed to her. I wanted her to have an unforgettable wedding at a Bulgarian church and a lavish reception. My assistant at the office, with whom we became friends, helped me with reservations for a restaurant, working on the menu, scheduling the church and civil ceremonies, sending out invitations (to all close friends I made at regional offices and Sofia's tax offices, Ministry of Finance officials, a family from the German embassy as our kids were going together at the Anglo-American school, and the groom's and my family), purchasing a wedding dress, ordering a cake, working out the details about Bulgarian customs during weddings, reserving a car, and hiring a photographer.

It was January 7, 1995. Sofia was covered with snow resembling a white lace. The bells at the Alexander Nevsky Cathedral solemnly sounded as we were all fussing and getting ready. My son stayed longer for the wedding and kept close to his grandma, talking lively and gesturing. Soon the limo arrived, and we headed to St. Nedelya Church on the square by Sheraton Hotel. The priest performed a typical Eastern Orthodox wedding ceremony, an ancient ritual performed three times for the Holy Trinity with crowning the couple holding candles the entire time. The civil ceremony was fast with witnesses called *kum* and *kuma*. After which, the wedding party headed to the restaurant in the Lozenets quarter of town for the reception. My daughter was beautiful. Her face was sparkling, and the white dress caressed her soft snow-white skin like a princess from a fairy tale. Her new husband was elegant, dressed in a tuxedo, standing by her with a wide smile on his face. The music was played by a DJ with a variety of folk and popular dances. It was truly an incredibly exciting and memorable celebration of my daughter's wedding surrounded by friends and family.

Tax Advisor for the International Monetary Fund in Russia

"Nina, here is your briefcase with materials for your meeting in the afternoon. I already checked in your luggage. Have a nice flight." My assistant hugged me as I headed to security on my way to the flight to Moscow. I had layover in St. Petersburg, but no time for sightseeing. My Bulgarian translators said that it was a beautiful city, and I wrote it down on my list for desired future travel locations.

Getting back on the plane, I noticed that the couple of men across the aisle from me were getting louder and laughing a lot. I did not understand how their mood changed so fast by drinking orange juice. Later, I learned that they probably had a bottle of vodka and drinking cocktails of screwdriver all the time. Soon we landed, and I was met as soon as I got through passport control by a tall, somewhat heavy-built Russian man.

"Welcome to Moscow," he said, extending his hand. "I am the Russian translator for the Canadian tax advisor. There is a car waiting outside to take us to your hotel. You have a scheduled meeting with the Russian commissioner at two p.m., which will give you about an hour to grab lunch. I will come to the hotel at 1:30 p.m., which will give us plenty of time to walk across to the ministry." With that, we headed out of the building where a ministry driver was standing in front of a black luxury car.

I was absorbing every detail of the trip from the airport to the hotel. It was February 1995, a cold winter day with snow on the ground, and soon I recognized from pictures the center of the city alongside the Moscow Canal. My host, the translator, was pointing out some important sites on the way, like the government buildings of the Russian parliament and the Bolshoi Theater. Shortly thereafter, the car stopped in front of Budapest Hotel, a well-kept Russian hotel a block from the ministry. I preferred Budapest to Metropol, where all advisors stayed, because of its proximity to work and still walking distance to Bolshoi Theater and Red Square. My reservation was for a suite with a living room and a good-sized bathroom. The place was clean and well maintained in its old state. I particularly enjoyed the space especially for my six-week contract with IMF. After soaking in the tub and unpacking, I grabbed my notes for the meeting and headed to the restaurant where I had the famous Russian soup borscht. The personnel were very polite, and I enjoyed practicing my Russian with them. I still remembered the language as it was a mandatory subject in Bulgaria for all middle and high school grades. But I could speak it mostly because of the time I spent living with the old man in Ann Arbor.

I headed to the lobby precisely at the time scheduled to meet the translator from the ministry and noticed that he was already there, appearing impatient, looking at his watch, and glancing in the direction of the restaurant. "Ah, here you are!" he exclaimed, and soon we were on our way for a very important and, for me, historic moment in my life. This was a different feeling from the one arriving in Bulgaria, where I felt at ease and very comfortable, as being at home. In reality, it was home as Bulgaria is my homeland. This time, I felt a solemn and intense feeling in the air as we approached the commissioner's office. A middle-aged man sprang to his feet as we were introduced by his secretary.

"Welcome to Russia. We are looking forward to your work as we understand that your advisory assistance to Bulgaria was superb." He was speaking in Russian, and the translator stood by in case of a need to clarify or explain, but I managed on my own, which made me very proud of myself.

"Thank you, sir. I assure you that I will extend to you all the needed tax policy and administration assistance to the best of my abilities. I will propose that I visit tax offices in Moscow and interview your managers and agents in the field to get a clear picture of what I need to address."

"There is no problem. My secretary will arrange for you any necessary appointments and meetings you need during your stay. How soon do you want to start?"

"As soon as tomorrow, sir. I am eager to start work as soon as possible."

"We like such attitude, and I wish you luck. For any future contact, please call my secretary. This a direct line to ensure you get a fast response."

"Thank you, sir. I appreciate your support." The man smiled, and I left his office feeling relieved knowing that my initial contact with the Russian commissioner was successful in planning my future work.

The translator led me to my office, where I met two Canadian, one Danish, one American, and one Swedish tax advisors. They all greeted me very warmly, and each one explained their role in the project. Everybody was on a contract with the International Monetary Fund with leave of absence from their government tax jobs, ensuring their return to their previous positions. The Canadian advisors were providing tax policy and administration assistance. One was in his thirties, and the other in late forties to early fifties judging from their looks. The younger Canadian was in Russia with his family and two children. "My wife let me take this assignment only under the condition that my assistant is male," he said jokingly, but I knew what was the real reason. Russian women, just like Bulgarians, were desperate for American and Canadian men at that time. He showed me the cabinets full of completed reports and analysis created in the last two years. The male translator who was escorting me was assigned to them. The American man was in his thirties as well, single, with a young female translator who was pretty and quiet. Later, he took her to the States and married her. The Danish and Swedish advisors, a younger male and female in her fifties, were on temporary assignments just like me, whose job was to outline changes based on their experience in Denmark and Sweden. It was a very good crew of professional people, very accommodating and friendly.

I returned to the hotel relieved and content that my first day at the ministry went well and was productive. I felt that I had a very good start. But I couldn't rest even though I felt exhausted. I had to go see the Red Square. Bundled up the best I could, I ran out the door into the icy cold street with more than twenty below zero temperature. It was supposed to be a short walk, which turned to be extremely long, as my eyes were filled with tears from the cold and my body felt the piercing arctic air. But I was determined to get there at any cost, and after a painful walk, I saw it, gigantic, solemn, and beautiful in the night. I stood in the middle of it, gazing at Kremlin, at St. Basil's Cathedral with its bright domes, and there was also Lenin's Mausoleum. I was freezing but exhilarated to be at such a historic and monumental place in the world. My elevated spirits from my successful first day on such an important and historic mission representing the International Monetary Fund in Russia added to my night sightseeing experience helped me return faster and easier to the hotel. It felt so good walking in my warm suite and indulging myself of taking a hot bath in an old-fashioned tub. I fell asleep with the TV on and did not move till the phone's wake-up call.

The commissioner kept his word of a speedy assistance as in the morning, I had a driver waiting to take me to a Moscow tax office located in the suburbs and considered to be one of the few revenue-producing locations. The tax manager was a tall, dark-haired man who greeted me heartily with a strong handshake. "Welcome to my office. I arranged for you to speak with my inspectors, after which we could discuss my operations." I thanked him for his hospitality and headed to a conference room where I met a young group of revenue agents all chatting and appearing to be in a good mood. I did not discover any different way of examinations than those in Bulgaria. The audits were boring and unproductive as they compared invoices and receipts to numbers on the tax returns without taking into account that the documents for the most part were not authentic and the real activities of the companies were not disclosed for tax purposes. These audits worked in the totalitarian system when all enterprises were state-owned, and the accounting was on cash basis, somewhat similar to fund accounting.

The tax manager knew exactly where I was heading. As we walked in his office and sat down, he looked me in the eyes and started to talk before I even said a word. "These newly rich company owners will never pay taxes voluntarily. This is something that bothered me from the very beginning of becoming a tax manager. See, I know under Communism there was no such thing as tax cheating. Everything was well run and regulated, and we had the so-called state control officials reviewing the accounting books of the government-owned businesses. Penalties were very strict for stealing, and everything worked like a clock. Now in this free economy system, owners are not inclined to pay taxes voluntarily, so what I do is summon them at the end of each month, and based on my observations of their lifestyle, I give them the amount of taxes they owe, which they pay without any objections. What I take into account is what cars they buy and own, where they live, the cost of their kids' private schools, etc. It's a small neighborhood, and everybody knows everybody's business, so it is easy to get information."

I stood in silence, not believing that this man applied his own indirect methods of taxation and that his employees just went through the motion of futile auditing. It was my turn to speak, and I explained to him the purpose of my visit as well as the work I plan to accomplish during my six weeks' stay. He appeared very much interested in the documented and much more precise indirect auditing, which seemed to be the only way to conduct examinations at that time.

"I am looking forward to your written reports. I feel that I am well respected, and people abide by my requests without any problems. I will be curious to see if my estimates will be close to what you propose to introduce as methods of auditing." Then he moved on to a different topic on which I was not going to express any opinion. My involvement was strictly tax advisory. "You know, Antonina, it stings that I need a passport to visit my parents in Ukraine. We are not happy that we cannot travel freely, and all the former Soviet Republics are like separate countries." I muttered something like "I understand. I don't like restrictions to travel." And with that, we parted.

On the next day, as I arrived in the office, I saw a tall young woman sitting at the conference table. I shared the office with all the other advisors, and there was a conference table in the middle for us to have discussions without leaving the room. She was a Russian revenue agent waiting to take me along on one of her audits. Glancing at her, I noticed that she looked preoccupied and worried. A driver from the ministry drove us to her audit site, which was an architectural firm working in a spacious apartment of a tall building. Moscow is a big city, and it took us close to an hour to get to the place. A tall young man greeted us at the door, and I could see the Russian agent immediately becoming frightened. Her eyes were directed at the handgun the man had on his holster. The color of her face changed to light pale, and she looked like she had a hard time moving. The man took us to a conference room similar to the ones that companies have in the States. There were piles of records on the table, which I curiously looked at. As soon as the door closed, the woman started to speak, "I am afraid of these people with guns. That's why yesterday, I called and secured a special agent to come and be with us while I am examining the records. He will be in shortly."

"You do not have to be afraid of the man with the gun. They carry guns for protection. I understand businesses in this part of the world and in this era are subject to attacks from criminals. I witnessed that in Bulgaria, not to talk about extortion when owners have to pay the mafia for protection." She was surprised to hear me talk like that. Somehow, she did not seem to know that this was common practice for businesses operating after the fall of Communism in countries from the former Soviet Bloc.

After our talk, she relaxed, especially seeing me calm and not concerned. We made ourselves comfortable, and she started to review the requested documents. Soon there was a knock on the door. She startled, but I told her to relax and stood up to open the door. There was a well-built young man in front of me, whom the lady recognized. She sprang to her feet. "Let me introduce you two. This is a special agent who is assigned to be with us today, and this is a representative from the Internal Revenue Service who is a technical advisor and assisting with our audits," she said, looking at both of us.

The young man smiled radiantly and extended his hand. "I am so pleased to meet you. I work with the Russian tax police, and I owe this thanks to your country's assistance. Our division was formed after we received training at your Georgia training facility for special agents, and we operate under similar policy. This is an unforgettable life experience for us learning tactics, strategies, laws, and ways of operating in a criminal environment." Needless to say, I was pleasantly surprised that IRS extended criminal investigation training to the Russian tax administration. I provided the Bulgarians with penalty code provisions of Title 18 and basic information about the functioning of CID, but they were far from organizing their own tax police. The Russian special agent went on to describe how they were trained side by side with the Americans and how incredible it was to be engaged in training exercises as a team. His voice softened as he recalled the bonding between all training participants and the comradery created during this time. Then he asked the Russian auditor about her concerns and went to interview the owner of the firm. Shortly thereafter, he returned and confirmed my observations that there was no imminent threat to the tax officials at this location.

After leaving, I had a chance to talk to the lady auditor about the exam procedures applied in all audits. As in Bulgaria, there was no formal training for conducting examinations. The requirement for the job was to have an accounting degree, and most auditors, being graduates from the old system, continued to operate in the same manner. She was curious to find out how I was going to proceed with her exam, and considering the time limitation, I gave her a crash course on interviewing the owner based on the provided records with explanations for the purpose of each question. I ended up working with this young auditor a couple more days, which provided me with great pleasure, as I was watching her conduct quite well her own investigation and obtain answers, clarifying the records piled up on the table.

Back at the ministry, I started to work on my reports for Washington and drafting a condense audit manual for the Russian tax administration. I was amazed at myself as I started to write in Russian without any difficulties, with very few mistakes corrected by the Russian translators. Auditing in Russia was no different than auditing in Bulgaria, so I used to a certain extent the materials I already had for the write up of the exam manual. By the end of the third week, I had a short version for use of indirect methods and was ready to meet the commissioner. It was a Friday morning when I walked in his office carrying a folder with notes for the meeting and the document I created in Russian. I started by sharing my findings from the visit to the tax office and the work with the tax auditor. Being as brief as I could, the meeting still lasted a few hours.

"I know about the tax manager you visited. That is why I needed to find out what you think of his methods. He operates in an unorthodox way, but it proves to be efficient. So you have a written proposal for a structured and more accurate audit, which I would like to review. You have to agree that my manager has the right approach of judging companies' taxable income by observing and obtaining information about the owners' assets and lifestyles."

"Yes, sir, that's correct. The thought process is right on point. My proposal is to train all your auditors and managers in adopting a process of indirect auditing with proper arguments and support documentation. I created an abbreviated version of an audit manual stressing primarily a uniform approach to auditing in applying such methodology." Having said that, I handed him the booklet, watching his reaction. He glanced at the title then quickly browsed through it. I could see his face beginning to brighten.

"This is what I need," he said in a joyful voice. "A report and a booklet of twenty pages which I can read over the weekend. I am sure you have seen the cabinets with reports created by your Canadian colleagues. I don't have time to read these voluminous documents. I need a brief shotgun approach to deal with a difficult situation. Thank you, Antonina. Make sure you ask my secretary on the way out to schedule time for you to come on Monday."

It had been a rough three weeks of working day and night, and I felt like joining the others from the office for some fun. The American was having a Friday dinner party, so I got together with the Swedish and Danish advisors, and we headed to the metro station close to the office. The Moscow Metro was just as glamourous as I imagined it to be from reading descriptions in travel books and magazines. The stations were of exquisite architecture with marble columns with styles of Art Deco with Gothic, Empire, and Russian elements. It was a spectacular museum of history projecting light, brightness, and happiness.

The American advisor's place was a three-story town house in a gated community close to the university. The first floor was called guest quarters or was intended to be for servicing personnel; the second floor was for entertaining, with modern kitchen and spacious living and dining rooms; and the third floor had three bedrooms all with separate bathrooms. The building itself was modern with high ceilings, a terrace on the second floor, and windows, allowing for plenty of light. "You will be housed in this complex if you decide to take on a project at the ministry," the host said jokingly. I just smiled, and we all headed to the dining room, tastefully decorated with a table display of delicious dishes and a variety of drinks. I felt at ease in this group, as if I knew them for a long time. I usually do not talk openly to people I just met, so I was surprised at myself on how comfortable it was to exchange experiences and stories of our lives. It was way past midnight when we headed back to the center of the city. I was a little leery about using the metro at that time of night, but judging from the relaxed and cheerful faces of everybody, I gathered that there was no need to be concerned.

Sunday was another amazing day, meeting up again with the team and visiting the famous Izmailovsky Market situated inside the walls of Izmailovo Kremlin, with beautiful displays of handmade crafts such as the matryoshkas (wooden hand-painted dolls within dolls), pottery, winter shawls, hats, books, etc. I always watched my spending with all the financial responsibilities I had, so I was content to buy an artistic, beautifully decorated wooden egg and had Russian *pirozhki* (dough filled in with cabbage) for lunch. It was another extremely cold day, so we did not explore more at the place even though this area had a well-known and much-visited park. On the way back, I stopped with the Swedish lady at a kiosk to see, at my surprise, that they were selling caviar and champagne. Needless to say, we treated ourselves for the evening.

On Monday morning, I got up before the phone's wake-up call and quickly got ready, dressing in my favorite suit. The usual Russian breakfast was at my door, which I savored with a cup of tea. I was eager to start the day as I was supposed to meet the IMF boss for the Russian project and the Russian commissioner for a feedback on the materials I gave him to review during the weekend. The cold air brushed across my face as I briskly crossed the street to enter the Ministry of Finance. The International Monetary Fund manager arrived shortly after me and joyfully shook my hand.

"Hello, Antonina. I am managing the Russian project. I am very happy that you could join us in working on this tax endeavor initiation. I have heard a lot about your work in Bulgaria from my friends at Treasury, and I am glad that we could borrow you to take a look at what the situation is here. I received your reports and read the document that you provided to the Russian commissioner. This is an outstanding work for such a short time. I need a person to assist with taxation in Russia for one year starting in September. After reviewing and evaluating your work, I determined that you are the perfect candidate for this position." I was listening in amazement as I did not expect this long introduction with offering me an extended tour starting almost immediately. The man had made up his mind and assumed that I would jump at the offer. I felt confused as I thought that this was going to be a short-term assistance since I was still on a contract with Treasury for another year. My face must have revealed my thoughts as the IMF official continued, "I talked with your Treasury bosses. They have no problem having you work for us, and upon completing your work here, you will be able to return to your job at the IRS. And of course, you need to talk to them as well."

I felt uncomfortable as I always saw through my work to the end, and there was still quite more to be done in Bulgaria. I did not respond as the man added that he was seeing the Russian commissioner to present to him his proposal for continuous assistance. With that, he left for his meeting with the Russian commissioner. My colleagues in the office overheard the conversation, and as soon as the IMF official left, each one of them congratulated me without asking if I agreed to take over this responsibility. The Swedish lady looked perplexed.

"I wish you the best, Nina. I was hoping so much to get this assignment."

"That was a surprise for me too," I responded. "And besides, I still have a contract with the IRS. There is a lot left to finish in Bulgaria for one year."

"But you heard that your Treasury bosses don't mind that you come here."

"I don't know," I responded. "I will need to talk to them when I return." She shrugged her shoulders, and everybody went back to work.

The Russian commissioner's secretary called me and asked me to see the commissioner after my IMF manager. *What a day*, I thought to myself, *with totally unexpected turn of events*. As in previous meetings with the Russian commissioner, I was accompanied by a translator whom I rarely used but felt more comfortable not being alone.

"Here you are!" the man exclaimed as the secretary led us to his office. We all sat at the conference table, and I waited impatiently for the commissioner to start speaking about my audit booklet. "Nina, you are a genius, learning in such a short time our accounting and tax systems and our methods of operation and creating an audit manual universal for all tax offices. This document is concise and clear to the point of how to conduct audits, as currently, nobody is tax compliant, and filling up these tax declarations has been a joke. I spoke to the IMF representative this morning, and he said that you are selected to work here for another year."

"Thank you, sir, for reading the manual and sharing your thoughts with me. I am happy to know that you find my work useful and applicable. I will be delighted to continue my work for the Russian tax administration, but I am still on contract with my employer, US Treasury. I will need to speak with my Treasury director and IRS manager."

"I understand, and this is the right thing to do. But we need you here, and if you decide to come back, we will build you a monument," he said this jokingly and made me laugh, as I knew that the Russians would build a monument for an individual deserving big recognition. "It is true, Nina. We will do that to acknowledge the value of your services." I thanked the man and returned to the office.

It was lunchtime, and we all headed to a nearby Russian café for *pirozhki*, which I adore. But there was a cockroach on one that the lady just brushed off. We all looked at one another and headed to the nearby McDonald's. Entering McDonald's in Moscow was different than anywhere I knew. To avoid crowds inside, they would let in only a certain number of people. There was a long line out in the street waiting to get in, but the service was fast, so the wait was not long.

Back at the office, everybody got busy in front of the computers (these computers were from Stone Age, huge boxes occupying the entire desks, having only Word and Excel). Before we knew it, it was Friday, and it was St. Patrick's Day.

"We are going out to an Irish pub. Come with us. It will be fun!" the American fellow shouted out, getting ready to leave.

"Sounds like a good idea. Detroit goes crazy on St. Patrick's Day," I responded cheerfully.

"Great, the Danish guy will pick you up at six."

Exactly at six, my Danish colleague arrived, and we headed to the pub. It was a walking distance close to the Red Square. I was pleasantly surprised as the pub looked like any Irish pub in the States—same setup, menu, and beer. The night went by quickly, and we were taking turns buying beer, so that made how many glasses? It was crowded, and you could hear only English. The rest of the public was American and English advisors in different fields and, of course, the traditional Russian girls, as my American colleague called them. "Watch, Nina, it's the same group of girls appearing at all places with Americans and English guys." My Danish colleague walked me back to the hotel. It was freezing outside, so once in the building, the heat hit me, and entering my room, I did not have time to even undress for bed.

The next morning, I felt chilled and feverish, but I wasn't going to miss going to the Bolshoi Theater with my Swedish colleague. We wanted to see the famous Russian ballet *Swan Lake*, with performance of world-famous ballerinas, but they were on strike (something new for the Russians as there were no strikes under Communism). We opted to see the opera *Otello*, choosing box seats close to the stage. Bolshoi Theater was a spectacular architectural and historical place, which I wouldn't miss seeing for the world, especially staying at a hotel only a couple of blocks away. I felt like being in a fairy tale observing the lavish gilt interior with red velvet draperies of the boxes, imposing huge crystal chandeliers, the paintings of Apollo and the Muses, splendid ceilings, astonishing architecture resembling nineteenth-century Italian theaters. I was sitting, not believing that I was at this world-renowned structure of beauty and art, where one could see famous ballet and opera performances.

Back at the hotel, my condition worsened. I was very hot with chills, weak and hardly staying on my feet. My American colleague brought me antibiotics, and a sister-in-law of one of my second cousins from Bulgaria who lived in Moscow immediately came with fruits and juices. Soon I dosed off but woke up around 5:00 a.m. with an awful pounding headache, burning with fever, and shaking. I called the American embassy in Moscow but was told that they did provide medical assistance to anybody except their own employees. Calling the Russian ER was not helpful as they promised to drive me to a hospital without guaranteeing treatment. It was getting time for me to get ready for work, which I had no strength to do. I stayed and worked in the hotel, advising everybody at the ministry that I was too sick, and it was not wise for me to have contact with anybody. Late in the afternoon, I got ahold of my IRS manager in Washington, DC, asking if I could return to Bulgaria.

"No, Nina, you are on a contract with IMF, and you cannot leave until the end of the six-week period. Work from the hotel. I'll be calling you there."

A female translator from the ministry came in shortly after that and applied cupping on my back; she was not afraid of getting sick. I survived to the end of my assignment, creating more audit procedural documents in Russian for the Russian tax administration.

The same black limousine with the male translator took me to the airport. I already felt relieved knowing that once in Sofia, I could see a doctor whom I trusted.

Maybe I was getting better on my own or the doctor prescribed me medicine that worked, but I was on my feet in a couple of days. My Bulgarian assistants were waiting to show me all the work they did in my absence, mostly relative to the start-up of the Bulgarian training center. The phone rang as we were talking; it was my Treasury supervisor from Paris.

"Welcome back, Nina. I want to congratulate you on the completion of your assignment in Moscow. Your work was deeply appreciated by IMF and the Russian tax authorities." Before I could respond, he continued, "I am calling also to inform you that the Macedonian Ministry of Finance has requested your assistance. I will arrive in Skopje, Macedonia, next Monday and will expect you to meet me there. Bring with you all documentation and manuals you created for value-added tax. I will mail you the invitation letter from their minister. Again, job well done in Russia."

"Well, thank you, sir. I will arrange for my travel right now."

Visit to Macedonia
as a Tax Advisor

My assistant was listening in, and as soon as I hung up, she asked me how she could be of assistance for my next trip. There were no flights from Sofia to Skopje. If flying, I had to go through Brussels, which meant a whole day flying and waiting at airports. So I decided to travel by bus. It was more pleasant seeing all the places on the way.

This was another trip close to heart as all my father's relatives lived in Skopje. Mom and Dad lived there after getting married in 1947. They both taught high school, but Mom felt uncomfortable in Macedonia as a Bulgarian. Since there were a lot of similarities between the languages, she said that whenever she wrote by mistake a Bulgarian word, one of the students would correct her. One night, a couple of Bulgarian doctors and friends of my parents got arrested by UDBA, the Yugoslavian police, and never came back. Mom got scared, and they moved to Sofia, Bulgaria. So did my grandparents, and the families of my two uncles and aunt followed.

The trip to Skopje was going to take me back to places where my parents lived before I was born. It was Sunday, and the passengers were mostly Macedonians returning after a weekend shopping in Bulgaria. Everybody was chatting joyfully until we reached the border, and a Bulgarian customs official came on the bus.

"Everybody, get off the bus. Line up with your luggage opened in front of you."

I watched people getting up and silently following the orders. Reminded me of movies from the war where people were lined up with their few belongings in hands. I got off the bus and stood at a distance behind everybody, holding my luggage. The Macedonian invitation letter was in my briefcase, and I was ready to pull it out in case one of the customs guys approached me, but they did not even look at me. The customs men started to confiscate shampoos, deodorants, and other toiletries of the people if they had more than one. After watching this painful search, I heard a man ordering everybody back on the bus. Once seated, people started to curse the Bulgarian border patrol, but the same scenario occurred on the Macedonian side, where the Macedonian officials confiscated whatever was left in people's luggage. That was the reality of crossing the Bulgarian-Macedonian border in 1995.

As soon as we were on Macedonian soil, the bus driver, knowing the stress these people went through, stopped at a café. "Here, folks, you can get coffee and go to the bathroom. The bushes behind the building to the right are for women, to the left for men." I waited on the bus until everybody returned, and soon we were zooming along small Macedonian villages perched on green hills with farms and gardens, with meadows of wildflowers stretching in the horizon.

Once in Skopje, I looked at the map, and the hotel being at a short distance, I decided to walk regardless of my luggage being heavy and not on wheels. On my way, I had to cross a bridge over the Vardar River, where I stopped to catch my breath. Looking at the water, I remembered my mother's story of how they used to have picnics by the river when they lived in Skopje. One weekend, they were sunbathing. It was hot, and Mom decided to swim. Mom was not a good swimmer and got caught in a current, at which time my grandpa jumped and saved her. I sighed, picked up my bags, and continued my walk to the hotel located on the other side of the river. Once checked in and situated in the room, I had an incredible urge to meet with relatives. The name Duridanski or Duridanov was unique, and the first person I picked and called form the yellow pages happened to be a cousin. I met him and his wife that evening in the old part of town over *chebachitsa* (grilled minced meat with special spices) and Macedonian brandy. It felt good being with family. We hugged and started to talk about our lives and the family's history. My cousin drew on a napkin the family tree going back to our great-grandparents from Shtip, a town in

Macedonia. It was an emotional meeting feeling right at home surrounded with family happy to see me.

Early morning, I showed up at the Ministry of Finance, eagerly
waiting in front of the building. Soon my boss arrived, and we headed
together for a meeting with the Macedonian minister of Treasury and
his deputy, the commissioner of the tax administration. The meeting was very cordial and relaxed. The two men were pleased to hear
about my Macedonian heritage, which made the dialogue easier and
productive. I spoke in Serbian and translated for my boss in English.
After sharing and recognizing that their tax issues were similar, but
not as severe as those in Bulgaria, the discussion moved toward the
subject of creating and implementing value-added tax, so crucial for
the economy of all European countries. Both the minister and his
deputy agreed that the value-added tax policy adopted in Bulgaria,
based on the Danish model, was sensible and that it could be applicable to their country. I had copies of all value-added tax materials,
including forms, tax reporting requirements, manuals for registration, auditing, and collection, which I left for them to review, so we
could discuss at our next meeting in a couple of days.

My boss and I left the office pleased with the initial meeting at
the Ministry of Finance in Skopje. His spouse accompanied him to
Skopje, and I joined them in the evening to attend a small art exhibit
with reception on opening night of a Macedonian lady artist. I love
art, so this was a special treat to get acquainted with the work of a
local artist and meet her personally. One painting named *A Dream*
impressed me the most since it was open to many interpretations.

The following morning, we decided to benefit from the day
off work and engagements and travel to Ohrid, a city known for its
beautiful lake on the border with Albania. This was another thrilling
experience for me as I knew this road well, traveled in the past with
my mom and for my senior class school trip. Arriving in Ohrid, a
picturesque town with old historic houses perched on hills with the
King Samuel's fortress at the top, I felt my heart starting to beat as
I remembered my first visit as a teenager when my cousin and her
father took me to the market and I received the most beautiful pair of
shoes on heels in white-and-crimson lacquer top. I could still see their

smiling faces showing me around and being so happy to provide me with a very pleasurable and heartwarming reception at their house. At the fortress, I entered into a dispute with a young Macedonian, claiming that King Samuel was Macedonian, but I dropped it. The borders between the countries had changed so many times in the course of history that it was not worth to discuss.

After a very refreshing and uplifting trip to Ohrid, we resumed our work in Skopje. My boss and I met with the Macedonian government officials early in the morning (at that time, working hours in Macedonia were from 7:00 a.m. to 2:00 p.m., no lunch break; people would have their big meal at home then rest and socialize in the evening). Both gentlemen were very cheerful, and from the expression of their faces, they were glad to see us. The conversation was again in Serbian language, as my Macedonian was not that perfect, even though I understood every word of it. There were other officials present. A lady comes to mind who congratulated me on speaking Serbian fluently after learning that I studied in Belgrade. Hearing that I was of Macedonian descent, she went on to discuss Macedonia's economic situation, saying that Macedonia was much better off in the union of Yugoslavia. Even though I tended to agree with her (I was in Macedonia at those times when people had everything in abundance, and now they were traveling to Bulgaria for basic supplies), I hesitated to engage in a discussion about politics by saying only, "I understand." Luckily, the conversation was steered toward a discussion of the documents that I provided in Bulgarian language (Bulgarian being so close to Macedonian and understood by most Macedonians presented no difficulty for the tax officials to review them). Both men expressed a desire to follow the Bulgarian practice of enacting the tax as they fully understood the policy provisions and were impressed with the audit control ensuring its successful implementation.

We parted like people who knew one another for a long time, and we all shook hands.

"Thank you, Antonina, for providing us with such important and valuable information. We will definitely act upon it," the Macedonian commissioner said as we were leaving the office.

My boss was very pleased with my simultaneous translation; he could tell by the body language and face expressions of our hosts that the meeting went very well. My trip back to Sofia was much more pleasurable as I joined people from the American embassy in Sofia returning from Skopje in their private vehicle. Since the car had the embassy's license plates, the driver just slowed down as we bypassed a long line of cars waiting to cross the border.

Last Year of Tax Advisory Assignment in Bulgaria

My son left for the States shortly after the wedding. Anabelle was back at school, and I continued to do what I liked the most, working with tax managers and their inspectors in tackling issues. While on my assignments in Russia and Macedonia my assistant informed me that the Varna office requested my assistance with VAT in the summer. That worked great as I could take along my younger daughter. As soon as school ended, we headed for the Black Sea, where we were put up at one of the Ministry of Finance lodging facilities. Every morning, a car picked me up and took me to Varna's tax office where I was immersed in cases with inspectors, encouraging and support-ing them in resolving a recurring issue of refund requests, the issue I anticipated would prevail when I drafted the VAT audit manual. My Danish tax colleague also followed with his translator, arriving from Sofia a few days later. We both left early in the morning holding meetings with managers and agents in the Varna office, assisting with specific questions and issues since the VAT law was enacted.

A few days later, a neighboring regional tax office located in Dobrich invited me to spend a day with them. The Dobrich region, known as the Granary of Bulgaria, is amazing in the summer with its golden wheat fields. After interviewing the regional manager, fol-lowed by a meeting with his tax manager, it was evident that their issues were no different than those in other regions; only the approach was geared toward the region's conditions and economic peculiarities. The outcome of my visit was very productive; extending on-site assis-tance as always proved to be very successful. My observation for both the Varna and Dobrich regions was that tax officials were very versatile in tax policy and administration for value-added tax, but they lacked experience in the field. My involvement at this point as anywhere else in the country was to provide them with confidence that they already possessed the necessary skills and tools to do the job.

At the end of the day, I would return to the hotel knowing that my daughter had fun on the beach playing with other children on vacation with their parents from the Ministry of Finance. There was a security guard at the entrance, so children could not leave the facility without being stopped. And the vacationers formed one big community where everybody knew each, so it was completely safe. My assistant was with her family, and I knew my daughter was in secure hands playing with her two boys. After dinner, everybody gathered in the club with DJ music, where the children danced and we, the adults, talked about work and the economy.

I had a couple of days that I was hoping to use for personal leave when a call came in from Dobrich that the Romanian tax authorities heard from their Bulgarian colleagues that I was in the area and requested that I meet with them for a day at the Black Sea by Romania. Of course, I was thrilled to take part in such assignment, which I cleared with my bosses from Treasury and IRS, but what made it more attractive was that I could take my daughter with me. She was only eleven at the time, but she had been around tax officials in Bulgaria and the States and was very well-behaved. The Dobrich regional manager picked us up early in the morning and drove us through the Dobrich region toward the Romanian border.

On the way, we stopped at a hunting lodge, which was astounding, with horns of deer decorating the entrance. This place was the pride of the region, well known to international hunters. Heading to the Romanian border, the Bulgarian officials informed me that the Romanian tax authorities would meet us at the border and would take us to the place of the meeting. The Dobrich regional manager assured me that his car would pick us up in the evening and that all details were worked out for me to not worry. Arriving at the border, we walked toward a black BMW, in front of which was a gentleman who waved at us.

"Welcome to Romania." He smiled, extending his hand. "It is an honor that you grant us this visit since the Bulgarian tax officials are raving about your assistance with training and materials prepared especially for them."

"It is an honor for me, sir," I responded, "to have this opportunity to meet with you and provide you with similar assistance." I was curious about the checkpoints on the road, and he explained that they were in the process of overhauling all their system, so in the meantime, the police was penalizing all foreign cars with unspecified fees.

My hosts were very polite and wanted to make it a pleasant visit also by showing me sights by the sea. On the way to the meeting place, we stopped at a Romanian vacation spot with cabins tucked among pine trees. Our final destination was a resort on the Black Sea. It was lunchtime, and our hosts treated us with a specialized Romanian fish dish. The conversation was in French, but they also knew English, for which I was glad because I could present to them the English version of all value-added tax materials and documents and, most importantly, the policy and the manuals. The Romanian translator spoke English. He glanced at the papers, after which he told the Romanian tax official that there would be no problem translating them in Romanian. During the four-hour-long lunch, I provided a short version of the Bulgarian value-added tax policy and administration, emphasizing areas of scrutiny and attention in implementation and application.

Anabelle was a good girl. After finishing lunch, she sat by the pool watching vacationers jumping in the water and swimming, laughing, and having fun. She loved observing people at the beaches of the lakes in Michigan ever since she was little. As a baby, she used to sit under an umbrella without budging, following with her eyes kids running and playing in the sand, boats in the water, or people swimming. I was so proud of her speaking French to the translator who was a young man; she studied French in Bulgaria at the Anglo-American school, and I could tell that she was happy to be able to understand and answer in French without problems.

Driving to the Bulgarian border was at a higher speed as we needed to get there before dark. As promised, we were picked up by the Bulgarian tax office driver and delivered to our lodging by the sea outside the city of Varna. This was an exhilarating experience spending a day in Romania with their top tax officials and accomplishing another important objective of providing a neighboring country of Bulgaria with valuable and needed information and materials.

Back in the capital, I spent a couple of days writing reports for Treasury and IRS, which I faxed later on Friday evening. Something incredibly moving happened earlier in the day. I placed a call to Washington, and the operator, hearing my name, began thanking me. "God bless you, ma'am, for coming to help us. Just wanted you to know that we are very grateful. May God grant you happiness and long life." With that, she connected me with my manager. This unknown woman was acknowledging the value of my help and expressing gratitude, and for me, it was like the voice of all Bulgarians. I felt tremendous satisfaction knowing that people knew about me being in the country and were thankful for my work and sacrifice. Yes, I sacrificed not being with my children and relying on my mother to bring them up, which was a big burden and responsibility.

"Hi, Nina, I know you just returned from a trip to the Black Sea and Romania, which I am sure was very successful as usual. I assume the reports are on their way?"

"Yes, sir, you will get them in a few hours today." I had a diary of my activity from my trip, which I explained in detail.

He was deeply impressed with my achievements at the cities of Varna and Dobrich, as well as the day spent in Romania. "Nina," he said in conclusion, "what is really valuable is the fact that you are providing advisory assistance in Bulgarian language, making it easy to communicate with the tax personnel. I am sure you can pick on people's reactions easier than an outsider. I am also impressed that you spoke French with the Romanians since I am sure they felt more comfortable than using a translator. In addition to delivering excellent results, the use of your language skills is definitely saving time."

"Thank you, sir," I responded. "I know that a phrase lost in translation could be critical or without meaning in this line of work. Sir, I need to talk to you about a delicate situation relative to my trip in Russia." I went on explaining how I felt that I could not abandon the Bulgarian project now that I have only one year to build a training center, which the Bulgarians could use after I depart and not seek much foreign assistance. I added that one of my personality traits is loyalty and that I felt obligated to finish my assignment with the IRS.

My manager did not interrupt; he just listened. And at the end, when I ran out of words, he said, "I totally understand. Working for the Service is like wearing an old pair of shoes which are so comfortable. That's why you are not ready to join the IMF project. I will let them know, so they can make other arrangements." With that, we ended the conversation. I knew that the doors to IMF were closed for me forever and that this was one of the decisions that could have completely changed my life. Then I remembered the lady operator and thought to myself that this was my destiny; I needed to finish what I started in Bulgaria.

Leaving the office, I bumped into a man in the hallway who looked at me and started to talk very animatedly without any introduction. "I am assigned to listen to your conversations. You are the most boring person on earth, only work, only taxes. I have a big headache now. Thank God your stay here is temporary." And he stormed down the stairs. I did not know what to think of it. Obviously, the man was listening to my conversations, and not knowing much about taxes was extremely bored. I shrugged my shoulders and headed home. The streets were empty by then, so I picked up my pace, arriving home late in the evening.

The next couple of weeks were busy with meetings at the ministry with the Bulgarian commissioner, whom I briefed on my work in Varna and Dobrich and extended greetings from his Romanian counterpart.

"We are very grateful that you take time to travel the country and extend assistance at various tax offices, and this time, your work at the cities by the Black Sea is much appreciated as inspectors completed their cases successfully and are equipped with knowledge for future audits. The theoretical aspect of your materials is fantastic, but you are also going above and beyond your duty by ensuring that our tax employees understand and know how to apply audit techniques from your manuals. Places that you visited are performing above projected expectations. Your approach has been unique from the beginning and is showing fantastic results. You are also contributing to a regional collaboration and cooperation. You know, I had a visit from the Macedonian commissioner after your visit there, and we agreed on exchange of information for all tax matters. He was particularly interested in your work with our tax officials in implementing value-added tax. Your diplomatic approach resulted in bringing the two countries together, which you know has been difficult because of former historical events and disputes." I was pleasantly surprised to receive such news, particularly being of Bulgarian and Macedonian descent.

Back at my office, my assistants were eager to discuss the plan for the follow-up work with the establishment of the training center and scheduling follow-up visits in other parts of the country based on requests from their regional directors. My schedule soon was filled up with weeklong training sessions for the fall in Pleven, Gabrovo, Blagoevgrad, Plovdiv, Kazanlak, and Stara Zagora.

Prior to my first training scheduled in Gabrovo, the commissioner called me and said that they signed an agreement with the Germans not to use any other foreign tax advisors for training. Then he looked at me and said, "We are not breaking the agreement. You will continue training as a Bulgarian."

I smiled. "It will work out," I responded, "since I was born here."

Summer was coming to an end. It was already August, and I left with my younger daughter and her father for Washington, DC, where I usually attended a two-week-long meeting for Internal Revenue Service senior managers working abroad, mostly employees of TAAS and representatives stationed at American embassies in Europe and Asia, with taxpayers' service for American citizens and assistance to foreign governments fighting tax crimes. We usually went to Michigan after the meetings so I could see my son and friends from the Service. This year, on the way to Washington, we stopped in Paris. I wanted my daughter to see the City of Lights. Our hotel was close to the Eiffel Tower, which we visited on the first day. A ride on a Bateaux Mouches on the Seine was in order, and then we had dinner close to the Arc de Triomphe. You can guess where we ate with an eleven-year-old—at a pizza restaurant. It was a weekend, and we had our bikes. The streets alongside Seine were closed for traffic, so we could cross a bridge and ride on both banks of the river after having a typical French breakfast of croissants, pastries, jam, and milk.

Being in Washington, DC, was always invigorating, meeting IRS people of high positions and hearing their speeches about IRS goals on the international arena. The IRS assistant commissioner for foreign affairs was retiring in the fall, and there was a retirement celebration for her. I was sorry to see her leave as she was very much interested in my work and always approved of my advisory methods. She believed as my manager and Treasury director that my unique approach of following through with assistance in the field was very effective for getting results and measuring the success of the program. During these meetings, I met the IRS commissioner, spent time with TAAS employees, and had interesting conversations with representatives to Japan, Rome, and France. TAAS had at the time advisors stationed in the Baltic countries, Romania, Turkey, and former Yugoslavia. Hearing stories about their activities made me realize that I was the only one working with regional and local tax authorities; they all never left their offices at the Ministries of Finance. TAAS showed a film of their foreign advisory activities, and since Bulgaria was not mentioned, my boss looked at me and said, "You are too busy working. That's why you are not on this film." My boss was also a diplomat as I knew that the TAAS employees who made the film were not happy with me getting this assignment. I overheard some of them talking. "She has been with the Service only eight years..." I didn't hear the rest.

I could take a breather once in Michigan as we stayed in one of the rooms in our rented house in Lexington by the lake. My daughter ate all the hamburgers and ice creams she wanted; we rode our bikes and stayed by the beach. We went to see my son in Holland; he was staying with friends enjoying summer break. I was so happy to see him. Every time being away and seeing him again, he seemed more mature. He grew into a very handsome young man, tall, with dark hair always cut in style. My son always cheered me up with his large smile and relaxed attitude.

Back in Bulgaria, I was hardly unpacked when the Danish tax official called. "Nina, we scheduled another weeklong value-added tax classroom training for government officials from Eastern Europe, including Ukraine and Belarus, at the ECD training facility in Copenhagen. It starts in September, and your participation is very much needed. I just got off the phone talking to your manager in Washington. They will arrange for your travel authorization. I know that you will accept, won't you?"

I couldn't say no; a couple of weeks later, I was on a plane for Copenhagen. Looking out the window, I was enjoying the sight of the little islands just before reaching Copenhagen. I loved the water, and the picturesque scenes above the country were welcoming. My Danish counterpart met me at the airport and drove me to a hotel where all the course participants were staying. It was midafternoon, and he offered to show me the location of the training center. He had a high position in the government and was primarily involved in policy making for value-added tax in the newly emerged free market economy countries in Europe. My specialty intrigued him as he made a comment that the best tax policy provisions in the world would not be effective without a proper implementation with strong audit control.

On the way to the training site, the man briefed me on the upcoming training scheduled in the following week, and I used the opportunity to take a glimpse of the city with sights along the way. We walked alongside the famous Nyhavn district by the canal lined with cheerful, colorful houses with restaurants and thriving with life of cheerful crowds. My host pointed out Amalienborg, the home of the royal family, and took me to the courtyard with the statue of King Frederick V in the middle, surrounded by four palace structures. The guards resembled the ones in England. On my way back, I had to see the statue of the famous little mermaid, inspired from and created based on a story by Andersen, which I knew from my childhood. And there it was by the harbor right in front of my eyes, surrounded by people. It had a sad expression, which I knew came from the real story of the mermaid's destiny. I continued my walk to the main pier and, from there, to the pedestrian section on Strøget

Street, considered to be one of the longest streets in Europe. It was a very lively street lined with houses, shops, cafés, and restaurants. I couldn't resist and stopped for a cappuccino, which was extremely tasty, definitely matching one from Italy. Back at the hotel, I organized my teaching materials and settled in for the night.

Teaching at the OECD center in Copenhagen was an honor because only the best instructors were invited to lecture there. Since my involvement in introducing value-added tax in Bulgaria, I became the auditing expert in Europe, having extensive knowledge of its policy as well. My audience were high-level government officials from Eastern European countries, including Ukraine and Belarus. I lectured in English, and each participant received simultaneous translation with headphones at their seats. The classroom setting was not designed for interactive discussions, but I was curious of what would be the response from my audience. My teaching tools were a flowchart outlining the topics and handouts providing examples and exercises with reference to their answers (Powerpoint came much later). While talking, I examined the participants' faces and felt very content seeing their interest as well as approval, especially when it came to specific case examples in reference to each one of the audit techniques. I knew I hit home when I noticed people nodding in consent of what they were hearing. During lunch breaks, I had an opportunity to get their feedback in person, coming to find out they all had the same, if not similar, situations with tax abuse in filing tax declarations for value-added tax. It appeared that what I predicted when I wrote the audit manual for Bulgaria was happening; filing tax returns for invalid refunds was a common phenomenon in the Eastern European countries.

My Danish counterpart joined in all conversations. During one of the breaks between classes he looked at me and said, "I told you, Nina, you are providing not only Bulgarian but regional tax assistance. Your contribution is on a larger scale, as by providing very valuable tax audit techniques across the entire region, countries in Eastern Europe will be successful in the value-added tax implementation, which will accelerate their ability to join the European community." I never thought of the regional impact that my teaching had; in my mind, I was extending my services to countries in need. What was peculiar was that I felt very much at ease communicating with these individuals speaking different languages but having the same goal—to be successful in building a tax system that would allow them to be equal partners of the European Union.

At the same time, Revenue from value-added tax continued to be steady in Bulgaria, which meant that my nationwide training, classroom and in the field, was successful. However, my assignment was temporary, and I needed to ensure that upon my departure, the tax administration could function on its own. With the concurrence of my bosses in Washington, I approached the commissioner about the formation of a Bulgarian training unit headed by a director and composed of highly qualified tax officials, such as a representative from the ministry's legal staff, the assistant commissioner, and senior inspectors. The assistant commissioner's involvement was crucial as he was originally not receptive of any changes of the system.

"This is a splendid idea, Nina. We know you will be leaving, and we need a qualified group of individuals to take over training upon your departure. I will provide you with a list of tax officials to include in the program. But how do you propose to do the preparation of a training center?"

"Sir, I will submit to my superiors a request to invite the Bulgarian training group of future instructors to the States, where they will receive on-site training. I am not sure how soon I will receive a response."

"This is a very pragmatic approach, and I thank you for your efforts to assist with our future operations. Please let me know as soon as you receive a response so that we can plan on our end details about the trip."

A month later, I was on a Delta flight to Washington, DC, with a group of Bulgarian high-level officials. We were scheduled to visit Internal Revenue Service training facilities in Washington, DC, and New York City. A Bulgarian translator working for the other Treasury advisor came along. The group consisted of the assistant commissioner and chief council, the future director of training, and a couple of other ministry officials. We had layover in Munich, and upon getting on the plane for DC, I knew something was wrong as the stewardesses started to serve drinks, not customary for economy class. This was the first time on a plane for some of the people in my group, so they panicked when we were told that there were technical issues and we had to get off the plane. They all calmed down, except for one man, who was afraid of not seeing his family again. The lunch vouchers were used in the Duty Free shop.

After a couple of hours' wait, we were told that the plane would not fly and that we needed to pick up our suitcases as we would be spending the night in Munich. I met with a Delta employee, and showing my credentials, I arranged for a dinner voucher and a stay at a hotel by the airport. The person scared of flying was not doing well; he used his lunch voucher on whiskey and hardly recognized his suitcase. But all was well in the morning after a good night's rest and a good breakfast. We were back at the airport in Munich heading for the States on the rescheduled flight.

I have arranged for the Bulgarian tax officials to attend a class at the IRS training center in Washington, DC, called Training the Trainer, designed especially for classroom instructors who get certified upon completing the program. We showed up early to find seats and to set up the translator's station. A week passed by quickly with daytime classes and evening and weekend sightseeing. A trip to the White House was a must; I could see the excitement on everybody's face glittering with joy as we entered the building.

Our next stop was New York City. We took a train to the Big Apple, where I arranged reasonable accommodations at a hotel with studio apartments at the tip of Manhattan. Taking a walk after settling in, we discovered a food store and stocked up with small items of groceries for a week. Some of the men had never cooked in their lives, so I gave them a quick lesson on broiling steaks and cooking eggs.

We had a scheduled weeklong visit and observations of classroom training for indirect methods at the IRS training center in New York City. There were a couple of metro stops to the facility, and I gave everybody the address as well as instructions to wait at the second metro station stop if we got separated. Nobody wanted to be left behind as they all stuck together when the trains arrived. At the end of each day, we walked back to the hotel, a few hours' walk, and on the way, we stopped at restaurants for happy hour. It was interesting to hear the explanations they provided for their interpretation of happy hour since that did not exist in Bulgaria at that time.

Back at the hotel, we gathered at one of the studio apartments to review what they learned and their impressions and feedback from the training. They all concurred that the material was very useful as it was universal and could be applied in Bulgaria. After the first few days, during one of our discussions, the lady from legal counsel said, "Nina, we are truly very grateful for the opportunity to train at the IRS main facilities in Washington, DC, and New York City, and we are grateful to you for making this happen. We will incorporate the IRS material in our textbooks to train more instructors as they do in the States, and we will keep the indirect training module. What I need to say is that the training was very useful, but you teach better because there is passion when you speak, which inspires us, and it's easier to understand you."

"I am passionate about my job," I responded. "I enjoy every aspect of auditing, tax law and research, conducting investigations, getting to know businesses' accounting systems, and discovering tax schemes. We have a network of specialized units, which assist with areas outside the scope of our job, such as engineering and computer assistance. We work closely with our Criminal Investigation Division as well as departments other than Treasury such as Drug Enforcement Administration. But what attracted me to the agency is their mission and principles of honesty, integrity, equity, diversity, inclusion, and fairness.

"Since my first day at the Service, I met dedicated employees committed to serve the public and fight tax crimes. There is cooperation between tax offices all over the country, and whenever there are activities in a different region connected with a local audit, agents get assistance from that region with whatever necessary actions, such as bank summons, interviews, tour of businesses, etc. IRS auditors are backed up by our legal counsel, and we have direct contact with tax attorneys who not only answer legal questions but also accompany agents and managers in the field. There is closeness between all IRS officials regardless of their position based on pursuing the same goal of serving the country. For me, working for the Internal Revenue Service is very satisfying considering that my life principles coincide with theirs. I hope this explains why I am passionate when I share my knowledge with you all."

Everybody was silent. I could see from their faces that I struck a chord, which was the feeling of belonging and responsibility for delivering to a cause.

"We have a long way to go, Nina, but we have a good start. Thank you."

The next couple of days was a weekend, and we literally ran through Manhattan, stopped at Central Park for a minute, and continued by catching a boat for the Statue of Liberty. It was a remarkable trip not solely for training purposes but also providing the Bulgarian tax officials with understanding of the American culture. Seeing them off, I returned to Washington, DC, to attend meetings with my bosses and submit my report for the visit.

Returning to Sofia, there was a continued need for work particularly on international issues of tax abuse with the new value-added tax. The RSR stationed at the American embassy in Rome was servicing the Balkan Peninsula, and this being my last year of advisory services in Bulgaria, I needed to leave the Bulgarian tax authorities with an opportunity to receive continuous assistance from the Internal Revenue Service available in the area.

"Nina, I am very grateful for this initiative" was the Bulgarian commissioner's response. "I will recommend that my assistant accompanies you to Rome."

Arriving in Rome on a Saturday evening provided us both with an opportunity to visit the well-known Trevi Fountain, which had a particular charm lit up at night. On Sunday, after preparing for our meeting with the RSR at the American embassy, we did a power tour of the city, visiting the Vatican. From there, we had a quick run to the Colosseum, the Roman Forum, the Pantheon, and Piazza Navona. Early morning, after a typical Italian breakfast of croissant with cappuccino, we headed to the American embassy. The RSR greeted us at the door and led us to his office. The assistant commissioner was prepared with specific cases of Bulgarian companies dealing in Greece and Turkey. The RSR listened carefully, taking notes of names, addresses, and suspected tax crime offenses.

"I appreciate your visit in person," he responded. "I will follow up with your request for verification of activities at places you mentioned. I hope you understand that I won't be able to get to it until next month as my calendar is full. Nina is aware that I have as well requests for assistance from our tax offices in the States, and there are deadlines for responses to them. Since you are here with Nina, our tax advisor, I will be able to fit you in on…" And he blocked days for checking on addresses and information provided by the Bulgarian assistant commissioner.

After a delicious pasta meal lunch, we headed to the airport, arriving that same evening in Sofia. Another successful mission accomplished for immediate and future tax assistance to Bulgarian tax authorities from the Internal Revenue Service.

The day for goodbye came sooner than I expected. My manager called me on February 14, 1996 (I remember the date as it was Valentine's Day), and informed me that there would be a replacement for my position with an advisor with collection background starting in April, which would give me enough time to wrap up everything pending, pack up, and head home.

Twenty-Four Years Later— in Times of Coronavirus

I woke up today thinking, *Another day staying at home, and hopefully, I would have enough energy to do something of value.* It was April 4, 2020, and the world was coming slowly but surely to a complete lockdown. Countries from all continents one by one were imposing travel restrictions, closing businesses and nonessential services, and ordering people to wear masks and keep social distancing.

It all started back in January with a deadly Coronavirus paralyzing the city of Wuhan, China. My husband, Mitt, who I met in 2011, and I had planned a vacation on a cruise ship with Oceania sailing the Pacific Ocean, leaving on February 8. I am describing this trip because nobody knows how we all are going to end up and what will happen next. The day of our departure was a regular day with very few cases of the virus sickness in the States, usually of people who recently travelled, so nobody thought much of it. The flight to Sydney, Australia, would have been long and stressful, so we stopped in Hawaii for a few days. We landed in Honolulu and sought out a taxi to take us to the hotel. Our hotel was across from Waikiki Beach, and I immediately noticed that we could watch from the balcony people surfing, bathing, and having fun. What I admired the most was the huge banyan tree. We walked up and down the beach and ended up stopping at a place by the water where we had a pineapple slush. We visited that same place for breakfast the following morning as we saw it serving fresh fish, and we both love fish dishes. As far as spending time on the beach, the water seemed cold to me, and I did not feel like swimming. For the first time in my life, I did not dip myself in the water being on a beach. I had a little sore throat and did not want to chance getting sick and not being able to get on the ship. We were informed by e-mail that they will be taking temperatures before letting people on board, so we knew that things regarding the Coronavirus were getting already a little bit serious.

Being in Honolulu, we couldn't miss visiting the Diamond Head Crater. We took a bus stopping close to the hotel and started our hike. We walked through a tunnel taking us to the center of the crater and winding up on a steep climb with amazing panoramic views. The crater itself was a pretty imposing sight, and the white lighthouse by the water was very picturesque. Once at the top, we reached the lookout and saw an incredible view of Waikiki Beach, with hotels alongside the ocean. Curious about the origin of the name? British soldiers in the 1800s took by mistake the glittering stones of the crater for diamonds, hence the name. We also discovered on our walk in the evening the International Market, which was a mall, and attended a typical local Hawaiian show with dancers and singers.

Our next stop—Sydney, Australia. The hotel was at the Circular Quay, which was very conveniently located by the Rocks, a walking distance to the opera house, the Sydney Harbor Bridge, the Darling Harbor with the wildlife zoo with a main attraction of kangaroos and koalas, and the harbor from which we took a ferryboat to Manly Island. It was an overcast day, and there were no tourists on Manly Island, but we walked from the ferry to the beach where we just sat and enjoyed the view. Water has always had such a peaceful effect on me; I felt that time stopped, being transposed in a state of peace and tranquility. Being in Sydney, it was imperative to see an opera at the unusual architectural structure of the opera house by the harbor. I have been very fortunate to see performances at some of the greatest opera houses in the world—Moscow's Bolshoi Theater, the Buenos Aires opera house, and now at the Sydney Opera House, where we saw *Don Giovanni*, the story of a seducer with numerous sexual conquests.

The flight from Sydney to Auckland was short, which gave us an opportunity to explore the downtown area by the harbor as soon as we unpacked at the hotel. The following day, we walked to Viaduct Harbor from where we watched the drawbridge open and the skyline of the city; it was quite of an imposing sight. Instead of taking a tour bus, we hopped on a local bus that took us to Eden Hill and to the other end of the island through different suburban towns. We ended the day by walking in a park called Auckland Domain, stopping to see a winter garden with fern trees and a museum. On the way back to the hotel, we checked the pier where our cruise ship had already arrived; it was a short ten-minute walk to the hotel.

The cruise started in Auckland. We always travel light, so we walked from the hotel with our carry-on suitcases and backpacks to the harbor. Yes, they took our temperatures, and we headed to our stateroom. I love Oceania ships where we always have a room with a balcony, and the service is impeccable, with gourmet food in all restaurants. First docking was at Bay of Islands, where we signed up for a tour to visit a glowworm cave. The peculiar thing about this cave was that the glowing worms on the ceiling of the cave resembled stars. Out of the cave, we walked on a small hiking trail up and down a hill. Then the bus took us to see kauri, thousand-year-old trees in a parklike setting. Last sight was the first stone house built by prisoners with salt water on the left side and fresh water on the right side.

Next docking was in New Caledonia, in Noumea, where we booked a trip to Amédéé Island, an uninhabited nature reserve island with a tall lighthouse and known for sea turtles and coral snakes. We could snorkel from the beach, and since I don't like snakes, I snorkeled by myself close to shore, very careful to avoid them. And there it was, a beautiful sea turtle that I would have loved to observe longer when, all of a sudden, I saw a colorful snake on the other side of it, so I swam as fast as I could to shore. I was also thrilled to see colorful fish. Mitko swam out and came back saying that he also saw stingrays, which I feared a lot. The next day, we snorkeled at Master Island, which is a resort with stilted houses in the water. Snorkeling for me at this place was very pleasurable and amazing, with colorful fish even close to the boat. I also saw a turtle. Mitt swam further out and saw a shark as well as numerous turtles.

Next port was Vanuatu, where we took a cab to the Blue Lagoon; the drive was through lush tropical vegetation and trees, and the lagoon was a pretty site nestled in a rain forest. Later in the day, we signed up for a boat trip to Paradise Cove, a place known for great snorkeling. It was an excellent spot with blue starfish. This time I held onto Mitt's bathing suit, and we swam over beautiful corals to the beach. There was a pole with a bag of bread in the water for feeding the fish, but I did not do it as I was afraid of attracting stingrays or sharks.

Early next morning, we docked at Lautoka, Fiji, where we grabbed a cab and explored on our own the first land beach. There were beach houses on the beach, and some curious vacationers popped up their heads to look at us. We found close to the pier a good spot for swimming and cooled off before heading back to the ship. They were taking our temperature every time we came back on board, and Mitt had a slight fever, which was very troublesome. They did not let us on the ship. I sat in a chair they pointed to me and watched Mitt pouring a bottle of water on his head. Thank God he was fine after that. The afternoon was also very exciting as we visited a Fiji village, watching a group of local people in costumes perform by singing native songs and dancing wild dances. Mitt said that I almost got cooked by the cannibals as one of them was making harsh movements toward me. LOL. I had one of their kava kava national drinks in small quantity, which supposedly numbs your mouth, but it did nothing for me. I suppose due to years of drinking Bulgarian grappa and American whiskey. Next, we stopped at a beautiful orchid garden at the bottom of the mountain Sleeping Giant, named after its shape with multitude of orchids of different shapes and colors. On the way to the ship, we saw an Indian temple but were not allowed to go in. I could not figure out why as I had been in Indian temples before. Suva was another place in Fiji where we docked at and where we decided to go for a hike in the rain forest. The lush tropical vegetation of trees, bushes, and plants was overwhelmingly pretty as we hiked by terraced pools, stopping at the last one to cool off. The water was extremely refreshing as it was humid and hot.

Bora Bora, the dream island and paradise on earth, was our next destination. And what else was there to explore on an island with turquoise blue water over amazing reefs except underwater marine life of multicolored fish? Snorkeling at coral gardens was amazing. Some of the beautiful fish we saw were parrotfish and butterflyfish. As I snorkeled toward the boat, I saw a stingray, which made me freeze for a second, then I swam as fast as I could to get on the boat. The second place where the boat stopped was full of stingrays and sharks swimming in groups. The guide went in the water to feed them, and everybody followed, except me and a couple of other people. I would go in the water infested with sharks and stingrays for nothing; even watching the tour guy playing with the stingrays did not convince me that it was a good idea. I just took pictures from the boat. The second day snorkeling was more like going on a private trip as we were accompanied only by two other couples. The guide gave us a tour around the island and stopped at the spot for snorkeling and swimming, where we were also served cocktails in the water as it was shallow. We were across from Matara Beach, so when we returned from the trip, we got on one of the local buses to spend the rest of the day there. It was a hot day, so I decided to float on my back the entire time in the pristine, beautiful blue water.

Last docking was at Raiatea Island, where we went snorkeling on a catamaran, again with a small group of people. Sitting on the side of the boat, I was admiring the different beautiful blue shades of the ocean. We had two captains and a lady with whom I was so happy to speak French. On the way, they were pointing out atolls, which were a remarkable sight amid the aquamarine, azure, and turquoise waters. We arrived at the snorkeling place and dived in as soon as the boat stopped. I was holding again on Mitt's bathing suit and went further out than where I would go on my own. The corals were beautiful, but there was not that much fish, so I asked him to take me back to the catamaran. I couldn't understand what Mitt was trying to tell me, but at one moment, I felt one of the guys pushing me forward. Once by the boat, the lady gave me a noodle; however, the current was too strong. The second guy from the boat pulled me up with a rope.

This was the last island we visited. What I omitted to mention was that American Samoa, Samoan Islands, and Mare Island, which were on the list to visit, refused to let us dock, and Huanini Island diverted us to dock at Papeete for customs inspection before allowing us to continue to Bora Bora and Raiatea. By that time, the Coronavirus concern was rising with more restrictions on travel. And every time we left the ship, a guy would take our temperature before letting us back on board.

We disembarked in Papeete on March 5, 2020, after our last delicious breakfast and walk on the deck. Our flight to LA was on the following day, so we stayed in Papeete at a local hotel. The address was at what looked like a private residence with a barking dog. Our taxi driver called the phone number from our reservation, and soon an all-puffing lady arrived, opened the door, and we entered in the front yard. She looked at our reservation and offered us another accommodation since the one we had booked according to her had no air-conditioning. Then she added that we were lucky that we were traveling the next day because tourists were supposed to get medical clearance before staying on the island. We ended up with a nice two-bedroom apartment on the second floor of the next-door building, freshly painted in white, with two terraces, one facing the water and the other the hills. It was an incredibly hot day. We unpacked the absolute necessities for the day and headed to the nearby store where we bought some food, milk, and beer for the day. We assumed that there was a beach across the street, but the water was not clean, so we walked a little further down the road to a restaurant with a pier where the water was somewhat more acceptable for a swim. I spent the rest of the afternoon watching French TV where there was nothing but a talk about the Coronavirus. They were showing areas in France affected the most from the decease, and in a period of four hours, there were around four hundred more infected people. There were no reports of other countries. I just could not understand how this virus traveled from China to France and was spreading so fast.

Our flight to LA was early in the morning and was very comfortable because we had the front seats in the emergency isle only by ourselves. I was surprised that I was the only one on the plane wearing a mask, disinfecting the seats and the air around us, and using hand sanitizers. It was the same on all our previous flights. I could sense people looking curiously at me, but I really didn't care, especially now, after listening for hours about this virus on the French TV.

We spent the night in LA at Hilton and took a flight home to San Antonio on the following day. We were not tired when we arrived home, and it didn't take us long to put everything in order. I even went grocery shopping. Watching the news, we were relieved to see that the Coronavirus situation in the States was not serious with about 1,400 cases of sick people nationwide.

March 8 is Woman's Day, a holiday in Europe, and there was a big celebration with all Bulgarian women in San Antonio at the newly opened Bulgarian restaurant Europa. I took Uber, not having to worry about driving in the evening, and was so happy to see the girls from the folk dancing group. I rushed to them, gave them hugs, and we took photos. There were over forty women, and some of the men delivered flowers for each one. The Bulgarian bread *pitka* was so delicious I must have had five pieces of it. There was a competition of selected women to paint a woman's picture with makeup from their purses, arrange products for a salad, and sew. I did not stay long and missed all the dancing later that evening, but it was the first day after we arrived from the trip, and I felt a little tired. As soon as the competition was over, I headed home, filling the Uber with bouquets of flowers. That was probably one of the best March 8 celebrations I ever had.

A lot happened since the gathering at the Bulgarian restaurant. We had been on stay-at-home orders for the last two weeks. Schools, theaters, restaurants, gyms, and all nonessential businesses had been closed. Schoolchildren and college students had been studying online. The number of contaminated and dying people with the virus had been going up dramatically from 1,400 sick last month to 270,000 plus and 7,000 plus dead. Hospital staff and patients shown on TV and Facebook were all in protective gear. There were daily briefings from the president about measures taken to fight the virus and the status of the current situation. Hospitals were badly in need of ventilators, masks, gowns, and medical supplies. There were new hospitals being built in New York; Navy ships were converted to medical facilities for the cities of New York and Los Angeles. Hospitals reported that there was a ranking system for who gets a ventilator based on life expectancy, so older people like me better not need one. And pictures from New York City, considered the epicenter of the epidemic, were scary with empty streets and overfilled hospitals, with morgues in tents or trucks with refrigerators. The entire country was affected one way or another with stay-at-home orders in most parts of the country. There were continuously sad stories of people passing away.

A Bulgarian woman visiting her son and his family in Pittsburg died in his arms, and subsequently, he was in intensive care on ventilator himself. A nurse lost three of her patients waiting to be assigned beds only half an hour after she checked on them. A man lost unexpectedly his father who was in good physical shape. The initial theory of the virus infecting only older people with other underlined health problems was not true any longer as there were younger people who lost their lives to it, the last victim being a six-month-old baby. Added to the crisis was the economic disastrous picture. The stock market had crashed from 30,000 to 20,000 points, and millions of people were unemployed or losing their businesses—a very grim economic picture at a time you are worried about the safety of your family.

San Antonio, Texas, was not suffering as other big cities, but numbers of sick and dead people was going up, which had called officials to stop activities in the city except shopping for food and medicine or seeking medical help. People here do not take this threat seriously, after all, most have not seen a person who has tested positively. The shopping malls were full with parked cars, and people were emptying stores and dragging toilet paper in big quantities (that has been a world phenomenon, which few can understand). But there was a sense of urgency as I heard that there was a shortage in freezers and guns. Last time we went to Target, I saw a few empty shelves, something I haven't seen since Bulgaria under Communism. What was curious was that very few people of the general public wore masks and glasses. We decided not to go out except for walks around the block as nobody claimed to know everything about this virus. It was supposed to be transmitted by saliva of people sneezing or coughing, but recently, it was discovered that it was airborne, with hospital rooms testing positive, which required more protection for hospital personnel. The six feet distancing between people when in public was supposed to be effective, but who knows? And not everybody observed it anyway, especially those hanging at the stores every day. Another theory was that virus does not like high temperatures, but it had spread to countries with warm climate as well. It was also supposed to disappear at forty degrees Celsius, but then why do people with high fever die from it? There had been descriptions of the sickness from people who survived. They said that at first, they had a little sore throat, low fever, and very shortly had difficulty breathing. The sickness had been determined to be extremely contagious as people could be sick without symptoms and infecting everybody they were in contact with. That was the main reason for states and cities to apply stay-at-home orders as a way to save lives. But the numbers of sick and dead continued to go up, and there was no prognosis for things to improve soon.

How was life when you follow the stay home order? At first, I tried to adjust by scheduling every day to do something productive, like play the piano, write my book, or paint. I even started to have piano and Chinese lessons online. Today we had a virtual folk dancing, and it was so good to see the girls from the group. I am so lucky to have my older daughter come and supply us with groceries; she is a real angel. Today is also my twin grandkids' birthday, and I saw them on FaceTime, but they looked sad. I know they didn't understand why there would be no big celebration but a cake at home. It was difficult for them to comprehend that something invisible had stopped people from going out. My son would also FaceTime me, and I see him with his wife and baby. I saw them today, and it was such a joy watching my sweet little granddaughter wave and smile at me.

April 5, 2020, another day in purgatory. No reason to rush. There was nothing going on. I was waking up a lot during the night and finally decided to get up at 4:30 a.m. The situation was very grim as the president announced during his briefing that the next two weeks were expected to be very bad. His exact words were, "A lot of people will die." According to the last statistics, the number of infected nationwide went over 300,000 and 1,000 more died in the last twenty-four hours. San Antonio, Texas, where we live, was not that critical with 364 sick and about 60 dead. However, nobody was sure about the real number of infected people, and that was the reason why most of the states ordered to stay at home. New York continued to be most affected with the president deploying the military with 1,000 men to assist with health care and other issues arising from the Coronavirus. Health-care workers from New York City appeared on TV to share that they were working for weeks without any rest. With tears in their eyes, they were talking about the most devastating experience being the loss of some of their colleagues.

Several cruise ships had been stranded in the last month with sick passengers on board. The last one, *Royal Princess*, reported today that two passengers died on board. We looked at each other without saying a word. We were so lucky to disembark our cruise ship on March 5. We both remembered how some people who were at the airport coming home were concerned about being sick. Since we came back, we took high doses of vitamin C, vitamin D, etc., and we gargle with alcohol, French vodka to be more precise.

It was exactly a month today, and we felt blessed to have been able to return from our trip without any issues. How am I enduring the stay-at-home in quarantine? Not too well, as I don't like restrictions in movement since my life in communist Bulgaria. I was starting to compare my life now deprived of freedom with the one I had in Communist Bulgaria, not being able to travel and not being safe. It was a very uncomfortable feeling of being encaged and restricted to move. The only pleasure I got was seeing the kids and grandkids from Kentucky, Michigan, and here in San Antonio on FaceTime and Facebook from their posting of pictures and videos. Seeing my daughter with her husband and my grandson from a distance when they deliver food for us was the highlight of my day in seclusion and reminded me of the meaning of life. They had been coming every week, and today they called early to let me know that the order they put in for food arrived and they would be coming over to deliver some items. My heart jumped with joy. I saw them through the glass front door, and after they dropped off the bags, I went out to wave and made signs at them that I love them. My eyes were filled with tears seeing them leave. Why? Somebody might ask. Because there are so many things in this world happening beyond our control or understanding that I cannot help but feel sadness of what might occur next.

April 12, 2020, today is Catholic Easter. We had breakfast with boiled eggs decorated with lipstick, deer sausage from my daughter and her husband, and feta cheese. It's so ironic that this virus is called Coronavirus on a day like Easter. This is a day for families to celebrate the resurrection of their Savior, and this year, it would be celebrated from a distance. I would be seeing my daughter and her family later today, waving at them after delivering for us Easter dinner. I saw my grandkids in Michigan, how they started their day on Easter morning, and I talked to relatives and friends overseas.

Bulgaria was on a complete lockdown; nobody could travel as a tourist in or out of the country. But people were not anxious. My half-brother, his wife, and his stepson; my relatives from my grandma's village; my friends from Sofia were all in good spirits. "Bulgaria has been through a lot during many centuries, and this will pass" was the attitude of all my close and dear people. My relatives on my father's side whom I saw during my brief stay in Skopje last summer were also doing well with all the family gathered close by and the younger ones taking care of my cousin and his wife. This was the couple I saw in 1995 when on assignment for a visit to the Macedonian Treasury Ministry. I stayed in touch daily with my cousin on my mother's side who lived in Vienna with his family. We were close from our childhood years as we all went together to the sea in Varna and Obzor, and I babysat him in the summer. Recently, he reminded me of how bold I was in those days. "Nina, do you remember when once you came to pick me up and a policeman stopped you saying that you are not dressed properly to which you responded in English, so he left you alone thinking that you were a foreigner?" Well, that was a close call because young people picked up in the street deemed not properly dressed were taken to labor camps. I don't remember how I was dressed, but I am sure it wasn't anything indecent. Seeing each other every day on WhatsApp, we talked about those days and shared information on what was going on at the places we lived.

I also learned more about my family history from my father's side. I knew the family was Macedonian coming from Shtip, but I knew nothing about my grandparents' story. After many years, I saw one of my cousins who lived in Germany and with whom we played together as kids at my father's funeral. She was a few years younger and was always looking up to me as an older sister. What I just learned from her was that our grandfather was very smart and, as a kid at the age of fourteen, was sent from Macedonia to study at the time at the prestigious university in Istanbul, Tsarigrad was the old name. Upon completion of his studies, he traveled in Bulgaria and decided to teach at Bulgarian schools. Our grandmother, who was from Chirpan, Bulgaria, came from a very wealthy family. Her father, our great-grandfather, was a merchant having businesses in Austria. He sent my grandmother and her sister to study in Paris, but shortly thereafter, there was an outbreak of the Spanish flu, sweeping away people in the millions. Our great-grandfather contracted the flu and passed away, which put an end to my grandmother's studies. My grandmother returned to Bulgaria and started to teach. It was at that time that she met my grandfather. After getting married, they settled in a village called Kriva Bara by the city of Lom on the Danube River, which they picked up as it was a place they could afford.

Ironically, years later, my mother who graduated political science went to do her student teaching in Kriva Bara and met my father who was also in her program. My grandfather at the time was the principal of the school, and my grandmother was taking care of the family—they had four children. After my parents' marriage in 1947, the family moved to Skopje, Macedonia, where the rest of our relatives lived. My parents started to teach and settled in for a long and peaceful life. Mom liked the outdoors, and they often had picnics by the Vardar River. All was well until one night, their close friends, both husband and wife doctors who were Bulgarian, were arrested, and nobody saw them after that. My mother got scared, and with a doctor's excuse, the families, ours, and that of my grandparents returned to Bulgaria. My grandparents went back to Kriva Bara, and my parents returned to Sofia. My father became an instructor at the University of Sofia, and Mom became a high school teacher in social studies.

I was born in 1949, which means that if they continued to live in Skopje, the events in this book would not exist. If we were in Skopje, I never would have immigrated as Yugoslavia was not behind the Iron Curtain. Yugoslavians always had the opportunity to travel and study abroad, and the country did not forbid practicing religion or Western music and entertainment. As a young person, I would have had access to music, art, and shows from the West, as well as having the opportunity to visit other countries freely and study anywhere I chose. My parents separated and divorced just as my father was advancing in his career at the university, because of what he explained to me years later was the influence of a bad company. My parents' divorce was the biggest gossip among the intellectual circles in Sofia. The process of separation was painful with years of court orders for eviction and disputes for the family apartment in which I lived with my mother. My father married to the sister of a well-known academician and became a very well-known professor in linguistics. He was a very intelligent and respected man with hundreds of publications in linguistics, receiving international recognition. But he did not stay in touch with me because of what a friend of mine explained was fear of losing his position. I still have a hard time understanding his thinking because I guess being raised by my grandmother, mother, and aunt, I would never stay away from the people I love.

Twenty-Four Years Ago—
Back in the States

It was an early spring morning in the year of 1996 when my older daughter and I headed to the airport escorted by a Bulgarian couple in charge of providing me services during my assignment. In the last week, I met all Bulgarian tax officials from the ministry, summarizing all accomplishments and outlining a plan for a continuous work in the direction I started. I also had brief meetings with members of the embassy and USAID. The previous night, we had dinner with my mother and aunt and felt uneasy leaving them behind.

The forty boxes of materials and clothing were already shipped, and we were traveling light with a couple of suitcases. My debriefing in Washington, DC, was short; I had been sending reports weekly, keeping in touch by phone and faxes almost on a daily basis, so there wasn't much to discuss about my accomplishments. The director of TAAS and my manager thanked me, and we shook hands. Soon we were on our way to Detroit, Michigan.

Back at the IRS office at the McNamara Federal Building in Detroit, I resumed auditing of companies and was surprised to see that compliance was worse from the time I left as tax promoter schemes had emerged, some completely illegal and others in a gray area requiring specialist's opinion. I got involved in an earned income credit project where the entire city of Dearborn was noncompliant, with accounting firms preparing bogus tax returns. An accounting aide helped me go through tons of tax returns, collecting evidence for assessing penalties, and it was worth it because the word got out and the abuse was stopped. At that time, the IRS was also becoming more efficient in tax return selections for audit. Just to clarify, IRS does not audit all individuals or businesses; the selective process identifies areas with irregular entries.

I got involved in a pioneer project at a unit called PSP for special programs (each state or bigger city had one), a unit responsible for securing tax returns for auditing for the state of Michigan. This project used a program called MACS, where you set parameters for certain issues and the system spits out all returns with abnormal tax reporting. Up to this time, returns were selected manually where senior agents were pulled from the field to spend time at PSP, picking out returns for audit. Working on the MACS project, I had the opportunity to get to know most of Michigan exam managers, ensuring that the flow of returns was more efficient and productive than in the old system.

My younger daughter soon joined us with her father staying behind. There was something very strange going on, which I could not figure out. Returning from my assignment, I was assigned to work at a regular exam group; the international group's manager was cold and said that they did not have a spot for me. My younger daughter returning home by herself told me stories that helped clear my suspicions. Her father was involved in a lot of affairs, but this was not his only betrayal.

"Mom, he made me write in my diary things against you, like you work for the Bulgarians and you carry a gun. Then my diary disappeared, and he bought me a new diary. I know he went to the American embassy the day that my diary went missing."

Of course, I thought to myself, *a diary written by a child will be taken as true.* There were already people at TAAS who did not like me because I was too young and too new to the IRS to head a project overseas. My ex-husband helped them get rid of me. Washington liked intrigues and gossip, as whatever my ex-husband achieved with my daughter's diary spread from the IRS to Treasury. I remember my last conversation with one of the Treasury officials who always praised my work looking confused, and as he was leaving, he said something like, "We thought the Bulgarians started to do things right." I attributed his remark to possibly the work of the newly appointed Treasury advisor to Bulgaria, but now I knew exactly what he was referring to. My daughter looked worried, but I assured her that it was not her fault. My IRS manager knew all my personal life story overseas, but now I had to share with her this new discovery.

"Nina," she said, "I don't know exactly what's going on in Detroit because I can also see the resistance of people here to let you at least get back to international. I saw your file before you came back, and there is nothing in it compromising your work. I suspect that this all was an oral discussion and order from Washington. I don't like this, and I will help you get back to your level if that is the last thing I do as a manager."

My daughter wrote a letter to the American ambassador in Sofia, apologizing for writing lies about her mother, which I was sure made no difference. I picked on my new routine knowing that in time I would get back to having a challenging position.

The three of us settled down. My older daughter resumed her studies at Wayne State University, and the younger started a new year in middle school. I sold the house in Lexington, Michigan, and moved to a condominium in Farmington Hills, Michigan. It was funny because I mentioned jokingly to the girls how I missed public transportation in Europe, coming to find out there was a bus service to Detroit and back with a stop around the corner from where we lived. I was also happy to see my son regularly as he decided to take a break from college and stay in the area for a couple of years. But I missed my mother. I talked to her every Friday evening after work, telling her about our new life arrangements. Long-distance calls overseas were still expensive, and I set up to hear her at the end of each week, catching up on news from both sides of the ocean. Our apartment had two bedrooms, and I knew I had to find a place for her and my aunt, if not in our complex, at least somewhere close by. I used the same agent who sold me my apartment to look for a one-bedroom apartment for them. It took a couple of days for her to offer me something that grabbed my eye; it was a senior complex for ages fifty-five plus on Walled Lake a few miles from me. The building had sitting areas with views of the lake where the women could read or have lunch if bored of staying in the apartment. There was a billiards room, which the girls liked immediately, and being on the lake, we could all sunbathe in the warm months.

The paperwork just needed my signature, so I walked over to the Century 21 office. The receptionist took me to the conference where I waited for my and the seller's agents. Soon the door opened, and a man in his forties with a funny grin on his face appeared. I didn't know what to make of it. He continued to stare at me and said, "I recognized your name. You audited me in 1988, and I did not know if your audit or the divorce I was going through at that time was worse." I knew this must have been one of my early audits because it was in the first year after training when I audited small proprietorships. But I also dealt with accountants representing the firms, so I had no idea who this guy was. After hearing the whole story, I remembered the audit and some of the issues, as well as the fact that the man paid for the extra assessed taxes without bothering his wife at the time.

Next thing I knew, he pulled a folder and asked me to look at his currently filed tax return. "Look... Can I call you Antonina? I don't want to go through this experience ever again. Please let me know if there is anything irregular that jumps at you." He insisted for me to review his return, and I couldn't refuse. There was nothing to look over; I could see even from a distance that the tax return was properly filled in, with nothing out of the ordinary. But what got me was the amount of money he grossed, and I knew that he did not have a degree, maybe took a few classes at college.

"Hey, can I ask you a question?" He nodded. "How difficult is it to become a realtor?"

"For you, it will be very easy. I will suggest that you take a month's course, and after that, all you will need is to pass a state exam for licensing. I will give you the information if you are interested. Let me know because my boss would love to have you work here."

"Thank you so much," I responded. "I'd like to give it a try, but it will have to be part-time and on weekends since I will continue to work at the IRS."

"No problem. We work with clients mostly weekends and evenings anyway."

I thanked him. By that time, my agent arrived, and we finalized the paperwork for the purchase of Mom's apartment.

Restless Spirit, New Challenges

My work at the IRS was not challenging, and I needed to add something to my life. It reminded me of the life of a high-level Bulgarian official from the Ministry of Finance who spent an year at Harvard University and, upon his return, lost his position and status. The man went to work for a private company and later managed to get back to his former status. The summer of 1987, I spent studying for the real estate exam by the pool with the girls, watching them swim and joke. My son also stopped by and spent the night with us, sometimes with friends, which brought me lots of joy. I had all my kids around, and that was what mattered the most. The real estate test was unbelievably easy. What was supposed to take all morning took me only one hour, and that was with double-checking all the questions and answers as I couldn't imagine that it was so easy. I shared with Mom my experience, and her response was, "Don't you have enough work already?" She was joking because I knew she loved every time I accomplished something new.

I traveled to Sofia to start making arrangements for both Mom and my aunt to come to the States. Arriving in Sofia, I met with a realtor and agreed on a price, setting a closing date for the sale of Mom's apartment. The contract was one page long with sellers' and buyers' names, property address, sales price, and a paragraph stating that it was an as-is sale without any other conditions. Notary public took only one day to research the title. It was a cash sale, and the lady arrived with banknotes hidden in multiple pockets of her coat; she did not want to carry a briefcase and risk to be robbed.

Then the issue came with the money transfer to the States. The banks at the time were not doing such transfers, and I definitely did not trust to leave the money in a Bulgarian bank. I witnessed a lot of banks go bankrupt and people losing everything overnight. One particular bank where the American embassy kept operating funds allowed for money to be withdrawn only to pay salaries.

"Nina, we can offer you a solution," the realtor said. "There is a businessman we know who could wire the amount to you from Turkey in exchange for a fee." I had no choice. We left on good faith without any paperwork showing that we were going to receive the money.

Back in the States, I had my mother and aunt settled in their new place, which they loved. But Mom was very worried that we were tricked and she would never see the money from the sale of the apartment. I was about to tell her that the money arrived just to keep her calm when the wire transfer came through.

That fall, I started to work as realtor at Century 21 some evenings and weekends. Somebody might ask how I can have another job working for the IRS. You can so long as there is no conflict with your IRS employment. For example, one cannot work for a CPA firm or open a tax preparation firm. The other condition is to inform your manager in writing about your intent to work outside the service with detailed description of what you will be performing and receive approval again in writing. I did receive an approval and started initially to take calls in the office on evenings and weekends. Soon I had a client base, which grew fast because I had a background, which helped me develop the best and most effective ways of servicing people.

Most realtors at that time worked from the company's offices, using their desk computers and office equipment and supplies. I knew that this was not the most efficient way of communication as people were busy, so I purchased a laptop and installed the MLS program on it. I started to see people at their homes at their convenience. On evenings and weekends, I invited them to sit in front of my computer and explained to them the entire search process. This was a very unique and innovative sales approach for the real estate business; I am sure that even today realtors do not educate their clients on how to purchase a house. I loved my new job and made many friends who later referred me to people they knew who were looking for a house.

And I was the only realtor in the office with a cell phone; everybody else was carrying beepers, which I found ridiculous. People liked the fact that they had direct contact with me; nobody liked to beep a realtor and wait for a call at an undetermined time.

What I realized was that people sometimes noticing houses for sale as they drove wanted information right away, which I could provide. Becoming a realtor, I also found out that my last realtor was not honest with me when she gave me information about the sales history for the apartment I bought for Mom. This list showed sales of properties in the area but did not show sales in the same apartment building. There was no reason to confront the woman at that time as I was not going to accomplish anything, but it just left a bad taste in my mouth about relationship with realtors. So much about honesty in people, which I already learned while working for the IRS. Not everybody is honest, especially where money or gain is involved. I was just glad that I had real estate knowledge to recognize if people were not decent. Real estate sales commissions were very lucrative—3 percent of sales price and 6 percent when a person sells properties over one million dollars. I easily reached that number and, to my surprise, started to make more money working part-time than at my daily IRS job.

During one of my assigned call days at the office, I met a family from the United Arab Emirates. They were in the process of relocating to the States, and they needed a home and a business to start their new life, as well as recommendations for good schools and universities for their children. I enjoyed their company as they were very educated with very progressive views on life about humanity, peace, education, and work. I was happy to help them settle in the area they liked with a good school system, and I also assisted them in purchasing a small gas station in partnership with another family that they knew in the area. The husband returned to sell his business and properties they had back home, and I marked on my calendar the date to contact the lady upon his return. It wasn't a couple of weeks later when I received heartbreaking news from the lady. She went home as a relative called and told her that her husband was sick in the hospital, but upon arrival, she found out that he already passed away.

The man was in his late forties, and nobody expected such a tragedy. I felt really bad for the family and did the best I could to console the woman and the kids. I am telling this story because it will lead to another phase of my life endeavors, an unthinkable undertaking.

The devastation was too big for the lady to be able to conduct a business at the gas station, which was supposed to be one of her husband's occupations. I was aware of the financial and operational status of the gas station, which happened to be in Plymouth Township, walking distance from where we lived when the kids were in high school. After giving it a few days of consideration, I thought it would be a good opportunity for my children to get exposed to business and make a few bucks for school. This was a business purchase only, and the price for its purchase was reasonable since the land was owned by individuals. It was a franchise of Amoco, which had control over management and the business operation of gasoline sales. They had sales reps who would pay visits to suggest that you drop prices to sell on volume rather on profit margin, which was not the best strategy for this location. Prior to taking over the business, I received an approval from the IRS that I could own and operate such facility, and I started to make preparations for this new adventure in my life. Yes, it was an adventure as I learned later that all gas stations in the area, or maybe the country, were owned by Middle Eastern males, and the sales of those businesses were dictated by somebody overseas.

I took personal leave from my work to attend a week's course for Amoco dealership licensing and took over the place upon my return. My mother and aunt went back to Bulgaria as my aunt felt very isolated not knowing the language or anyone she could talk to except my mother. There was no internet at that time or other ways to watch Bulgarian TV or be in contact with her friends and other relatives. Getting into the gas station business was a very big decision, and I did not have Mom to run it by, so I just moved forward entering a world totally unknown to me. I believed I could handle it. It wasn't a huge place; there were four pumps on each side of a building, which was a convenience food store, with a cashier's enclosed area with bulletproof glass. The security system was wired to signal the police upon pressing an alarm button from under the register's counter. Since this location was in a nice area in the suburbs and in a neighborhood I knew that I did not have much concern for safety.

The Amoco training course was helpful because among other things, I learned that the big theft was not done by customers but employees and suppliers. I had employees at the gas station, which at the time was open twenty-four hours—a young girl working the register, another somewhat older working part-time and was in charge of ordering purchases for the store, a high school boy, another young guy studying at a trade school, a high school teacher working on weekends, and a truck driver working nights. With all these personnel, I originally thought that I would have to just monitor the operations, do the record keeping and banking, and keep an eye on gas pricing. By the end of the first month, I knew things were not going okay. I was heading for financial crisis, realizing that I would have a hard time keeping up with gas purchases in the thousands of dollars every week. According to my record keeping, sales were stable but cash was missing. I called on a company to install security cameras outside and inside the store, especially over the cash register where I could see the ringing of purchases. The cash register in itself was programmed with buttons for the most purchased items, such as cigarettes and drinks, and was connected with gas dispatch with a monitor recording the level of gas located under the counter.

First weekend with the cameras, I watched the schoolteacher open the register, take money, and stick it in her pockets. This money was never returned to the register. The worst part was that when I showed her the tape and told her that I would hold money from her pay to make up for what she took and that she was fired, she became angry. That blew my mind, a schoolteacher being a thief and belligerent on top of it. Late afternoons, friends of the high school boy would come in, take whatever they wanted, and leave without paying. Another confrontation resulting in firing the guy, who was on top of everything, threatening to complain to the police for not being paid for the day. I withheld money from the guy working the night shift because of missing merchandise. The truck driver viewing the tape became vulgar and started to curse. My IRS training came in handy as I preserved my composure and calmly told him that if he did not leave, I would call the police. There were missing cigarettes during the shift of the part-time young female. I took her off working the register, which made her furious, and that led to her dismissal as well. I was left with the young female and the guy from the trade school.

My older daughter hearing about all the problems and how the family was heading for ruin offered to help. She learned the business and its operations really fast and discovered that the ordering was in bad shape; there were a lot of outdated sodas, which were included in the sales price of the station, as well as on the shelves, pushed to the back of newly ordered items. The female who stayed was not happy that she had a supervisor at the cash register as well as for ordering and receiving goods. A day after my daughter started to work regularly at the station, she announced that she was quitting, which was fine; it saved me the trouble of firing her. She appeared the next day as if nothing happened.

"What are you doing here?" I asked.

"To work," she responded.

"But you quitted yesterday" was my response. You can guess her reaction. She zoomed out, slamming the door behind her.

Luckily, my request to Amoco to close the night shift was approved. My dear daughter worked during the day; she opened every day at 6:00 a.m. until the guy came from his classes to relieve her at 6:00 p.m. It was rough because Amoco allowed only two days in the year to close the station for holidays.

My life was like nothing I could imagine; I felt like in a whirlpool as my days were swept by with continuous tasks. I got up at 5:00 a.m. and rushed to my daughter, who had already done a drive by the other stations, checking the sales prices, and had made coffee and baked cookies at the station for the early-morning customers. Upon arrival at the station, I would change the sale prices on the cash register and the pole outside (it was done manually at that time with a big stick switching the numbers) if necessary. That was critical for the profit margin as I tried to keep it at 10 percent contrary to Amoco expectations of 2 percent profit, which would have not provided me with enough money to pay the high rent. If there was enough time, I had coffee with my daughter and greeted some of the customers.

From there, I dashed to my IRS office in Detroit or to an appointment with accountants or business owners. My manager, who was an elderly lady, often left me to replace her while on vacation or away, which gave me an opportunity to assist other agents with their audits. I had my own cases with challenging issues as well such as companies creating layers of partnerships and corporations between related individuals, operating in different states with foreign bank accounts, making it difficult to trace the flow of money, or companies that liquidate and reopen at different locations under other corporate names, with irregular transactions in liquidation and start-up of a new business, which in reality was the same as the old one. During the day, I loved solving puzzles, doing extensive tax law research on Lexus and disentangling schemes created by masterminds for tax evasion.

On my way back from my IRS office, I would call my daughter and stop at the stores to buy supplies, cigarettes, and sodas mostly as those items sold fast. Back at the station, I used to take care of banking and record keeping, but what I enjoyed was the time spent with my daughter having late lunch, more like supper, and catching up on things from the day. Surely enough, there were stories of delivery drivers who tried to cheat by miscounting and entering wrong amounts or numbers on the invoices. My daughter used to stand by the door and check off every delivered item, which stopped any attempts to steal. Most of the customers were local and would stop by to purchase a few items and say hi. My daughter used to cater to all of them by having special orders of produce, food, and drinks, such as chocolates, dairy products, etc., and I used to bring flowers. The gas station became home not only because of the long hours but also because of the contact with people who appreciated the special attention and service and were comfortable sharing personal stories. There were only a few instances when younger females tried to walk away with a gallon of milk or something else without paying, but these were rare cases. The more serious was a complaint of a woman who claimed to have fallen on the snow by a gas pump and hit her head. Luckily, the cameras showed that this was not true, and the police, whom she called, warned her not to make false accusations as this was a crime. There was also a man who filed a claim with the state stating that his engine blew up because of the bad gas he purchased from us. He was not aware that we could not purchase gas wherever we wanted; this was only Amoco gas, monitored and supplied by only one dispatcher. This incident went away, but because of it, I knew that we could easily be a target for fraud and deceit.

Trying to hire help proved to be impossible. The couple of women who claimed to be hard workers were not trainable, and my daughter had to let them go. We used to leave around six when our only employee arrived. We ran to the gym since at least we had some relaxation for a few hours. I kept in touch with Mom, informing her of our crazy, new life. I was happy to hear that she and my aunt were thinking about coming back to the States and that my aunt already had a visa. My aunt, however, was not healthy, and shortly before their travel date, she passed away. I tried to conceal my tears in front of people, as I was at the station when I learned about it. We had a futon in the back room by the supplies, so I went there mourning and thinking of all the times with my aunt as a child. I was devastated that I could not spend more time with her, like take her to get pedicure (lately, she was not able to bend down) or go for walks. Mom arrived by herself, crushed by the loss not only of her sister but also her best friend. She lost a lot of weight and had episodes of feverish shaking, which doctors could not diagnose. I knew it was tremendous stress, and with time and care, she was back on her feet.

Sometime in April 2001, our evening employee quitted, and that was for the best as he started to steal as well. I stood dumbfounded watching a tape of ice delivery that disappeared during the night, as well as customers stopping by and warning me that somebody was at the store at night, taking merchandise out to a car. I took over the evening shift until closing with Mom keeping me company. Looking back, I don't know how I made it, but this is what I am. I do not exasperate when times are difficult but rather stay on course until I finish what I plan. During one of those evenings near closing time, a young Asian man walked in just before closing and stood by a counter with coffee and fountain drinks. I was with Mom locked inside the partition with the bulletproof glass. The man had his back turned to me and ignored my questions about helping him. I knew I was in trouble and was ready to push the panic button when one of our regular customers, an African American young man, walked in with his usual big smile. The other man ran out the door, which confirmed my suspicion. My customer stayed until I closed the place, and we all left together.

We found a replacement, a young man in his early twenties, who was thrown out of his parents' house without a penny and had no place to go to. He was scared and seemed very sincere. I guess I never stopped being a teacher, and I could not turn him away when he walked in the station, asking for help. With a pay advance, he found a room, and I was picking him up on the way from my IRS office so he could work evenings. However, because of prior problems with employees, I did not want to chance having any more issues and stayed in the station during his shift. Keeping this schedule was extremely hectic when on top of it I was also approached by people referred by prior clients with requests for real estate help. I remember being tired, collapsing in bed at night, but not stressed out. By that time, there were added incidents, which made me wonder about our lives and safety at the station.

One day, entering the bank, I noticed a policeman standing by the door, which seemed unusual. Coming to find out there was an armed robbery in broad daylight the previous day. The bank was a block away from the station, and that was very disturbing. I knew that we could be attacked next. This event was followed by a robbery at a gas station not far from us, which occurred at night when the place was closed. All these incidents plus the crazy schedules my daughter and I had made up my mind that we had to get out while we could. Still working for Century 21, I put the gas station for sale, asking the same amount that I bought it for.

It was September 11, 2001, when I woke up later than usual in the morning and jumped out of bed, worried about how my daughter was doing at the station. The phone rang as I was getting ready, and it was my daughter yelling, "Mom, a plane hit one of the towers in New York City! Turn on the news!" She added in a calmer voice that she managed fine in the morning, so I could go to my work at the IRS. I told her to relax and that I would be there as soon as I finish my scheduled appointment in the morning. After hanging up, I turned on the TV, viewing a terrifying sight of the last floors of the second tower blown up and burning.

Being late, I rushed out the door and drove to an appointment I had at a CPA office in Dearborn, Michigan. The representative for the company under audit met me at the door and took me to a conference room where I prepared to work. She started to talk about the incident in New York City, that this plane malfunctioned and hit the towers. "Yes, that's a big tragedy," I responded. "So many lost lives on the plane and in these buildings." The lady sighed and left the room. I was about to call my manager when my phone rang, it was my son.

"Mom, are you in Detroit?"

"No," I responded, "I am at an accountant's office in Dearborn."

"That's even worse, Mom. Don't ask questions, just pack and leave. Call me when you are out of Dearborn."

There was an urgency and worry in his voice, which made me anxious. I grabbed my computer and briefcase, heading out to inform the accountant that I needed to reschedule. Going to the parking lot, I was struck to see cars all over the place going in all directions, not observing street signs or traffic lights. Dearborn was known to be the most populated Middle Eastern community outside Beirut. The signs on the shops were all in Arabic; there were Arab bakeries and restaurants, and some people, usually women, living there did not speak English. I discovered all that when I worked on the earned income credit project and spent a couple of months in the city. I managed to get out of Dearborn by taking side streets and headed toward Ford Road, on the way to the gas station. Traffic seemed to be normal here as I headed west of the city. I felt somewhat relieved, and I called my son to let him know that I was out of Dearborn going to Vanesa.

Arriving at the gas station, I saw cars lined up for gas twisted in circles and filling the entire place on both sides of the building. There was a big commotion with people all over the place, some on top of their pickups with gas tubes. My daughter met me at the door with a frightened face; her voice was trembling. "Mom, there has been an attack on America. We are at war. Terrorists took over two planes, hitting the towers in New York. A lot of people died." I hugged her and rushed in. My younger daughter was also at the register with her husband; they were both sweaty, helping out people who seemed to be in exasperation. In a couple of hours, we were out of gas, drinks, and food. All that was left were gum and chocolates. The kids wrapped the gas pumps with signs "Out of gas," and we sat down to evaluate the situation.

I called my office in Detroit, learning that my manager dismissed everybody for the day. There was no word on what to do. We had extensive audit training, but nobody thought of preparation for war. That made it difficult as I was hoping to receive some kind of information and direction from my office coming from the Treasury Department. Calling Amoco dispatch, I did not get any answers either, except that there would no deliveries for a while. Then everything was quiet. The streets were empty, there were no cars or pedestrians, there were no signs of life in front of people's house, and it became spooky, not knowing what to expect. This was one of the moments in my life when I felt desperate. I looked at my daughters. They were distraught; their eyes were expressing fear and confusion. All of a sudden, I felt very tired. The inability to plan or make a decision on top of the crazy last few hours totally exhausted me. I nodded at the girls that it was time to go home.

There was not a single customer the next day. I took the day off to spend it with my daughter, and we just sat in anticipation of something to happen. Gas stations in the Detroit metropolitan area were owned mostly by Arabs, which I discovered at a few Amoco meetings. By now, it was announced that the terrorists were of Arab origin from Al-Qaeda. I was sure that the Arab-owned gas stations were possible targets for revenge. A few people from the neighborhood peeked in to see if we were okay, making comments that white Caucasian women did not have to worry. There were no incidents of violence at any of the gas stations. What was disgusting was that one journalist managed to air a picture on TV of Arabs in Dearborn celebrating, which quickly disappeared, and that was never mentioned again or commented about.

Life resumed in a few days as normal as it could be expected, and we started to go about our daily routines. Nothing out of the ordinary happened for the average American who worked with kids going to school. There was one shooting incident at the federal building with a man opening his briefcase and shooting at a security guard, but it was an isolated case and not an organized terrorist attack.

In September 2001, there was an event worthy of mentioning, and that was the birth of my first grandson. My younger daughter decided to be an adult, leaving home at the age of sixteen. I kept thinking that she would come back home as I didn't think she would like being a waitress serving people when I treated her like my princess. I was wrong. She stayed in the area with her boyfriend, but she never mentioned that she did not like her new life. I used to visit her at Denny's restaurant where she worked, looking at her face for signs of desire to return home. She became pregnant at the age of seventeen, and I remember taking time off at lunch while working in Detroit to get them married at the city hall. My grandson was born on September 20, 2001, a healthy baby growing up later to be a sweet, lovable child.

The following winter, Mom had a hard time being bedridden with acute osteoporosis. The extreme cold temperatures were affecting her health, and after discussing it with my manager at the IRS, I decided to move us south to a state with a warmer climate. There was a clause in the government rules for a transfer due to hardship because of a necessity to take care of a family member. I took this decision also upon the recommendation from Mom's family physician, which prompted me to act fast on selling not only the gas station but also our house. Selling the gas station proved to be close to impossible because of tricks played by prospective buyers of Arab and Indian descent. The outcome of the first sales offer was mind-boggling. The conditions included training of the guy's brother prior to closing date. The people seemed to be sincere, so I sold our house, and we moved to an apartment. It was a few days prior to finalizing the sale when the buyer's attorney called and said that they need to review also the company's tax returns. I had nothing to hide, but as soon as they had access to the returns, I received a call that the tax returns did not show a profit they expected to see and therefore were backing out of the deal. My explanations that the year-end adjusting entries were for amortization of covenant not to compete and bonus for my daughter whose duties increased were in vain. I realized that I was used to provide free training as the buyer owned a gas station, which was not profitable.

My next buyer of identical situation as the first one gave me the same offer, only this time I was prepared and made a clause in the contract that the sale was based only on financial records without a provision of tax returns. Sure enough, prior to the sale, the buyer asked for tax returns and backed out of the deal. This time, he lost his deposit, which was only 3 percent of the sales price, but I wanted to make a point. The second similar experience seemed fishy, and I started to believe that all these people were connected and that I would have a hard time selling the place. I knew some gas station owners from Dearborn from meetings organized by Amoco and went to see them. My suspicions were confirmed; I was being deceived in believing that I would sell the station even at a loss because there was a sheik who was directing not only the gas station operations in the Detroit area but also their sales and purchases. That explained the similarity in the offers I received so far.

I went home thinking that I needed a strategy to outsmart that guy. In the next few weeks, I received more offers, which I knew were fake. One was through a realtor who could not provide records for the financial ability of his prospective buyer to purchase a station. An offer also came directly from a gas station owner who claimed to be serious since he did not use an attorney. And a third offer was drafted by an attorney of an Indian descent man. I accepted all offers, which was not a standard practice in real estate. To my surprise, I was approached by another Middle Eastern man who owned a few Amoco gas stations. What I did would not be done in any normal real estate or business deals. I showed to the last buyer that I already accepted three offers, warning him that for him to acquire the station, there should be no conditions and no games. It worked. The sale materialized at a much lower price than the one I originally paid, but we were out of this place. A week later, the transfer of business ownership was done by an Amoco rep. Being a business major, I knew it was not correct to enter in four contracts for the same property, but I had no choice. I started to think that even my attorney was against me as he assured me that the contract with the Indian guy was fine, and I signed it without reading it in detail. But there was nothing regular dealing with these people. There were big smiles on my and my daughter's faces when we left knowing that we were finally free. We did not have one day off since I took over this gas station, and we were exhausted.

Without giving it a second thought, I requested and received personal leave from my IRS job. My mother was also very tired from all nerve-racking situations at the gas station. We all needed a vacation, and that was the first thing I did—book a trip to Cozumel, Mexico. Cozumel was a paradise after the turbulent years of owning a gas station. The sun and the water always had a very calming effect on me, but this time, being at the beach was the best cure for my exhausted mind and body as I lay on the sand without moving for days. Some of the American tourists, knowing a couple of Spanish words, would pass by saying jokingly that I was probably *borracha*. Mom enjoyed the beach and the freedom of eating and drinking whenever she felt like—it was an all-inclusive resort. After regaining some of my strength, we rented a jeep and drove around the island, stopping at all beach pubs and a park with iguanas. There were iguanas at the resort too as one day my daughter was stopped in her tracks, running to the room, by an iguana crossing in between the beach houses. I remember the delightful feeling of the breeze brushing my body and smelling the fresh scent of beach vegetation along the coast. Slowly I came to life, enjoying the colorful Mexican culture and food, the sunrises and sunsets over the sea blinding my eyes with their beauty.

One evening, at the dinner table, I made a comment that in Cozumel, there were tourists from all over the world, but there were no Russians. As soon as I said that, I overheard two couples and an elderly woman at the next table speaking Russian. I was curious, so I turned around and asked them where they were from.

"We live in the Dallas area," responded one of the ladies. "But we are from Ukraine. And you, where are you from?" They invited us to join them at their table, and we spent the evening talking about our lives. The families immigrated first to Kansas and then moved to Texas because of job transfers. The one lady was a musician, and her friend was a doctor, which led to interesting topics and discussions about music and medicine. I shared with them that after our vacation, my daughter and I planned to take a trip to Arizona and Florida to search for a place to relocate somewhere south.

"What about Texas?" my musician friend asked. "Stop by us and see if you like our area. We live in Rockwall, a city about twenty miles east of Dallas, by Lake Ray Hubbard." She continued by describing the house market, the location of the city on a hill overlooking the lake, their daily routine, the neighborhood where they lived, and the Dallas community. I listened with great interest to her stories of life in Texas, feeling very close to this woman. We definitely had common experiences as immigrants from the same region, but it was more like being with a long-lost friend. We have not considered up to this point Texas as a place to visit and possibly relocate to. Listening to my new friend, I made up my mind. Texas would be our first stop on the list when we travel south to figure out the most suitable place to move to. We exchanged addresses, and a month later, my daughter and I rented a car to take this very memorable road trip from Plymouth, Michigan, to Dallas, Texas.

We were both in great spirits, relieved from the gas station ownership ordeal. The music in the car was turned up high; we were joking and laughing. It was evening when we arrived in Rockwall, Texas, looking for my friend's house. Coming from Michigan, we were struck by the nice homes, which up north would be very pricey. My musician friend was happy to see us and made us feel very welcome. After a very tasty Russian dinner, we agreed on a time to meet on the next day and headed to our hotel, La Quinta. The hotel was new, and after settling in for the night, we sat out on the porch enjoying the warm Texan air. It was September, and it was still very hot. My lady friend took a couple of days off from teaching music at school and lessons at home to show us around and help us decide whether we would stay and buy a house in the Dallas area. After showing us new houses in Plano, which was one of the prestigious areas to live in at the time, I looked at her and said that I would prefer to look into the Rockwall house market. I liked the drive on the bridges of Lake Ray Hubbard with a view of the city on a hill, especially attractive at night. We found the perfect house in the Shores community, with swimming pools, tennis courts, a golf course, and a clubhouse. I thought I was dreaming as such a place would be beyond my means in Michigan. The house was a new two-story colonial with four bedrooms, two living rooms, a study, and a dining room.

Returning to Michigan, I completed the paperwork with my manager at the Service for hardship transfer and packed for the big move. Saying goodbye to my son and young daughter was not easy, but what comforted me was that they could always come to see me and even move with me if they decided to do so. After all, that was one of the reasons I bought a big house. What I will never forget though is the crying of my daughter, Anabelle, on the steps of the apartment building the day we left; I never thought that she would be so sad since she left home a couple of years ago and had a family of her own. That scene brings tears to my eyes until today. It was something that I never anticipated or was prepared for.

Move to Texas—
Final Destination?

It was in September 2002 when we made the big move to the south. I rented a mailbox instead of using the house address for a change of address because I did not want to come across the Arab men with whom I broke contracts for the sale of the station. The manager at my old Century 21 office told me that the realtor representing one of the Arabs threatened to file a complaint at the real estate board in Lansing against me, but since I left, this threat faded away.

Arriving in Rockwall was like moving to a different country for a lot of reasons, not only because of the climate but also because of the people, the culture. It wasn't before long that we met and got to know all neighbors on our street. I bought for Mom a bench for the porch, which made her happy talking to people passing by. In Texas, we discovered the *howdy* was accompanied by hanging around and having a conversation, which Mom loved. My daughter signed up for classes to complete the requirements for entering in a nursing program at Baylor University, which she always wanted to study. It was a pleasant surprise to see that tuition was considerably lower, and the college was not that big of a drive from the house. We did not drive much in Dallas as the highways were intimidating compared to the ones in Michigan. Lanes were added on the right side, later disappearing, and drivers in the city were not that friendly to let you in. One trip to the car insurance off I-75 north from I-30 was enough to convince us that this was traffic that we needed time to get used to.

I contacted the IRS union (yes, federal employees, not management, can belong voluntarily to this union, which assists them for the most part with administrative issues) and got in touch with one of their representatives. The man was very pleasant and accommodating. He came to see me in Rockwall and followed up on the paperwork that I submitted in Detroit for my transfer. Hardship transfer was a very agreeable policy for families in need of relocating in cases of sickness or marriage. The downfall was that employees of higher grades would lose all promotions down to grade 11, and they would need to wait for an opening as there were no open hiring spots all the time. It was in March 2003 when I received my assignment as grade 11 agent in Desoto, Texas. That was a big drop from being a tax analyst for foreign governments, but it did not affect me at all. It was a long drive, but I was happy. I was in the right place where Mom was much better. My daughter was very successful in getting through the classes she signed up for, and I was back to work with the best agency in the world.

My manager was a very straightforward and pleasant person to work for as she valued hard work and dedication. My colleagues were all friendly and made me feel soon a part of the team. In the next five months, there were vacancy announcements for revenue agents grade 12 and 13, which I applied for, and I was selected for both positions, first as grade 12 and then grade 13 agent. The process involved application for the announced vacancy, review of my documents by a managers' panel, a face-to-face technical interview, and selection based on a very strict criteria. I still remember one of the questions being identifying the code section for accumulated earnings tax, which I stated without hesitation to be 531.

As a grade 13 agent, I was assigned to an exam group in Dallas managed by an African American gentleman, who recently moved with his family from Wisconsin. Apart from my new challenging inventory, I became the right hand for my new manager, replacing him when he was out of the office, resolving group's issues, and helping agents with their cases. A case of my own that deserves mentioning was with about forty million dollars of adjustments for two years in a roll. It all started with an amended individual tax return with three million dollars decrease in income due to bad debt originating from partnerships. There were procedures to follow for high-dollar amount refunds, which also led to examination of multiple number of partnership tax returns, an audit scope beyond our division of Small Business Administration. The interview with the representative for this case lasted eight hours. My manager was also present when after receiving a general information and records for the source for the claimed refund, I discovered a forty-million-dollar adjustment, asking a very simple question, "Sir, what is the reason for having almost the same dollar amounts of deductions for two consecutive years?"

"I am sorry. We made a mistake. The deduction should have been taken only in the second year."

After receiving this unbelievable explanation leading to immediate adjustment in the first year, I turned my attention to the second taxable year, which required examination of a number of partnership tax returns created solely for loans to different companies going subsequently out of business. Since such examination fell under the jurisdiction of the large and midsize business unit, I needed permission from upper management to proceed. Presenting facts obtained from my interview, I had no problem convincing tax officials at higher levels the it was crucial to continue the examination. The stipulation was, however, that I would need to develop the case and complete a detailed report with facts, tax law research, and arguments with final governments position. My research and the entire write-up of the case was fifty pages long, which led to an agreed report by the taxpayer with adjustments close to another forty million dollars. The controller for the partnerships formed by family members was aware of the situation from the start of the audit.

"Nina, my client told me to take everything possible to the limit but to ensure that there are no criminal charges."

Indeed, it took me an extensive research to formulate the government's position, which placed the adjustments as technical and not due to a criminal act.

Amid all the involved issues at work, I managed to take a couple of trips with my daughter, one to Costa Rica in the winter of 2004 and another to Bulgaria to join my mom for a couple of weeks in June 2004 (Mom spent that summer in Sofia). I always plan and have fun activities with my kids while on vacation, and the Costa Rica adventure included horseback riding with a French woman guide, where we rode up the mountain and descended by the beach (the scary thing was that the Frenchie led us in a tunnel full of bats, which I did not recognize without glasses). We hired a cab for the day for only one hundred dollars that took us, among other places, to a jungle with monkeys jumping all around looking for food and a beautiful secluded beach with crystal blue water. On the way to observe a volcano, we stopped at mineral water natural pools. And of course, we danced Latin dances with instructor by the pool.

The trips to Sofia, Bulgaria, were always very special, and the one in the summer of 2004 was not an exception. This particular time was more exceptional than before because it was my last vacation with Mom, which I didn't know at the time. Arriving in the city gave me always a warm, peaceful feeling, and seeing Mom was very comforting. She went out of her way to bring back my childhood memories by getting up before us to bring us *mekitsi* (deep-fried pastry) for breakfast; lunch was *kebapcheta* from the tastiest place in town. We were scheduled to spend a week at the sea, and Mom was at first reluctant to join us, so I tricked her to come by saying that the resort was prepaid. I will remember forever the week at Sunny Beach's newest Helena Hotel. Mom was very sociable, and we sat under the umbrellas trying to remember German in order to communicate with German families on vacation. I can still see her face lit up with happiness enjoying the view of the sea, the walks alongside the beach, and the joyous atmosphere all around us. The place itself was fabulous with incredible oil paintings, crystal chandeliers, and marble columns. Mom was always beautiful even at her old age, and she dressed up for lunch and dinner in very feminine and attractive dresses. We all returned to Sofia in very elevated spirits.

The next few days before my daughter and I left were very enjoyable—going to the nearby food farm market, cooking special meals, walking in the nearby South Park in Sofia, which got its name because of its location at the foot of Vitosha in the south part of town. There was also a reunion with my cousin Nikolai and his family at a dinner, which lasted for hours. I haven't seen him since I escaped from Bulgaria, and I still remembered him as a cute little boy. I was sad leaving Mom behind, but she was coming back in September, and I knew that time would pass fast with my busy schedule at work.

I loved the autumn in Dallas as summers did not end as in Michigan and other states up north. Christmas was around the corner when we received very happy news from my cousin Nikolai that they would take us up on our invitation and spend the holidays with us. Nikolai was the son of my mother's brother and the closest family alive on her side. Christmas had a special meaning this year, when we cooked together with Nikolai's wife, Didi, the traditional Bulgarian Christmas Eve and dinner meals and told stories, catching up on our lives for so many years. This was their first visit to the States, so a trip to Vegas was in order. What I liked most was seeing them amazed at the city that never sleeps, full of life and action at all times. Watching Nikoleta, my niece, having the best of time flying on an imaginary carpet gave me tremendous pleasure, as well as everybody's excitement on a helicopter ride over the Grand Canyon and seeing the show *Mamma Mia!*

Life Without Mom

They say that life is a collection of good memories, and this was one of them, surrounded by family during the most special season of the year for the celebration of the birth of Jesus. My cousin and his family left for their home in Vienna, Austria, shortly after New Year, and we resumed our daily lives.

There were newly hired agents at my office, and I was involved in their training, giving lectures and preparing them for fieldwork. My daughter resumed classes at the community college, which was her last semester before starting the nursing program at Baylor University. I was extremely proud of her being admitted to such a prestigious university with a scholarship for excellent academic performance. One day, which I will never forget, I received a call from the emergency room at Rowlett Lake Pointe Hospital. It was February 7, 2005, a chilly and windy day. Mom fell while taking a walk by the house and broke her hip. I flew to the hospital and called my daughter on my way. We both rushed to Mom and understood from the emergency doctor who examined her that it was serious and that she would be admitted to have a surgery on the same day.

Mom went on her usual morning walk around the block when she felt dizzy and, since she was close to the house, decided to hurry up. That was when she fell. It was on the ring road in the complex, so a car stopped and called an ambulance. They admitted Mom, giving her pain medicine, and we all waited for hours without anyone coming or the nurses knowing what was going on. I finally called the surgeon's office only to find out that he had appointments all afternoon and that he was not scheduled to perform any surgeries on that day, maybe the next one. They operated on Mom the next evening, and the surgeon assured me that everything went fine and that she would have physical therapy the next day. He did not tell me that there would be a family doctor assigned to her and that I could talk to him only in the morning.

The next day, my daughter and I went about our usual schedules when I received a call from the hospital that Mom was in extreme pain. I hastily arranged for necessary work to be done by the trainees and peeked in my manager's office to tell him that something was not okay at the hospital. I found Mom with her face swollen and twisted in pain. The nurse told me that they increased the dose of the medicine, but it did not help. There was nothing in her chart showing a scheduled physical therapy, and there was no doctor available to let me know what was going on. Mom was placed on blood thinners, but I did not know that there were different blood thinners for specific treatments. On the second day after the surgery, the floor nurse informed me that the doctor ordered MRI because of possible lung embolism. That same evening, Mom was transferred to ICU, and there was no change in her condition for the next couple of weeks. They gave Mom an oxygen mask, which she didn't like and was taking off. Mom was always a very strong person, and deep inside, I believed that she was going to get better.

I stayed by her bed, holding her hand, when one day, she looked at me, saying, "Nina, I have $1,000 saved in my closet just in case I don't make it." My face cringed as I couldn't imagine Mom passing away. For me, this was absolutely absurd. Mom knew me well and did not want to pursue talking about it, so she changed the subject. "Nina, I want you to know that all I wanted was for you to be happy." Ever since then, these words have been on my mind, bringing me the worst of sorrow.

It was a Sunday, February 13. I cooked stuffed peppers as I wanted to take them to Mom when the phone rang from the hospital. "Your mom is waiting for you. She would like you to bring her hot dogs." I already packed the meal, and thinking that this was better-tasting than hot dogs, I thought to buy them next time. Mom ate my stuffed peppers, but I could see that she was not that happy. I still hate myself for not buying the hot dogs on that day. Her nurse walked in the room as I was explaining to Mom why I did not bring the hot dogs and pulled me to the side. "Your mom told me this morning that she could feel that she will die. I have been a nurse for a long time, and every time a patient said that, they passed away."

"My mom is different. She will make it" was all I could say.

February 14, 2005, is a day I would always remember as the darkest day in my life. I do not like Valentine's Day anymore because bad things happen to me on this day. It was early morning, and I was getting ready for work when the phone rang. "Ms. Danoff, your mom has taken turn for the worse. We had to put her on respirator. Her state is critical, and we advise you to inform the family."

Things started to spin in front of me. I hardly managed to sit down and yell out to my daughter, "Your grandma is not well! Call your brother!" I was in denial. Even seeing her lying helplessly with respirator over her mouth did not convince me that she was going to leave me.

"She has a 20 percent chance of survival," I heard the lung specialist tell me, and I thought that 20 percent was enough for a strong woman like my mother to survive.

This week was like a never-ending nightmare. My son flew in from Michigan with his fiancée, and during his stay, we had another scary incident when Mom was hemorrhaging. They had to perform an emergency surgery in the middle of the night. My son kept reading passages from the Bible, and in a couple of hours, they brought her in; she made it. Mom was hanging on, and I had this strong feeling that she would come out of it, even starting to plan how I would arrange for her the downstairs bedroom. We knew she could hear what was going on as when my son told her that she better get well because she needed to teach his fiancée how to cook *musaka*, she smiled.

The following Sunday, we went to pray at the Bulgarian Protestant Church in Dallas. I stood up and prayed and cried so hard that tears were falling down my face, drenching my blouse. The pain at this moment was intolerable. My son stayed a week, and since there was no change in Mom's condition, he returned home.

Mom's birthday was coming up. It was always a happy occasion, and we always celebrated it. This February 27, 2005, was a sad day as my daughter and I stopped at the Mexican restaurant in front of the hospital to have a drink to her health. On February 28, we stopped to see Mom before work and Vanesa before classes. She was lying motionless, but her eyes were open for the first time in the last two weeks, staring intensely at the ceiling. I panicked and observed her in silence, waiting for some movement, but she did not budge or even wink. Her blood pressure was very low, 60/40, so I ran to the nurse telling her that there was something very wrong.

"This is normal for her state," the nurse responded in a calm voice. Hearing that, I left knowing that there was a busy day ahead of me at the office.

It was 4:00 p.m. when my daughter called, crying hysterically on the phone, "Mom, Grandma is dying."

I dropped the receiver and ran into my manager's office. "Sir, I need to leave. Mom, I am losing her." I felt so helpless and disoriented. The man called a woman from the office next door, who lived close to my place, and she drove me to the hospital.

Entering Mom's room, I could see a couple of nurses at the front desk; the area was all empty except for Mom's partition. My eyes traveled in that direction, and I saw my daughter crying softly with a priest at the head of the bed. The numbness I felt is not possible to describe. I felt paralyzed, not knowing how I took the next steps toward the bed. I was in tremendous emotional pain. My heart was turned inside and out; my soul was screaming in desperation. I dropped down on the floor by the bed, shrieking with my hands up in the air. What I still remember was the passive and totally oblivious behavior of the nurses. They were sitting at the nurses station as if nothing was going on around them. I knew somebody walked in and started to explain procedures for funeral arrangements, recommending a funeral home in Rockwall. "Will this be acceptable for you?" a distant voice asked. I waved, not fully conscious of what he was talking about.

Then I felt a hand and heard the voice of my Ukrainian friend, "Ninochka, be strong. I am here."

We buried Mom on March 5. There were two services, one by a Russian Orthodox priest and another by the Bulgarian Protestant priest, who was surprised that the two services had the same prayers.

My son held me strongly in his arms, my older daughter's face was covered with tears, and my younger daughter was kneeling down by her grandmother, crying desperately. Back at the house, my neighbors gathered, bringing food and drinks. There was little talking; everybody ate in silence, which brought me a little peace. It was the children and their presence that pulled me through the next couple of weeks. My son and my younger daughter returned to Michigan, but my grandson stayed with me. My younger daughter was still very young and had a hard time settling down. She ended up splitting with her husband and was in a new relationship with a guy in a similar situation as hers—no education, no job skills.

Life continued around me like nothing happened. Mom used to keep busy with thinking of different tasks and things to do, and all this stopped the day she left us. Nothing mattered anymore. The spring of 2005, she wanted to travel to Bulgaria earlier than usual, and I had a ticket for her to leave on the day of the funeral. How strange life was as everything ended in one second.

I started work and was doing mechanically what was expected of me without being truly conscious of what was going on around me. The presence of people somehow soothed me and helped me make it through the day. Everybody at work was very considerate and tiptoed around me as they knew there was nothing to say to relieve a pain like this. They left sympathy cards and books for dealing with a loss of a loved one, but I knew that the psychoanalysis of the stages of grief would not apply to me. This pain of losing Mom has not diminished until today as there isn't a day that I don't think of what went wrong and what I could have done to keep her alive. I couldn't bring myself to go to the graveyard for months after the funeral. Every time I tried to head out that way, I would stop the car and stare.

Summer went by when I decided to apply for a frontline management training program and was admitted to it. By then, I managed to visit Mom usually after work and talk to her about my life, about my grandson who was living with us, about my daughters at home and in Michigan, and about my son. I felt so peaceful sitting on a bench by her grave, telling her everything that was on my mind and in my heart. I knew she was watching over me and the children, and the day I heard the news about my upcoming management training, I went to thank her for giving me the opportunity to work in an area I enjoyed.

The training by itself was very useful as it dealt with practical issues and behavior models to be considered in dealing with people. Taking walks after training with exceptional colleagues by the California coast somewhat eased the pain of Mom being gone. It was by the water after classes where managers/instructors continued sharing their experiences of dealing with employees and union reps. It was a three-phase training, and I completed the first one in the fall of 2005.

The Loss of My Dad

It was the evening of December 5, and I was at home enjoying the company of my two daughters and grandkids (Anabelle came to visit with little Jason who was only four months old). It was my half-brother calling from Germany.

"Nina, there was an accident. Dad was hit by a car when crossing the street by the apartment building." I just stood speechless, waiting to hear the rest. "He passed away. The funeral will be in four days."

I mumbled something like "How is this possible? Okay, I'll see you in Sofia. Will book a flight now."

My daughters overheard me, and both looked at me with eyes wide open, expecting to hear bad news.

"Dad passed away. I need to travel to Bulgaria," I said, gazing into space.

"Mom, I'll come with you. I don't want you to be alone on such a long trip."

So my older daughter and I traveled to attend my father's funeral. We booked a flight for the next day and sat in silence the entire time on the plane. I was not close to Dad as with Mom, but I got to know him in the last twenty years. I called him every weekend and loved hearing his wise words. I knew he was getting old as he had a hard time hearing, so I let him speak, and everything he said made sense. My thoughts jumped to Dallas. I left instructions for my younger daughter before leaving, but I had to find a way of calling her. My cell phone did not work outside the States.

I recognized my brother who met us with his wife at the Sofia Airport. I met him before once for lunch while I worked in Bulgaria, and we stayed in touch on Skype since then. He hugged me, and we all headed to my uncle Peter's house, where my cousins Vesselka and her brother were expecting us. My father was the distinguished linguist Professor Duridanov, and there was a flag lowered at the University of Sofia in honor of his memory. The funeral was attended by professors and academicians. I was surprised that some of them remembered me as a little girl. I also met other family members on my father's side. One was Uncle Ljubo, whom I did not like as he was in favor of my parents' divorce. He still appeared to be spiteful, looking at me with his squinting eyes. I met his son and family for the first time, and they seemed to be friendly. My aunt was also alive, but not well to travel from Chirpan. I met her daughter though for the first time. I haven't seen Vesselka since we were both very young, and I was happy to reunite with her. Her brother, whom I met for the first time, was very religious and very friendly, giving me a Bible in Bulgarian language.

Dad was given an honorary spot at the front row of Sofia's cemetery. I watched them lower the casket in the grave, thinking how stupid were all the feud and legal fights he had with my mother to get the apartment. We all will die one day, and the only thing we can take with us are the memories of the life we lived. We all have choices, but the one that is most gratifying is to appreciate and love the most valuable of God's gifts—family and friends. Dad must have been reflecting on his life the day he died as there were pictures of me and us when I was a child in front of one of his bookcases.

There was a snowstorm on the morning that we traveled back, and our flight was delayed, which caused us to miss our connecting flight from Frankfurt to Dallas. I knew there were scheduled training classes and managers whom I had to replace during the holidays, so I managed to call and let them know that I would be late. We spent the night at a hotel at the airport, which I remember had central heating, but it was so cold that we had to run hot water in the tub and the sink to stay warm. We were both relieved to reach Dallas and be home where my younger daughter was waiting for us. She left to be with her boyfriend for New Year, and we resumed our lives. This was the first Christmas without Mom, but we gathered enough energy to make it memorable for my grandson.

It was a couple of weeks since we returned home from my dad's funeral, and I still could not sleep more than a couple of hours at night, which at first I thought was from the jet lag. Losing both of my parents in one year was taking a toll over me. Mom's loss was unbearable, and with Dad gone, I felt a pain even though he was not in my life until I was a young adult. One of the senior agents recommended seeing her doctor, and with prescribed hormone treatment, I went back to feeling better, at least physically.

Exam Group Manager
in Houston

Being in the FLRP, I was continuously acting for one of the three managers in downtown Dallas, which gave me an opportunity to meet and interact with all agents. My second classroom training was in Philadelphia, which dealt with the use of computerized programs to evaluate agents and writing reports. I was happy to meet again some of the participants from the first phase of training in California. After classes, we explored the city, amazed at the history it had to offer. The place was considered the birthplace of American independence, taking you back to eighteenth-century houses in the old town with remarkable sights such as the Liberty Bell, Independence Hall, and the National Constitution Center in the Independence National Historic Park area. I was in awe visiting all these places where freedom was first declared and won.

Returning to Dallas, I came across an announcement for a group manager opening in Houston, which required relocation. I applied for the position and had an interview with the Houston territory manager and a couple of Dallas managers. I noticed how the Houston territory manager, an African American lady in her late fifties, was nodding and smiling when I responded to the interview questions. A few days later, my manager, with his boss, the Dallas territory manager, called me to his office, and as soon as I entered they both smiled and invited me to sit down. My manager looked at me and said, "Congratulations, Nina, you have been selected for the management position in Houston, that is if you are still interested. This is a big opportunity and a promotion."

"Sir, I will be honored to accept this position, and I thank you for all the assistance you provided me in gaining experience for it."

I started the following day to make preparations for our move with filing all paperwork for the transfer, arranging for movers and the sale of the house, and spending a week in the Houston area picking a house. My daughter's graduation was coming up, and that was an extremely happy event, after which she had to study for a state examination. The graduation ceremony was in Waco, Texas, and her father and brother arrived, as well as one of her friends from Michigan. I watched my daughter in a graduation gown feeling so proud of her succeeding in reaching her goal of becoming a registered nurse ever since she was a child.

The move to Houston was in two stages as I wanted to replicate my house from Dallas and make it homey. I purchased a house under construction in the Woodlands, which was bigger than the previous one as I wanted one with definitely enough room for all the kids. We rented an apartment, and I was at the building site every day, resolving construction issues, for example, the fireplace being on the wrong side of the room. The house was finally completed, and we moved in on New Year's Eve. It was raining, and I had boxes piled all over the place. Luckily, they were labeled and stored in the rooms they belonged.

It took time getting used to the new community as I missed Dallas and the fact that Mom's grave was in Rockwall and I could stop every night after work to talk to her. The city of the Woodlands by itself was unique with tall evergreen trees hiding shopping centers and businesses, with bike paths on all roads. There were numerous parks with playgrounds, pools, and tennis courts, which we explored and later visited in the evenings and on weekends. My daughter passed her state exam and started to work at the eye surgery unit of Baylor University, something she always wanted to do, to be a nurse in a specialized area. I found a childcare center for my grandson, and every day on my way to work, I sang to him the song "You Are My Sunshine." He used to smile and try to join in. I always rushed in the morning getting us both ready to leave, and on that one day, as we were walking to the car, he looked at me, took me by the hand, and said, "Grandma, listen at the birds singing." I still remember how I stopped in my track realizing that my grandson noticed the beauty of nature and was asking me to slow down and enjoy it with him.

My assignment was challenging as agents in the group had the worst of overage cases because they lacked direction. A senior agent was with neglected cases as the prior manager had her work cases of newly hired agents, and the latter could not get better as they were not encouraged to work independently. It was in the first month of my appointment when my territory manager requested that I do a full review and evaluation of a probationary employee (there was a year of probation after hiring during which agents were required to work on a successful level). The agent was close to the end of this period with months of poor performance, which was not priorly addressed. With the dismissal of this agent and objective reviews of the work of other agents, I received the reputation of being the new sheriff in town. What I wanted to accomplish was to awaken in the agents a desire to be successful in completing their assignments alone, which was going to help them grow and get promoted. I knew I had to do extensive detailed case reviews of all agents, providing them with instructions on how to proceed step-by-step in resolving their cases. I felt like being a high school teacher again with teaching, following up, and evaluating performance on a daily basis. I still remember the initial reaction of one of my senior agents receiving an okay evaluation rather than one she was used to get with marks exceeding fully successful performance. She stormed in my office, fuming, "I can't believe these grades. You can't do this. I never had such poor evaluation since I was hired." She started to jump, holding the piece of paper in her hand.

"It's an accurate evaluation of the state of your work. I used a computer software program, which requires addressing specific areas and assigning grades accordingly," I responded. "I know you have been working lower-grade cases for the newly hired agents, but that was not your job, and it was not helping them either. You will need to concentrate on your work, follow the guidance I am providing you for wrapping up these cases, and you will be fine." With that, she stormed out; I felt bad as I did not expect such reaction from a senior agent.

Analyzing the state of the group, I was convinced that there was something lacking in the training program of these people. My intentions in holding the first group meeting were to start a work relationship with them based on cooperation, trust, and their desire for success. Subsequently, as I discovered that the group was operating in a completely ineffective way, I called for an emergency group meeting at which I brought up specific points which I encountered in my reviews that had to be corrected in order to move forward. What I decided to do was use the first evaluations as a teaching tool without including them for their annual evaluation. It wasn't long before that I gained the trust of my agents as they started to be more proficient, working independently. I kept my door open, inviting them to share all their concerns and questions. My agents were all smart individuals who needed guidance, encouragement, and support in overcoming difficult tasks. I was happy seeing them confident to head investigations of fraudulent requests for refunds from research and development issues or attending conference meetings with groups of accountants and attorneys, winning arguments with proof of tax law provisions and court cases.

What I enjoyed was my appointment as representative of the IRS to the Houston CPA society, and as such, I participated in discussions enabling accountants to understand the audit process and better assist their clients in compliance with tax law. I used to take with me senior agents who gave presentations with live cases on issues encountered in the field with comments for importance of gathering correct information in tax return preparation. It was a tremendous pleasure to see one of my agents receive an award for providing best taxpayers assistance during his audits. I was also lucky to have a brilliant young African American secretary who always completed all office matters and reports ahead of time. Apart from that, he was an invaluable team player in assisting my agents and myself in designing graphs and tables for examination and performance reports.

The summer of 2007 was more relaxed as we settled in our daily tasks and enjoyed the parks and the pools on weekends. There was a happy occasion that occurred in August 2007. We received a wedding invitation from my son; the date was set as September 15. I felt so much joy. My son was starting his own family. "Your brother is getting married!" I cried out as I entered the house. "I am making arrangements for our travel right now."

My daughter took the invitation from my hands and smiled. "That's great, Mom. I am happy for my brother."

My son met us at the airport with a big smile and drove us to the hotel where we were staying with other guests. The wedding was on the next day at a golf course in a private ceremony, and I was very emotional watching my handsome son and his beautiful bride. The newlywed couple went on honeymoon the next day, and we stayed a couple of days more to enjoy the beautiful beach in Holland, Michigan.

Returning to Houston, I received an added responsibility to oversee and regulate the building operations of all IRS units—exam, taxpayer's service, and collection. One incident comes to mind about a day when returning from lunch I saw an ambulance in front of the building. I came to find out one of the taxpayer's service employees believed that a guy poked him with a poisonous needle while he was assisting him with forms. I personally thought that the employee was overreacting, but nonetheless, he had to be checked with confirmation that he was okay. The real challenge in performing this duty came with preparation for Hurricane Ike. I still remember when on a sunny Thursday morning on September 11, 2008, I received a call from Dallas headquarters to prepare the office for the storm. That meant all computers, printers, phone lines, and sensitive materials had to be safely stored and secured. The challenge was with taxpayer's service employees insisting that they were still open to serve the public and could not spare personnel for other activities. It was just the mindset of people that was something beyond my understanding. It was my secretary and agents who stepped up to help me with preparing all IRS offices in the building in a wake of a hurricane. My responsibility lay beyond the physical preservation of IRS property but also to ensure the safety of all employees. In issuing guidance to managers of the other units, I was hoping that they all had plans on how to stay in touch with their employees. Everybody in my group was very much connected as a team, and we developed a call system to stay in touch during and after the storm.

Driving home that day, it was a perfect weather, sunny and nice. Nobody could tell that such a tremendous storm would hit the next day. I found my daughter and grandson at home and suggested that we head north before it got bad, but my daughter, being extremely conscientious, wouldn't leave because she was on call. We had no choice but to prepare for the hurricane. The storm was expected to landfall the next day, and I informed my neighbors of it. We headed to the store, stocking up with canned food, water, candles, and lighters. People on the street started to board their windows and invited us to spend the next day at their houses until the storm passed. But we decided to stay home, and on Friday morning, we pulled the mattress from my bedroom to the family room and placed it against the staircase away from the windows. We filled the bathtubs with water and placed vital supplies on the kitchen counters.

On the evening of Friday, September 12, the TV news stations were providing update on the movement of the storm approaching the Texas coast. It was expected to be a huge storm hitting the entire Texas coast and getting deep inland. We watched how it first hit Galveston with people who decided to stay on the island and got trapped in it. "Write your Social Security numbers on your arms and foreheads" was the instruction of the police to people they could not get to. Tears rolled down my face as I knew that the Social Security numbers were necessary to identify their bodies. Just as we were watching, the power went out, and it became pitch-dark. There was a tremendous cracking noise outside, accompanied with a torrential rain banging on the windows. I managed to call my employees and made sure they were all at safe places then cuddled with the kids on the mattress. The noise was tremendous, sounding, as if trains were coming down the street. The heavy pounding on the roof felt like trees probably were falling on it. I went a few times to the window to see if the water was rising to cause a flood. Then I fell asleep; I was so exhausted with the preparation of the office building, worried about the safety of employees and neighbors, and getting us ready at home that I crashed. My daughter was pushing me trying to wake me up, but I was dozing off, fighting to stay awake. She called her brother and father in Michigan and stayed on the phone with her father till morning until it started to clear up and we could see outside. There were trees on roofs of all houses in the back of the house, but ours seemed intact. I ran to the front of the house and saw a tree from across fallen on the street between ours and the neighbors' house—that was pure luck. My neighbors across the street were on the porch, and I went out to wave, letting them know that we were all right. Later, I found out that a tree fell and hit their house on the window of their bedroom. Luckily, the boarding saved them.

The next couple of weeks were unbelievable as the place looked like it was bombed. There were trees blocking roads, damaged homes, and stores and gas stations closed. This storm was so powerful that it brought seashells to the parks around us. But something good came out of this—the storm brought communities and families together. Since there was no power, everybody in our street stayed out till bedtime. The first couple of nights, neighbors from about ten houses took out their meats, and we barbecued and ate in one of the cul-de-sac areas. We all talked and shared stories from our lives, work, and trips. The children played hide-and-seek, tag, and football. My daughter and I started work in a couple of weeks, but we still had no power and were taking showers and getting ready in the morning on candlelight.

The first day back at the office, I had to take my grandson with me, and I noticed how tense he became when he saw there was light and the TV in the reception area worked. I had no idea that the storm had affected him emotionally. I could tell by the way he sat in front of the TV, glued to the screen, that he was beginning to realize that certain things in life, even simple ones, couldn't be taken for granted.

We got our power back at home after three weeks, which made us extremely happy. By now, the city was cleaned up, and one couldn't tell that such a disaster struck just a few weeks ago. Things at work resumed with instructions on how to deal with businesses and individuals greatly affected by the hurricane. As much as I took pride of my team of agents who became highly motivated with great work ethics and skills, there were issues at upper management level beyond my control. I had a great respect for my territory manager as in the beginning she was supportive of my work, praising all the accomplishments made by the group. Then her attitude changed; she would call and yell about something that made no sense and hang up. She came to my office unannounced and pulled cases from agents' drawers while they were in the field to write them up for lack of documentation or other deficiencies. She did the same to other managers, and at one meeting with the area director, a couple of male African American managers expressed their feelings of inability to do their work because of her daily persecution. I knew that this was heading for trouble, and I tried to steer the conversation in another direction, but I did not succeed.

A few days later, my territory manager paid me a visit and called me to the side, "Nina, I know that some of your colleagues talked against me at the meeting with the area director. I need you to tell me the names of those managers." I couldn't believe my ears. I left Bulgaria because of fear for improper treatment at the workplace, and it was happening to me in Houston.

"I can't do that," I responded. "Maybe the individual who informed you of such occurrence can give you more details."

"It was the area director, Nina. He is my boss, and I can't ask him of such thing. I thought I could count on you." With that, she rushed out, and I knew that I was in trouble.

"Nina, the reports you provided were not correctly color coded." Again, there was no discussion but hanging up of the phone. I walked up to my secretary who was preparing for me all kinds of repetitive reports with different headings and colors that she requested. He took out the directions, and we both saw that there was nothing wrong with the report that was provided to her. It was impossible to work in such environment. I remembered a speech at one of the management classes. "If you all new managers come across a supervisor who is a tyrant, you need to know that things will not get better so the best thing for you to do is seek to work at another place."

"This is what I need to do," I told myself and checked out the managerial announcements.

Starting Over in San Antonio, Texas

I applied for a few positions, a transfer back to Dallas being one of them. At an interview for a managerial position in Dallas, the area director asked me, "Why are you seeking to relocate back to Dallas, Nina?" I knew better than to give him the correct answer, so I mumbled something totally irrelevant. After this occurrence, I noticed another announcement, which grabbed my attention; it was for a promotional manager's position in San Antonio, Texas, where the territory manager was a person I knew—it was the manager I had in Desoto, Texas, my first assignment since I moved here from Michigan. This lady had become my mentor since then, and while in Dallas, I frequently ran by her ideas about my future. I had a face-to-face interview with her and a couple of other managers on the phone, and I felt good driving back home that evening.

A week later, I was informed that I was selected for the position in San Antonio. I had a couple of months to wrap up things at my office in Houston and move to San Antonio. My agents in Houston were not surprised that I was leaving. They knew about the difficulties I had with my boss, and no matter how much I tried, it was going to end up badly. The peculiar and bizarre thing was that my annual evaluation was outstanding; however, I did not trust my Houston boss. Her behavior and attitude were irrational, and I knew I had to leave as the stress was affecting my health. My blood pressure was getting high; I was getting weak and unable to work as I used to. My agents were applying also for positions out of her territory to avoid further repercussions after my departure, and all of them, with the exception of a couple, were picked up to work in other units. It was well-known that the Houston territory manager not only rattled managers with excessive and unreasonable reproaches but was also following agents in the field, counting hours they spent at work and comparing them to their time reports and travel vouchers. It was also her habit to pick up their uncompleted cases for review to grade them down.

My daughter at home was aware of the issues I had at work and she could tell by the look on my face as I walked through the door that I got the job in San Antonio. "Congratulations, Mom. I know how much you need to get out of here, and this position is promotional. I am proud of you." I looked at her with a worried look as she continued, "I would like to stay here. I like my nursing job at Baylor, and since you will move in March, Jorden can finish the school year here."

Leaving a manager's position meant to complete departure evaluations for all employees and wrapping up all administrative tasks for the group. I couldn't imagine all the paperwork accumulated in the past two years that I needed to go through and pack or leave for the next person. We still were not completely automated and kept hard copies of procedures or exam issues. I knew I had to find a place to live in San Antonio, and a lot of options were coming to mind, but I knew that I did not have much time. I spotted on the internet a very promising real estate agent, and I scheduled time to meet him at the hotel where I was planning to stay. I knew nothing of the city, except learning that it was preferable to be on the north side of town at a distance possibly not more than about twenty miles to work. I wasn't even sure if the hotel I selected was in a nice part of town; it was Staybridge Hotel by La Cantera shopping center, which later I found out was the best mall. My real estate agent was prompt and very knowledgeable. After giving me a tour of the city, we sat in front of a computer to set desirable parameters of price, location, and type of housing I was looking for. I wanted to rent at first, but soon I discovered that it was more expensive to rent than buy a house. I was also amazed to see that used homes in my price range, not older than two years, were in a pitiful state. On the third day, we started to research new properties driving up highway 281. Houses recommended for this area were in the Stone Oak neighborhood, but as soon as I saw the heavy traffic in that direction, I decided to check communities with new houses in the opposite direction. I immediately liked fox grove, with a park like entrance. There was also a community pool and basketball court for my grandson to play. There were a couple of spec houses, and I picked the one that looked more spacious with a small park area in the front, which later on I found out was a mountain for bats. The house was a ranch, which suited me perfectly since I planned to live by myself with the kids from Houston visiting on weekends. There was also plenty of room for my son and daughter from Michigan when they decided to visit.

After a farewell dinner organized by my agents, I focused on getting my personal belongings packed and ready, picking a few pieces of furniture, a couch and a table set. A Bulgarian family, former neighbors from Rockwall, came to drive the small U-Haul truck I rented, and friends and neighbors on my street formed a line, handing one another kitchen and other items to wrap and pack, which I set aside to take along. It was an amazing sight watching about ten to fifteen people work in synchronized manner. There was a special box that contained gifts from my Houston agents and college; there were also cards wishing me well, as well as those saying that they admired my courage to pick and leave. I knew that all managers were on high blood pressure medications, and I was heading that way if I didn't leave.

We arrived in San Antonio in the evening, and the first thing we did after unpacking was go to a store for mattresses. On the way, I noticed how beautiful TPC Road was with its wildflowers and cactuses. After loading up the U-Haul with the new mattresses, we stopped to grab dinner at BJ's Brewhouse and not late thereafter crashed for the night. Everybody left the next day. I looked around, and all of a sudden, I felt a big emptiness. It was a new city again, and everything was unknown. I felt like starting over again, sleeping on the floor with a few essentials. I knew that the line of work would be the same as in Houston, but there were other factors, such as the dynamics of work at the new location and the peculiarities of people in my new group. In my previous move from Dallas to Houston, I discovered that people both at work and at home were different, ranging from driving habits to cultural peculiarities which was exhibited in their approach to work. My neighbors in Houston were mostly from other states and countries, bringing with them ways of life and culture from where they came from, whereas those in Rockwall were all from the area with true cowboy attitude and lifestyle. It was in Dallas that my daughter and I learned to dance two-step and dress in cowboy outfits from boots to shirts. All I knew about San Antonio was from demographics that it was around 70 percent of Latin origin.

March 9, 2009, was my first day in the San Antonio office with my new revenue Agents group. Their previous manager retired, and I could sense that they missed her, especially the female agents. I already knew that the new group of people assigned to me expected to hear about my work ethics; they also needed information about my and the Gulf States Area expectations. Arriving at work, I found out that all agents were in the office. I met my secretary, a Latino male of my age, and asked him to arrange for a group meeting. I watched each one of the agents arrive with somewhat anxious facial expressions.

"I don't want to take much of your time," I started, "but I would like to meet you all. I am sure some of you have heard that I was a manager in Houston. I would like you to know that I feel privileged to be your manager now. I also learned about the management style of your previous manager, and I don't anticipate major changes in the group's operations. I would like to stress that am a believer of the effectiveness of teamwork, and whatever new methods, technology, directives come our way, I would like to hear from you about your opinion for best ways to adopt them. In the next week, I would like to meet each one of you to get to know you and see with what I can assist you in reaching your goals." After reviewing and discussing the handout of the managerial expectations, I could see from the agents' faces that they were relieved.

"Mrs. Danoff, welcome to our group," spoke one the female agents. I nodded to thank her, wished everybody a successful day, and dismissed them.

With all agents in the office for the day, I managed to schedule individual appointments in the upcoming week. It took a couple of days to get access to all programs, so my secretary pulled for me the group's business reports as well as each agents inventory with detailed information of each case status. As I expected, most of my agents were of Latino origin, which I loved as I was going to brush on my Spanish. My secretary appeared to be diligent, taking notes as I went over his duties and workload. Getting him on board was crucial as all the daily and monthly reports, case assigning, distribution and closing of casework depended on his timely actions. And I made him feel a part of the team when I told him that he was not only my secretary and that he would also need to assist agents with all administrative requests about their cases. I quickly figured out that in San Antonio people liked to talk a lot, and without being rude, I asked some of the agents to let me work as I needed a lot of catching up to do. I liked to know them all personally, but that could wait after a brief introduction and share of interests. I knew that the reports would show the state of each one's work and needed areas of my immediate attention and involvement. The group was not in a bad shape. A couple of my senior agents were involved in training, a few were in the process of getting through different phases of training, and some were fully trained.

My biggest challenge appeared to be my senior agents. One of them was involved in the training program flipped and, for no apparent reason, cursed out trainees, which led eventually to her early retirement. Another senior agent could not resolve old inventory months after returning from training, and providing her with an honest midterm evaluation expressed dissatisfaction not in direct confrontation as in Houston but I overheard being called names and sensed her disagreeable behavior. Then there was a belligerent senior agent challenging all Gulf states area directives for changes in casework. And the fourth senior agent was transferred from a Houston's group for abusive transactions. This agent was a former manager who was required to step down because of mistreating employees. So it turned out that these people who were supposed to provide me with assistance were in need of my undivided attention.

In the course of the next months, I attempted to include these agents in the group's life by providing them with special assignments, as the one with participation in the UBS tax evasion project. This approach melted somewhat the ice, but since the two agents I selected for the project were eligible for retirement, it didn't take long for them to retire. Somehow, the requirements of the small business program for efficient case resolution did not go well with them. The belligerent agent transferred to another unit, leaving the group with agents eager to learn and advance in their careers. My primary objective with this group was the same as with the one in Houston and, prior to that, as a tax analyst and a teacher, to help people grow and feel fulfilled by setting objectives and reaching their goals. As a manager, I believed that it was degrading to check on agents if they were in the field, what time they arrived or left, because reviews of their cases showed of how much time and effort they put in their assigned work. Working smart was my motto, which my employees adopted under my guidance.

IRS offered a flexi place program allowing agents to work from home, which I supported and approved all my agents for it. I remembered how much time I wasted in the old days as an agent returning to the office when my appointments were cut short. This program was expanded, called maxi flexi, which expected agents to work continuously each day from 9:00 a.m. to 1:00 p.m. and the rest of the remaining hours were worked at the agents' ability or discretion. The new program suited my group perfectly as I had agents with children whom they had to see off and meet after school. There were also situations where agents were more efficient evenings and nights. One of them used to text me at 5:00 a.m., letting me know that a completed case was on my desk. I had my computer turned on till late at night, and I could see another female agent working at 9:00 or 10:00 p.m. I welcomed this type of scheduling as it permitted agents to work at times when they were more efficient and relaxed. My philosophy was that when people were in charge of their schedule and had no personal issues, they performed better.

Working as a team was another theory I fostered and applied for bringing agents closer together and enhancing learning. Having an open-door policy as in Houston brought to my attention what was needed most. Tax research was a critical area not taught well in training, so I organized a workshop taught by two of my agents, versatile in tax research using Lexis and Westlaw. I could see agents smiling being able to do their own research after the workshop. I particularly enjoyed visiting agents in the field and sharing my experiences with them by providing guidance for effective interviews, examination of records, and documentation. I observed with pleasure how my agents developed their cases and gathered the information they needed to resolve issues ranging from farming to international activities. There was a case for food aid to Africa where my agent, after getting the entire background for the business, asked, "What is this high transportation expense for?"

"It's for bribing officials to let the trucks through" was the answer.

There were interesting businesses and issues that the group came across, a lot of them dealing with farming and hobby loss. One case that comes to mind was where an agent, by asking the right questions, resolved a case setting precedence for horse racing activity as hobby loss in San Antonio. With that frame of mind where my agents became motivated with a drive to succeed, they soon gained skills that made them competitive and eligible for promotions. I wasn't that much surprised when I spotted some of their names selected for interviews for higher grade revenue agent positions. At that time I was acting for my Territory Manager and became responsible for interviewing and selecting agents nationwide for promotional assignments. The process was very involved; agents were classified in tiers after being picked from a computerized government program and interviewed locally or by phone. I was not alone in conducting the interviews; there was an interview panel with a couple of other managers on the phone. I did the interviews for my and other agents from the office, being proud of how they handled the questions, which guaranteed them securing the positions they applied for. I also hoped to get agents interested in management, providing them acting opportunities, and I was very pleased when two of my male agents with excellent technical knowledge approached me, expressing an interest in a management career. From that day on, I provided these agents with all necessary training, encouragement, and support in getting the necessary knowledge and qualifications for such a position. I exposed them to the use of all managerial tools and engaged them in participating in all management processes and tasks. My reward for the time and energy I put in helping them was their acceptance to the frontline management program and seeing them completing it successfully.

A few words about my secretary. He was not interested in growth. He was efficient with what he was doing, and his work was usually done by noon. Sometimes he exhibited a strange behavior like accusing another secretary of being racist and then having to excuse himself, especially after finding out that the woman was also Latino. We had numerous talks about correct behavior, which I knew he had a hard time dealing with. And I knew it took him a while to get used to the idea that I was his manager. The important thing was that he was efficient and very supportive of the agents' work. It took me a couple of years to bring my group in a shape that I envisioned—highly trained, capable, and motivated agents, ready to take on any challenges in the exam program.

Before going any further, I need to mention that after my move to San Antonio, my daughter who was visiting from Houston every weekend one day announced that she would like to move with me and my grandson. I was very sad just thinking about leaving Vanesa in Houston, but I didn't mention anything because for me her happiness and her career at Baylor Hospital were more important. We agreed that Jorden would come with me, and I already checked the schools in the area for his transfer. I decided to have the kid enrolled in the neighborhood elementary public school as I was not impressed of what I observed in the private schools. I wasn't ready to sell the house in the Woodlands though; I bought it for the family, for the kids to have a place to visit and feel comfortable. I wasn't sure at first how long I would stay in San Antonio, so it made sense to rent rather than sell the Houston house. After futile attempts to rent it furnished, I ended up selling all the furniture at very low prices. It was only furniture, but I bought it for the Dallas house when Mom was alive, and it had a meaning for me.

The lesson I learned here was to never get attached to things—houses, furniture, etc. My life was turbulent and full of surprises to try and make a home at any of the places I chose to live. Having that in mind, I bought a house in San Antonio suited for one person for temporary living. But it was still okay for the three of us, although the bedrooms for the kids were small.

My daughter moved with me in June 2009, the weekend when my younger daughter was getting married. They already had a child together, and it made sense for them to legalize their relationship, but she knew that there would be hard times ahead of them since neither of them had education or skills to support a family. I did not attend my younger daughter's wedding but rather organized the move for my older daughter and grandson to San Antonio. We rented again a small U-Haul truck, and friends and neighbors gladly ran over to help again with packing and driving the truck. My daughter is a very hardworking young woman. Soon she unpacked all the boxes, and the place looked as if we lived there for a while.

We were slowly getting adjusted again to a life in the new city, discovering meetup groups of different interests, taking trips. The happiest moment for me was to learn that my daughter found a job at an eye surgery clinic like the one she worked at in Houston. Best time of the day was coming home from work and having dinner with Vanesa and Jorden. Summers in San Antonio last a long time, so evenings, we used to go to the pool or the gym, while weekends were reserved for all day activities. After touring the city and the neighboring villages and towns, we started to attend cultural events, which San Antonio offers all the time. Joining a hiking group, we discovered all the beautiful parks in the area and fell in love with the nature this city had to offer. A Ukrainian group offered celebrations of religious and other holidays, including picnics at a ranch in the hill country or swimming in the Comal River in New Braunfels. It was at this group that I came across a Bulgarian lady with young twins married to a Ukrainian man. Through her, we met Bulgarian Americans of a Bulgarian group that offered interesting activities, such as a weekend Bulgarian school for children, which my grandson started to attend. My daughter and I joined folk dance and folk singing groups, meeting for practice once a week and performing throughout the year for fundraising and holiday celebrations. The Bulgarian community was very friendly; they offered us a very warm reception and made us feel very welcome. For me, it was a great pleasure to watch my grandson exposed to Bulgarian culture and learning about his heritage. I could see his face light up when there was an invitation for the public to join in folk dancing, and he never hesitated to join in with other people. I felt good in the company of my newly met friends, feeling at home away from home, so I opened my house for a once-a-month cookout with Bulgarian dishes prepared by a Bulgarian man and his father, both culinary experts, who later opened restaurant Europa serving all kind of European dishes.

Our life in San Antonio started to be more regulated and pleasant. We found everything a person could desire, except a church where we felt comfortable. We missed the Serbian church close to our old Woodlands house, and after our move, we made a few trips there. The Serbian priest was a down-to-earth and devoted man who united people of Eastern Orthodox religion from different Eastern European countries as one big family worshipping and celebrating holidays together. What impressed me was that he took my grandson to serve at the altar the first time we met him. The church itself was built on a farm where kids loved chasing or being chased by geese. There was lunch served after Sunday service, followed by soccer games, with band performers and singers on evenings of special church holidays. We couldn't find a similar place to worship in San Antonio. We attended a couple of times services at the Greek and Eastern Orthodox churches, but the atmosphere was impersonal. We prayed at home and, on holidays we placed icons on the kitchen counter and lit candles.

I used to take my grandson hiking on days when my daughter preferred to be home, and that day on September 3, 2011, was not any different. We joined a meet up group called San Antonio Outdoors for a hike in Fredericks park and soon took off on the trails. This group walked at a fast pace—they were running rather than walking—so I was always the last. I remember commenting to a woman how I would prefer a more relaxed approach to hiking, pointing out at a group resting by the side of the path. "Look, won't it be nice to stop and enjoy nature rather than running and be over with it in an hour?"

As we approached the group, a man looked at me and asked, "Are you French?"

"No," I answered. "I am of Bulgarian descent."

"You are kidding," he responded in Bulgarian. "So am I." I came to find out we were actually neighbors in Sofia. "Do you know another interesting thing?" I just looked at him, waiting to hear his answer. "There is a guy here, a friend of mine, who went to the same high school as you did. You probably know him." He called his friend, and we scheduled to meet on Monday, Labor Day, at Barnes & Noble bookstore. I was curious to meet this man with whom I could talk about the old school days, classmates, and teachers.

I arrived early and sat on a bench in front of the bookstore. It was a nice, sunny day, and I enjoyed the sunrays warming my face and body. Then I saw a man close to my age matching the description of my old classmate walking toward the entrance with a rose in his hand. It did not strike me as odd because European men like to honor women with flowers for no reason. I was right that I would enjoy meeting this man as I liked talking about the carefree high school days, our classmates, and teachers. He was in a different class right next door to mine, but I did not remember him as I was not interested in boys at that age. I just liked having fun dancing, going to parks, hiking with my classnmates. The following Friday was this man's birthday, and I accepted his invitation to attend his birthday party at a Mexican restaurant. My neighbor was there with his wife, as well as a bunch of other colleague doctors of theirs. I saw this man a couple of times after that, enjoying his company as he was very well-read and knowledgeable not only in his specialty of medicine but also in literature and art.

My birthday was approaching, and I was looking forward to seeing my son, my daughter-in-law, and my new grandson, who was only five months old. This was the first time I was going to see the baby, and I made sure I had everything for the little guy, from a car seat to diapers. We were in Turkey on vacation when he was born, and

I was looking forward so much to spend time with him. Gathering my children around me has always been a big thrill, and I could hardly wait to have them home at the kitchen table, laughing and having a good time. My daughter and grandson already knew my Bulgarian male friend, but I felt uncomfortable sharing this with my son. To my surprise, my son was happy for me to have a companion from my high school. My younger daughter could not come to any of our gatherings as she could hardly survive, left alone travel. A year after getting married, she got pregnant again and had twins, a boy and a girl. Children are a gift from God, and the babies were beautiful, but I knew that her life would become even harder with more children. Thinking of her and the way she lived in poverty always broke my heart. But I knew deep down that one day she would turn around and see that education is what she needs for herself and the kids to have a future. I never lost faith, and I prayed every day that my smart young daughter realizes that she needs to have a better life, a life which can be earned by returning to college.

Career in Senior Management

It was August 2011. I was in the office reminiscing about all the accomplishments and hardships in my life when I felt that I still needed more challenges. I knew where to find them—in the job announcements of USA jobs website. One ad grabbed my attention—senior management training program. After my overseas assignment, I knew I had to get back to being involved on a larger scale of the Service operations. I could not resign myself to the setback I suffered in my career because of my ex-husband. I will never forget the interview by phone with the assistant area director and other senior level managers, which involved strategic business-related questions for resolution of management issues. Once finished, I walked out of my office, still shaken up from anticipation of the interview questions and ensuring that my answers were right on point and correct. My agents were not surprised of my decision to look for a more demanding position as I taught them to always look for new challenges and growth opportunities.

My training in the program started in September in Denver, Colorado, and was spread out for weeks at the time to last roughly ten months. You would expect a senior management program to be boring, but it wasn't as it had practical aspects and real-life situations from the perspective of a senior management position. Of particular interest for me were models of change management with scenarios of various settings inspiring productivity as well as ways to motivate people with different mindsets and personalities. Lewin's change management model, ADKAR model, Bridges's transition model all came into place when learning how to assist employees to embrace change and let go of resistance for fear of the unknown and of failing. Communication theories as the one developed in the DiSC model provided insight of how to identify different traits in people and how to deal with individuals described in four categories of behavior and mindset.

Our training group consisted of about twenty managers, and we all took a test to discover which was our predominant communication style—dominant, influencer, conscientious, or steady. I came to find out most of us had dominant and influencer traits, but that was not to say that there were certain aspects present from the other categories. I found this fascinating as I was already applying most of the suggested approaches in communicating with employees after figuring out their personality traits. Role-playing of theories outlined for management styles were also used, stressing the importance of styles to adopt and styles to avoid. I already had enough exposure to different styles of managing and found out that my management style was democratic as I believed in teamwork and freedom of expression, visionary and that of coaching as I never ceased to teach my employees. We also had fun projects, such as attending a presentation of a wild horse taming and breeding provided by an individual who demonstrated his approach to receiving desired results of taming by creating trust and cooperation with this very free-spirited animal. The comparison was clear; working with difficult individuals is possible by treating them with respect and dignity. And because the entire training was interactive with role-playing and participation, it was easy to conceive how all theories of communication and successful management apply to the workplace.

The most incredible part of this training was engaging in physical exercises, pushing ourselves beyond the limits of our comfort zone. It was a sunny day in December 2011, the ground was covered with snow, and we were told to dress warm with jackets and boots to participate in outdoor activities. We traveled to the exercise camp, which I noticed was next to a hospital. Here we were provided with special gear and shoes and led to the field with the equipment. It was an unbelievable sight as it looked like a place for circus acrobats training. There were high poles I would estimate at the height of telephone poles with boards across them for crossing, swinging bridges, zip lines, and more. I knew how to climb steep surfaces from the times when I was a kid in my grandmother's village, but I was afraid of heights. I chose to try a pole that after climbing to the top, you had to jump over to reach another pole. Climbing up was no problem, but once on top, I could not bring myself to do the jump. We were all tied up to a professional when performing exercises high up in the air who could catch us if we fell, but I still couldn't bring myself to leap in the air as a monkey. So I tried the balance beam placed high up in the air, which I reached fast going up a tall pole, but once on the top, I noticed that the rope parallel to it was not close enough to grasp in case I lost my balance. I wanted to climb down, but the lady to whom my protective gear was attached to told me not to do it; it was dangerous. So I sat down on the beam and scooted toward the other end. Once in the middle of the beam, I asked if I could jump— imagine a jump from a telephone pole. I heard the lady saying okay, and I threw myself to the ground.

We all worked in teams, so there were five of my colleagues and the lady who grabbed me as I landed down. They all had very worried faces. I was not afraid of jumping down, but looking at them, I realized that I must have been in danger. I hugged them all, thanking them for saving me, and headed to something that I thought I could do—zip-lining. Once brought up to the platform, I sat down on the chair, but nobody told me to brace myself, so the impact of going down was so hard that I heard my neck snap. Luckily, nothing broke; I was just sore for a few days later. Leaving the place, I came across an individual in a wheelchair and asked him how he got hurt, and he said that he fell from one of the poles. Well, I was glad that it was over with. Somebody had a video of us participating in different exercises, but I was not on it. I suppose not to scare upcoming training groups.

There was also a practical aspect of the training involving a long-term senior management assignment, and after the second phase of classroom training, I knew that I would be assigned to manage a territory. I should mention that the year after I left Houston, their exam territory manager, after numerous complaints and problems, was forced into retirement. I heard from my former employees that one of the managers had a heart attack, and many others were with poor health due to stress of working in a hostile environment. The new territory manager was from Louisiana but was retiring in a year, just about the time when I was eligible for a senior management assignment. So it did not come as a surprise to me when the manager in charge of training called and offered me an assignment in Houston. By that time, the two agents in my group were trained to take over my position in San Antonio. I knew that such decision would cause the least disruption for the group's operations having one of their own lead them and assist them.

In August 2012, I left for Houston to prepare for my upcoming assignment. The ironic part was that I was going to work in this spiteful woman's office, having her secretary as my secretary. *Another twist of destiny,* I thought to myself. It was a weekend, and I went to check on my rented house and visit my neighbors in the Woodlands.

"I told you she was mean to you because she was jealous and afraid that you would take her place," said one of my neighbors from across the street of my old house. "See, it happened. You took her place." I smiled and left to get ready for the upcoming week.

The current territory manager met me at the entrance of the building and provided me with a security entrance card to the floor. Entering the building and walking in the office on the exam floor, I came across familiar faces, some curiously looking at me. I nodded and smiled at everybody, following my host. I checked the organizational chart prior to arriving. I already knew that there were no changes in the managerial staff, and most of the agents were the same from the time I left Houston a couple of years ago. The first couple of days I spent in analyzing reports, reaching a sad conclusion that Houston was on last place in the Gulf states area with the worst possible performance results. There were groups with 99 percent failing rates. The territory manager gave me a brief description about the background of the agents. They were all fully trained, and these were fallout cases dating back to the old territory manager's time. The direction given to the agents at that time was to pursue new issues and research more and more, trying to prove fraud. She also warned me that the union was very aggressive and breathing down her neck, so she did not take any action in changing any methods of operation, letting things continue without her interference.

I knew that I had to address all employees—managers, agents, clerical staff—in a territory meeting to set things straight in informing everybody the direction I was taking and what my expectations were in following the directives of the area. Pulling everybody off the field was not going to matter at this point as the situation was so bad that one day was not going to affect any work results. As everybody settled in the conference room, I noticed the union rep with her notebook ready to take notes and build a case against me. I had a run with her while I was a manager in Houston, but her allegations to protect the couple of agents who retired were groundless and quickly dismissed. My speech was inspirational and motivational; my goal was to reach the heart of my audience and awaken their desire to succeed from the time they were students to the time they chose working for the Service. I looked around the room. There were no conversations; all eyes were fixed on me in expectation of my speech. I took a deep breath and started.

"Good morning, and I hope it's a good morning for everybody as we are all gathered here to establish a union—a union which will help us develop strong ties, professional and personal, in reaching the same objectives. Most of you know me as I used to be a group manager at the north office and probably know something about my principles and beliefs. But what I want you to hear first is my story, which will help you understand why I think the way I do and why I value certain traits in people, such as honesty, integrity, professionalism, commitment, loyalty, strive for excellence, and success.

"I was born in Bulgaria in the family of intellectuals, and my desire to learn was from a very early age. Bulgaria was Communist at the time I was growing up, and people were poor. That was not the worst part. What was bad was that there was no freedom of speech, of artistic or scientific expression, of travel. Western culture and civilization were attacked to be decadent and were forbidden to study, discuss, and definitely follow. I escaped from Bulgaria when I was nineteen and arrived in America with a suitcase and $20."

I went on to explain briefly my life in pursuit of personal development and growth and how proud I felt when I was selected to be a part of the most respected agency in the world for their fight against crime. "I chose to work for the IRS because of the organization's principles of fairness for all, commitment to excellence, integrity, ethics, honesty, and trust. Those principles coincide with mine to serve the public in an honest and fair way and to have strong professional ties with my colleagues in treating everybody with respect and dignity. I am sure you share my views and that this was the main reason for you to select working for the Service." I shared some of my personal experiences as an agent in the early days, as well as those days as a tax analyst, assisting foreign governments after the fall of the Berlin Wall, such as the one in my native country, to establish tax administrations based on the IRS model.

The room was silent, Everybody was staring at me with eyes wide open. I continued by addressing the challenges that I knew I had to overcome together with them in Houston.

"So how are you going to be different from the territory manager who retired?" the union rep yelled out.

"For one, I intend to bring back the confidence in people that they are not only capable of doing their work but that they also need to seek new opportunities. My approach will be that of a leader showing you all the road to success. I believe that if I could help whole regions succeed individually and as a country, I would be able to have the same results with you all here. I saw the Houston business results, and they are poor, but I am going to work with you to correct that. We all need to work together in identifying areas of deficiency and necessary measures to correct them, whether you need additional training or direction to turn things around."

At that point, people became livelier. I knew they were concerned with the concept of direction, which the union rep immediately brought up.

"I intend to get involved by working with all of you, especially those experiencing difficulties, but the process will be different as you will also provide your own input on how to proceed in resolving your old cases. It will be a joint effort of managers and agents." I knew my speech was a success because I spoke from the heart; I was sincere and was able to convince the majority of my listeners of my good intentions. I knew the pain these people suffered working for years under autocratic management, and I felt so good knowing that I was given the opportunity to revive in them the belief and the desire to be successful.

I chose the worst performing groups and asked their managers to schedule meetings with the agents and their secretaries. This was extremely beneficial and valuable as I needed to gain their trust by working in small groups, permitting me to identify causes for poor performance. As I suspected, reasons for inability to perform ranged from lack of training in certain areas to lack of confidence and, in some cases, boredom. By introducing concepts of open communication without fear of repercussion, teamwork, and inclusion, I encouraged managers and agents to express their opinions and formulate plans of action on their own. Training seminars were organized to provide additional training in research, documentation utilizing computer programs, and common issues for the area. Managers and agents became confident in expressing freely their thoughts about direction they deemed necessary to take in case resolutions.

My guidelines issued to agents and managers were to close all overage cases, with little to no additional work, because it was a disservice to the public to keep businesses and their owners under audit for years. These were cases with tons of documentation without conclusive statements and no reasonable explanation for having them open. I felt like being in Bulgaria again as it was a grim situation with the exception that these people all went through extensive training. I had to create and adopt a plan geared not only toward a fast improvement of cases but also to boost employees' morale. Designing tables of all problem cases by group with mutually agreed upon actions with set days for completion was my first step. However, follow-up and holding further discussions was absolutely necessary to determine if the plan was working. Since my assignment was remote, once back in San Antonio, I spent days and weeks on the phone talking with managers and agents, verifying the progress they made, and agreeing on last technical work to finish their assignments. I could feel from the tone of their voices and I could see from the computer reports that my personal involvement worked.

Having the green light to use their knowledge, people started to feel satisfied and happy with their work. The accomplishments they made in a short time gave them courage to move forward and be successful. There were also agents who requested to be transferred to groups where they would be more effective or those who needed detail assignment out of the group because being an agent in the same grade level for a long time wears off. This was all a part of my strategy to engage people in developmental tasks, providing them with meaningful application and use of their talents.

Here I would like to mention how impressed I was with an African American male secretary selected for the position from the Wounded Warrior Project with arm injury. The first day I gave my speech addressing the whole territory, he walked up to me and said, "I have never heard about an individual like you. You are a great inspiration to all of us." I asked him about his goals and what it was that he wanted to achieve. In a way, he reminded me of my first secretary in Houston, who graduated from college and was working as legal assistant to counsel. The man looked at me and responded, "I would like to be one day a territory manager like you." This meant to me a lot as I realized that I helped another person aspire for a better future. I sat down and outlined for him the process, stressing how he would need to sign up in college as soon as possible.

At the end of my territory manager assignment, my area director asked that I complete departure managers evaluation for the managers of the Houston territory as this was going to be a true appraisal for the performance of their groups and for the timeliness in performing reviews on the agents. I pushed that task for three months later as I wanted everybody to succeed before grading their work. The group evaluations were a very involved process taking at least a week. I was delighted to provide excellent scores to the first couple of groups. There were issues with the third group, which was my old office, and the problem stemmed from the fact that the manager could not bring himself to evaluate his employees. The individual was technically very smart but was not comfortable grading people.

This was another case of misuse of talent as there were a great number of opportunities in the Service where individuals could be effective and successful. My monthly reports to the area were describing all my activities with detailed description of my work and that of my managers. It wasn't long before the area director called me and gave me the great news.

"Nina, whatever you did is extremely amazing as the territory manager for PSP, who is very hard on grading or giving compliments, called me and exclaimed in admiration about your business results. PSP was the unit analyzing and summarizing reports, grading the state of each territory in the area."

All the case closures took time to get through the system and show up in the current reports. It was a tremendous feeling to learn that I succeeded to turn around a huge territory like Houston from being the worst to climbing up on the scale of success. In reality, the numbers were just a mere reflection of how everybody reacted to my call for forgetting the past and looking forward to a successful future of achievements in an atmosphere of respect and appreciation.

It was toward the end of my assignment, but I was still involved in providing all managers with evaluations upon my departure, extending it into a seven-month territory management position. Upon returning to San Antonio, I found my group just as intact as I left it. The agents who I left in charge continued to operate in the same spirit of teamwork, cooperation, and aspiration for accomplishing all tasks with constantly shifting priorities. It was time for me to catch my breath before engaging in new ventures.

My Fight with Breast Cancer

February 2013. It was time for my medical checkup exam for which I still went to Dallas.

"You have a little lump on the right side," the doctor said. "I will give you orders to have mammogram in San Antonio."

I never had mammograms and didn't think much of having one. Back in San Antonio, I visited the nearest radiology clinic, and after the test, I sat in the waiting room watching TV and feeling bored.

"The doctor would like to see you." A nurse walked up to me and pointed toward the doctor's office.

"That's good. I wanted to talk to the doctor anyway" was my response. "But that is not good. Doctors talk to patients only when there is a problem," she answered. At that time, I realized what the problem might be and became very apprehensive about any news I was about to hear.

"Let me show you the results from the X-ray, which give me a concern," the doctor said. "You see these lined-up four dots. This is usually an indication that there is a cancerous process. I will have an order for you to have a biopsy in the next couple of days. There is another office down the street where you will need to go to."

All of a sudden, I became numb. Having no questions, I walked out and headed to the reception area where they scheduled me for the biopsy procedure.

I had the biopsy scheduled on February 15, wanting to have a celebration at the office and at home for Valentine's Day. I celebrated all holidays with my group with tacos from the neighboring restaurant, but this time, for Valentine's Day, I also bought chocolates. For a while, I forgot about the upcoming biopsy, listening to the joyful chattering of people around me in good spirits. My appointment on

February 15 was later in the morning, so I went first to work to be distracted from what I was about to endure. The doctor performing the biopsy was female of Slavic origin and was very comforting during the procedure while I had tears running down my face. Then it was over. I slowly got off the table when the doctor spoke.

"I took out all the tissue of the connected dots," she said. "I believe you will be all right."

I can't really describe what I felt because it was an extraordinary sensation of something unpleasant and distant. The results were negative, but upon the recommendation of the doctor who performed the biopsy, I saw a surgeon to eliminate any doubt for further issues. The original mammogram showed more dots, not connected at the time, which could become "active and cancerous," her exact words. The surgeon was a middle-aged man, short and slim. After viewing the mammogram, he immediately recommended surgery, which my male Bulgarian friend, being a doctor, insisted on me having. The two of us planned earlier a trip to Asia, which I was looking so much forward to, envisioning lands of incredible sights with unearthly beauty and extraordinary landscapes, encountering people with colorful and mysterious customs. I looked at both the surgeon and my friend and said, "I'll have the surgery, but it will be after the trip."

Exploring Hong Kong—the Flagrant City

February 23, 2013. It was an incredible flight on ANA as sitting in the first row of economy class, I felt like being in first class. The last weeks seemed like a bad nightmare. The service was impeccable because of the extreme politeness of the Japanese stewardesses; the food was also excellent. We had a layover in Tokyo, and I couldn't help but grab a couple of souvenirs before the flight to Hong Kong. Our hotel was in the district of Kowloon, which I selected as it was in a night market location where we could go out any time of the day or night. I knew my jaw dropped as I saw the room size, two single beds with just enough space to walk between them, and a small path leading to the bathroom. But it had a huge window overlooking the market with colorful lights of Mandarin advertising.

The adventure started the following day. We had it all planned in detail. After a breakfast at the market of noodle soup and scrambled eggs, we rushed to catch a boat, and on the way, we ran across people doing Tai Chi in a park. Once off the boat, we took a tram to the famous peak overlooking the city of amazing sights from the harbor and a skyline of a great number of skyscrapers. Stanley was our next stop since we both enjoy the sea, and this was a seaside village with a very attractive coastline, considered to be the affluent part of Hong Kong with famous beaches. Then on the way back, we were attracted by a noisy, picturesque fisherman spot called Aberdeen. We couldn't help but hop on a sampan boat of the Tonka people. Following was a visit to a Chinese temple, in front of which I stood in admiration with an open mouth. I had to participate in their ordeals, so I lit big sticks with incense and paper for wishes with the smoke going to the gods. This city had a public escalator going through downtown from which you could view restaurants and shops and people in their living rooms. We hopped on it and picked a place for dinner.

The next day, I remember running through the city as we took the subway, followed by a long walk and a skywalk to the pier of Macau. I still remember admiring the vast green areas full of flowers before reaching the pier. Taking a jet boat over to the island was an excitement on its own. Once there, I noticed that there were limos from the casinos transporting all passengers, so we ended up at the Wynn Casino, where I lost all seven dollars. What I wanted to see was the famous temple where I rubbed one thousand Hong Kong dollars on a wall for luck and happiness. The last adventure for the day was a trip to Lantau Island, from where a cable car took us to see the biggest Buddha dominating the mountain hill.

This visit to Hong Kong will always remain in my mind as a trip opening my eyes to a different world full of surprises, with colorful scenes, beauty, varied unexpected sights, like the fisherman village against the skyline of the skyscrapers.

Bangkok, the city of fairy tales

Our adventure started on the evening of our arrival, with a fabulous dinner on a deck of our hotel Navalai by the pier of Chao Phraya River. A ride on a public riverboat took us to a fairy-tale land starting at the Temple of the Emerald Buddha, where I was met on both sides of the entrance by the statues of two exquisitely decorated demon figures. Once inside, I gazed in amazement at the Buddha statue made of jade and in a gold robe. I felt like being in an enchanted world of unearthly beauty as we walked in the court of the Grand Palace. My eyes wandered around and stopped at the royal residence building with a quadrangular dome and attractive architecture of Renaissance style. I moved toward another building, Phra Mondop, which was shining in the sunlight with its green and gold mosaics, to view sacred scriptures written on palm leaves referred to as the canon of Buddha. Further ahead was the Royal Pantheon building with two golden pagodas and a row of very colorful demons guarding the building.

Back on the river at the west bank, majestically and glamorously standing, shimmering in the sunset, was Wat Arun, the Temple of Dawn, decorated with Chinese porcelain and distinguishable with colorful spires. And I definitely had to see the reclining Buddha at the Wat Pho temple, made of gold and being extremely long, forty-five meters. Taking off my shoes, I kept running from one end to the other, trying to capture in my photos every angle of it. It was hot, but there was closely monitored dress code at the entrance to the temples, so I had to zip on and off the leggings of my pants. I knew there was more to see, so there it was, Wat Kanlayanamit, a giant temple, with its enormous golden seated Buddha inside it.

Back on the riverboat, we traveled to Chinatown, where the Golden Buddha stood, built with 5.5 tons of gold. Grabbing a *tuk tuk* to the river was a cultural experience in itself. I heard before of the colorful life alongside the canals, and we headed toward a pier with private boats. Taking a ride on the canals was more like entering another world, passing by small houses, more like huts on wooden boards, with tropical vegetation and flowers around them. There were floating markets on boats, so I waved at a woman to show me the things she was selling from her boat; she had the most colorful and beautiful fans.

Angor Watt, forgotten civilization

I call it elephant country because while in Hong Kong, I dreamed of being there riding an elephant. Arriving at Siem Reap, we observed an interesting procedure at passport control. After filling in three papers and providing them pictures, our passports were passed on to eight individuals behind desks, one next to the other. After returning the passports, they took our pictures again. Arriving at the hotel, which was by the night market, we quickly dropped off our luggage and went out to explore. The place was jam-packed with massages offered in the street, restaurants, music, people hustling and bustling, motorcycles, *rameaux* (*tuk tuk* with a motorcycle in front and a carriage in the back).

Early in the morning, we headed to one of the most famous world wonders, the Angkor Wat temple. A spectacular sight was in front of us as we arrived at the grounds of the temple. The Angkor Wat is a building standing by itself, creating a mysterious and pious feeling. Built in the middle of a jungle, Angor Watt is dedicated to the Hindu gods and is the portrayal of Hindu mythology. I was in awe, in admiration of numerous bas-reliefs on the walls, a testimony to the important deities in Hindu religion as well as revealing celebration of major events. I was immediately attracted to explore first the grounds where we walked through ruins of structures with bas-reliefs telling ancient stories and massive sandstones. A lost civilization, I couldn't help thinking if this was a sanctuary, a temple complex, or a lost city stretching outside the temple. We came across giant tree roots engulfing parts of the ruins and admired bas-reliefs of sculptured beautiful women figures. Then I spotted the elephants. An elephant ride was an experience that I was dying for. Next thing I knew, a guy provided us with a ladder to climb up to the top of the elephant. What an exhilarating experience.

Thinking about Cambodia, I also remember the trip to Tonlé Sap. It was an usual sight to watch alongside the river rice paddies and houses on stilts, as well as supermodern homes. Once at the lake, we hired a private boat and soon arrived at a floating village where about 2,200 people lived on boats (rafts floating on empty barrels with roofs). There were families with children and dogs on these boats looking like shacks. I was amazed to learn that there was a floating school and a floating store where we bought food for the children. What was striking was that these impoverished kids looked happy, laughing and playing.

From Cambodia, we swung by Chiang Mai, another paradise on earth in Thailand. The drive to Doi temple and the Mae village reminded me of hiking on Vitosha Mountain in Bulgaria, but the vegetation was lush and tropical, and the multicolored plants and flowers were breathtaking. Walking up three hundred steps to Doi temple, which was a replica of the Emerald Buddha, was invigorating. Once at the top, I gasped at the view of the exotic colorful gardens. What comes to mind were the gorgeous rose and fern gardens at the winter royal palace. Mae village had a flea market displaying local and handmade souvenirs with a narrow path up and down a hill and leading to a waterfall with flowers of different shapes and colors.

Traveling back to the States, I remember staying at the most modern Marriott Hotel with the best service in the world being in Hong Kong by the airport. We were transferred to the hotel in a limo with drivers in black tuxedos. The room in marble and fashionable design had a spectacular view of the harbor and the mountains. Across from our room was a hospitality lounge with the tastiest gourmet appetizers I've ever had and high-quality drinks. It was a nice way to say goodbye to Asia.

It was March 4, the day before my surgery. I took the day off and started my morning later than usual. It was a little past eight when I stepped in the shower and heard a loud thump noise. Then it was repeated. *Must be the neighbors building something,* I thought. By the third time, I felt something was wrong. I wrapped a towel around me and dashed out of the bathroom and my bedroom looking to the left in the hallway. The front door was busted and was on the floor, and glancing to the right across, I saw the big TV from the family room missing. Without giving it any thought, I ran toward the front and noticed on the porch a smaller TV and my grandson's laptop. At that same time, he came back—a guy of medium height, a little stout, with Latino features and darker complexion. He stopped in his tracks, and I started to yell on top of my lungs, "Go away!" He did not leave at once. He stood in front of me, and I suppose he was surprised to see me home and was contemplating what to do. It must have taken him a good few minutes before turning around and rushing to a small black passenger car parked in my driveway, which I was not in a state to identify.

Then I realized that I was lucky because it was only him. You see, leaving my bedroom, I did not look to the right, and there could have been somebody else in the kitchen and dining area. I called 911 and then my daughter's fiancé. I dressed in a hurry and ran to the neighbors on both sides. One did not open, and the other said that he was washing dishes and had the music on loud, so he could not hear anything. Back at the house, I sat in a bewildered state, not completely aware of what just happened. I knew that San Antonio had the most gated communities not for only extremely expensive houses as in Dallas and Houston, and I started to understand why. Our subdivision was not gated. I knew of robberies in gated communities when I bought the house, so it was not really something that concerned me. A gate would stop a crime but not prevent it was the way I thought at the time.

My daughter's fiancé arrived shortly, he must have been driving very fast coming from his work downtown. He gave me a hug and called on people to repair the front door and the lock. It was much later when the police arrived to take a report, and that was the last I heard of them; there were no investigations or an effort put in tracking this guy. I managed to collect myself and headed to my friend's apartment, where I spent the night before my surgery.

March 5, the same day we buried Mom eight years ago, I was thinking on the way to the hospital. I had another biopsy, and this time, they said that one of the floating dots was cancerous. The radiologist had placed some sort of a plastic cup over the area marked for surgery, and soon they rolled me into the operating room. My Bulgarian friend sent me off with my favorite songs from the Asia trip—a nostalgic instrumental piece called "999 Roses." With dried tears, I listened to the song, envisioning how I was running by the green areas with flowers in Hong Kong on the way to the quay for Macau. The surgery, called lumpectomy, lasted a couple of hours, I was told. It was more emotional than physical pain of what I remember. The cancer was diagnosed as stage 0, referred to as noninvasive, and I was told that meant that the cancerous cells were statutory and not affecting other healthy cells. What was disturbing was that when I saw the surgeon after the surgery, he said in a calm voice, "I removed the cancerous cells, but one was very close to the healthy tissue, and you will need another surgery or an extensive treatment."

Another surgery was out of the question, so he referred me to a clinic where they said that the doctor prescribed seven weeks of daily radiation plus taking tamoxifen drug for five years. This seemed to me as a very aggressive treatment for stage 0 cancer. I started to research treatment options, and after a couple of weeks, I came across an innovative approach used at the cancer center of the San Antonio University Hospital with three weeks of daily radiation without any additional drugs.

Meanwhile, talking to my Bulgarian friend one day, he looked at me and said, "We are going to the gun range." I bought myself a revolver and took a class of theory and shooting. I passed the exam, giving me a license to carry a gun, which I have in the house always close to me. Listening to the recommendations on how to react in case of invasion in your home, I thought, *How easy to speak. I'd like to see you meeting face-to-face with a burglar in your house.* I just knew that a situation like that could take you in a completely different state of mind, not being able to rationalize.

I continued to work during the radiation treatment, but there was something very emotional every time I had to have it. A secretary at work and another manager accompanied me a few times, which gave me comfort. Sitting in the waiting room, I could see patients in bad shape, skinny, pale, some in wheelchairs. What helped overcome gloomy thoughts in this depressing place was the receptionist, who would give hugs and had kind words for everybody. I felt weak toward the end; I knew the radiation was taking a toll on my body, as I was walking slower and not feeling well. The day of my last treatment, I headed to the gym's pool, grabbing a lunch from the café. I sat under the umbrella, gazing at the water, which was so attractive. I thought I'd go in, but I could hardly swim half a lap. My fingers were getting stiff during the next month, which the doctor at the cancer center could not figure out why; this was not an expected side effect. Continuing with my work and life at home, I started to put behind me that experience as another bad dream.

Unplanned Wedding
and Retirement

My Bulgarian friend and I planned and booked a trip to Europe in the fall, which I was extremely excited about. It was somewhere mid-June when we met to talk more about the trip when my friend told me, "Sit down. I need to tell you something." He appeared calm but was with a serious face. "Nina, I have lymphoma. They discovered it from the gastroscopy test, which I had the other day." I couldn't comprehend right away what he was saying. "They told me I have an year to live. It's a stage four cancer," he continued.

I sat in disbelief but quickly recovered, feeling an urgency to act. "I'll spend the night with you if you don't mind, and I'll take you in the morning to my doctor at the radiology department of the cancer center." I felt that I could not leave a close friend to face this alone. I knew exactly how devastating the truth of learning to have cancer could be, and his sickness was far more dangerous than mine. We went straight to my doctor in the morning (his doctor could not see him till late that evening), who directed us to the right sector of the hospital dealing with blood cancer. I watched him flinch from the painful bone marrow and cardiology tests to get him ready for extensive chemo of five months with bone marrow transplant at the end. The first chemo was stressful as we both watched the drugs injected into his veins; the procedure took about a couple of hours.

A few days later, he called me at work and asked me to dinner. Arriving at the RIM Shopping Center, he stopped in front of Jared jewelry store and came back with a wedding ring. He gave me a ring of friendship the Christmas before, but we never talked about a serious relationship. Going to his apartment after dinner, he carried me over the threshold. We celebrated with a glass of wine, and once the idea of being married again sank in, I called and let my children know. He lost his hair after the second chemo, was nauseated, and could eat only certain food. But I kept him company, and his spirits were up.

We decided to marry on the day we met, September 5. The wedding was at the Westin La Cantera Resort, in an intimate atmosphere with closest friends and family—our witnesses (*kum* and *kuma* in Bulgarian language) were my Bulgarian neighbor doctor and his wife, a lady psychiatrist from the same hiking group, a couple of doctors (the woman was very supportive while I was going through my own cancer treatment), our book club hosts (the lady was a very talented artist, and her husband was an editor and expert in English literature), another Spanish-speaking couple, and my older daughter with her husband and grandson (my older daughter and her husband married a couple of months earlier in Hawaii and adopted Jorden). I enjoyed the company of my new son-in-law; he was very considerate, reliable, and loving. He was the same man who flew to my rescue when my house was broken into. The ceremony was performed at the restaurant by a chaplain from the VA Hospital. My new husband took out a Bible, placed a gun over it, and swore according to Macedonian tradition to protect and love me.

The ties I had with this man went beyond our high school years at the same school. His father was of Macedonian descent like mine. Both of our fathers were professors with offices at the University of Sofia not far apart; our mothers were from the same western provinces of Bulgaria about fifty kilometers apart. We further found out that our sons went to the same college and that prior to meeting in San Antonio, Texas, we lived in the same cities in Michigan and Texas during different times. There were a lot of coincidences of family history and travel, which made me believe that meeting him was not by chance. Most couples start their married life with testimonies of loyalty, trust, and respect in health and sickness; we started ours with swearing in supporting each other first in sickness and then health.

Our routine was the same every morning. We woke up to an upbeat Serbian song and rushed to the medical center for tests and treatment. There were a few weeklong hospital treatments, the first one at the university hospital. I had a bad experience from leaving Mom alone at the hospital, relying on doctors to do their part, so this time I stayed with my new husband, sleeping on a cot by his bed side. Every time they brought a new bag of drugs, I compared them with those of the doctors' orders; I knew the nurses were not happy with that at first, but then they accepted my involvement as a way to educate me about the different phases of treatment. This first stay at the university hospital was emotionally difficult as he was placed on a floor for extremely sick people, and the woman across the hall passed away. I tried to lighten up the atmosphere with music and food, which I knew he liked. And I made him take walks around the hallway.

We also planned our honeymoon, and the day after being discharged from the hospital, we flew to Cancún, Mexico. Staying at Iberoamericana Resort brought us back to life, him physically and me psychologically. Our room was by the pool with a waterfall on the side, close to the beach, and we had welcome gifts from the hotel. For a moment, we both forgot the cancer and the rigorous chemo treatments. The sun, sandy beach, seawater, fresh air, and soft wind breezes healed our hearts and our minds for a while.

Upon our return, another set of chemo treatment with a week stay this time at Methodist Hospital followed. We already knew what the best cure amid these horrifying treatments was. We booked a trip, and this time, we chose Brazil. The doctor looked at us and said, "His platelet count is very low. I do not advise any travel."

"Come on, Doctor. I don't want to die here. I'd rather be at a beach. Please give me transfusion," my husband pleaded.

The flight to Rio de Janeiro took all night, but we slept on the plane and were ready to go to the famous Copacabana as soon as we unpacked at the hotel. It was the beginning of October, and the sun was already high in the sky, warming the tremendous sandy beach. There were people exercising, some running, and the small cafés alongside the sand were starting to open. Here I had the best churros in the world for breakfast and the best coconut drink at sunset. The statue of Jesus was majestically standing on Corcovado Mountain, overlooking the city and providing a feeling of peace, tranquility, and security. An eventful train ride with musicians entertaining with lively Brazilian music on board took us to the top of the mountain, and after climbing some two hundred steps, we were at the feet of the statue, which was an imposing figure of Jesus with spread-out arms as if to embrace the world—the sensation was very powerful and enticing. The panoramic view from the peak was spectacular, offering scenes from the beaches, Sugarloaf Mountain, Tijuca Forest, Guanabara Bay, the famous Maracaña Stadium, the enormous size of the city, and the Atlantic Ocean disappearing at the horizon. Equally beautiful scenery was offered by the Sugarloaf Mountain from across the Corcovado Mountain.

What made Rio unusually beautiful was the presence of the large rocky peaks dominating a rain forest, which blended with modern life. We also experienced Búzios, a city down the coast with more amazing sights like the one from our villa at a resort on a hill overlooking the water. The resort was terraced and decorated with lush tropical vegetation and flowers. Opening the door of our unit, I could see beyond the balcony flowers of violet, pink, red, and yellow colors with the beautiful blue ocean in the distance. "Wow, that's so beautiful!" I exclaimed and then noticed a bottle of champagne with a congratulations card on it. It was easier to face the upcoming visits to hospitals after spending time at this enchanting country.

The following month, we continued to alternate chemo with travel and visited Cancún a couple more times. December was the big month as all the prescribed regular chemo were completed, and it was time for a cell transplant. That involved hooking my husband to a machine with numerous tubes and getting his blood to circulate in the process of which healthy cells were collected then frozen and, after another very aggressive chemo, were reintroduced in the body. In those days, my husband was completely exhausted and could hardly cross the street on his own. After the completion of all procedures, we went home, but I kept an overnight hospital bag in the car because if his health worsened, I had to be prepared to take him to the hospital right away. There were about a couple of weeks of critical period with low blood count and extreme weakness, but miraculously, my husband responded positively to the transmission. It was around the Christmas holidays, and I gathered the family with my daughter's and his son's spouses and kids for a big Christmas celebration.

Since my husband's sickness, I was working mostly online, having left one of my agents in charge of the office for face-to-face meetings with agents, taxpayers, and administrative work. I kept in touch with the group on a daily basis, discussing their casework with tax issues and work in the field. Whenever necessary, I stopped at the office, but working online proved to be as effective. I did all case discussions and agents' evaluations and had ongoing communication with them and my manager on a daily basis from my computer. My group was functioning just as efficiently as when I was in the office, which was a very rewarding observation. I have created a group where people were self-sufficient, being successful by working independently. Moreover, the agent whom I trained and supported to be a manager and acted for me proved to be an excellent leader.

January 2014, the beginning of a new year, giving my husband a chance to recuperate (he was in remission, and the memories of my breast cancer ordeal were starting to fade). My husband started to go to work for a few days a week, and I returned to being more in the office. I knew my secretary's personality. He wasn't that comfortable with other people managing the office; he was more relaxed when I was there. I resumed visiting my agents in the field, admiring them for being skillful in interviewing and gathering information for their cases. There was a taxpayer who worked as a private contractor in Iraq whose tax return was reporting almost no income and, in the middle of describing dangerous situations with bombing, provided financial information missing from his tax return. "We lived in the green zone," he said. "That was the only safe place, but it was expensive." And he gave my agent the expenses he incurred for rent and living while in Iraq. "You won't believe this," he said, "but I was in a room full of cash."

I also assisted agents in dealing with angry accountants and taxpayers. In a meeting with a representative from Dallas, the man threw a paper across the table, at which I immediately reacted. "Did you just throw this paper?"

"No, ma'am. The wind blew it."

We were in a conference room. I looked at his face, which was turning red. "I will suggest that there is no more paper flying," I responded, "or we are going to complete the audit right now."

In another case, a taxpayer, in an effort to avoid the tax issues, had called to complain about the agent, "Your agent caused damage to my door by taping a summons. And he was driving a car far more expensive than mine."

I let the man speak for about half an hour, making incohesive and unfounded accusations, and when he stopped, it was my turn to speak. I did not respond to anything but rather asked, "Sir, would you prefer that my agent issue a report with the information we have, or will you provide more records listed in the summons?" This ended the case without any more questions.

There were also negligent individuals who ignored reports for additional due taxes all the way to collection, seizing their assets. All the years that I was with the Service, I always believed that people need to be helped in meeting their tax responsibilities rather than punished. There were some who were classified as tax abusers, but for the most part, the American public wanted to be compliant with the law. Some reacted as soon as learning about mistakes on their tax returns and were thankful for the professional treatment and information to avoid future issues. Others ignored the reports and responded when collection was at their door. I was on friendly terms with the collection manager who shared my ways of work with the public, and frequently, my group assisted collection with review of last-minute provided records.

With all this going on, I still had aspirations for more challenge and traveled to Washington, DC, for an interview for a senior manager's position in appeals. Regardless of my excellent presentation demonstrating knowledge not only of appeals but also the exam division and my impeccable work track record, the one selected was an appeals officer from their own unit. Reflecting about this incident, I remembered one of the senior managers saying that for her to advance in her career, she was taking positions at locations that nobody wanted. Was I ready to travel the States to places I would never want to be at? After leaving Michigan, I had a few nightmares of being back at the Detroit office, promoted but unhappy, looking at the ice on the Detroit River. I could not imagine living again in severe winter climate conditions driving in snow and blizzards.

Both my husband and I were through very tough times in 2013, which we overcame by embracing life at its best by traveling to incredible beaches and places with amazing views and panorama. There was no need for much discussion; we booked a cruise to French Polynesia to celebrate life and experience some of the world-class resorts of islands with indescribable beauty.

April 5, 2014, here we were in Papeete, the capital of French Polynesia. My eyes were wide open as we circled the island over the multicolored, beautiful blue waters and landed at one of the world's renowned capitals. It was a different world of colors, sounds, and beauty. Met by performers of Tahitian music and dancers, we soon were at our ship named *Marina*. Our stateroom was gorgeous with modern decor, with balcony and showers for two and a bathtub. I am mentioning that because bathrooms on cruise ships are usually small. Across the pier was a market with flowers of different shapes and colors that I have never seen before, local vegetables, fish of different colors, handicrafts, and of course, the well-known black pearl jewelry shops of the region. Walking in a park alongside the beach, we came across a dance instruction class with local people and tourists dancing, which I immediately joined. This place was so invigorating and so full of energy and beauty.

Our first stop with the ship was Moorea, where we went hiking in the mountain. After being fed with delicious local fruits, we headed up a tropical jungle. The guide provided a very interesting information about the life on the island, demonstrating how the locals use natural resources for anything they need in their life. There was a shampoo flower, the secret for women's long, thick, healthy hair, and vine branch was providing water. The view from the top was astounding, with lush greenery all the way to the sea and small white houses, barely visible, toward the bottom of the forest. It was a steep path through amazing tropical vegetation, but being a rain forest, it started to rain, making the hike somewhat difficult for some of the people who were slipping and getting covered with mud going downhill.

I got up before sunrise as we approached the next island, Huahine, known as the garden island because of its green tropical foliage, where we got to experience typical local food served on tables in the water close to the shore, Tahitian dancing, and demonstration of breaking a coconut. Cook Island was memorable for a safari with off-road vehicles whose guide introduced himself as Useless, a nickname from his wife. As far as the population of the island, he laughed. "We told the Chinese that we will eat them, so they gave up the idea of buying land here." The island itself was surrounded by a lagoon extending deep into a reef, which I admired on a Muri Lagoon cruise and snorkeling tour.

But the most beautiful and famous island was Bora Bora. As the ship approached, there it was, a majestic mountain with two peaks surrounded by a lagoon of translucent green and azure-blue seawaters. For the first time, I saw villas in the water, something I knew from videos and reading books. I was still apprehensive of snorkeling, so we took a glass-bottom boat, viewing the most colorful and diverse fish I have ever seen. There was also a stop for the brave ones, not me, to swim with lemon sharks and stingrays. Another place worth mentioning is Rangiroa, which was a stunning sight with its pink sandy beaches.

I took this paradise home with me, and as I resumed my daily life at the IRS office, I began to reflect on my past, reliving some of the most eventful moments of my life, trying to figure out if I needed to continue pursuing my career or retire. At the age of sixty-five, I could retire probably with somewhat lower pension, but was it really worth it to work any longer? It was a lifetime decision because I did not want to retire and return to work after a few months for whatever reason.

By August 2014, the thought of retiring was very real as I made a calculation if there would be enough in my retirement funds to live without being a burden to my children. *I can make it,* I thought to myself. Then I called my manager. "Sir, I have an important matter to discuss with you or, better said, to announce to you. I would like to retire as of December 1 this year." He seemed surprised, because usually, people at the IRS plan years ahead of retirement. Besides, I was looking into promotional assignments not that long ago. His response was very encouraging and receptive of my decision, which prompted me to proceed with making arrangements for the big day. It was a big surprise for my agents as well. My agents also did not expect me to announce a retirement so soon. I summonsed them for a meeting at which after glancing at each one of them I started to speak slowly, in an even voice: "I am retiring as of December 1, this year. I feel that I already gave you tools to advance your careers, and after giving it a lot of thought, I decided that it is time for me to start a new chapter in my life. I would like to paint, to play the piano, to ride my bike, and to take walks first thing in the morning. I would like to travel to places I have only read about in Africa and Asia. I would also love to travel by train in Europe to all these countries that I couldn't go to as a teenager." I could see that the original faces of concern started to brighten up; they knew exactly what I was referring to.

"You need to write a book of your life" was a comment of one of my agents, and that gave me the idea of sharing my life story.

My retirement party was very emotional as agents from both exam groups in the office, other managers, my first and current bosses, and my daughter with her family were present. That day was a very special day for me as I was saying goodbye to my big family— my colleagues at the Internal Revenue Service. I was observing the happy, cheerful faces of agents, remembering my early years as an agent, when I was so excited and happy to be a part of a very important and respected agency. But it was time to make ways to the young.

I have lived a full, rich, and colorful life with experiences ranging from life under communism to the continuous pursuit of growth and happiness in the land of the free. My new home, America, is the only place on earth where people from all parts of the world can realize their dreams and potential. I was smiling as I was listening to the happy chirping voices around me, knowing that I did my share of contributing to our society by impacting the lives of so many people in their search for success and self fulfilment.

About the Author

 The author was born and raised in Bulgaria during the Communist regime. Growing in a family of intellectuals—her father, a professor, and her mother, a high school teacher—she develops a love for books at an early age. Witnessing and enduring injustices of the Communist system, she escapes at the age of twenty to the Free World and settles down in America, her new home.

Years later, with the fall of the Berlin Wall, she returns to Bulgaria as a tax consultant from the United States Treasury with a mission to fix the broken system and clear the road for the country to join the European Union. She is passionate about education and spends all her life teaching and inspiring young adults and colleagues at work to follow their dreams and achieve their goals. Whether a high school teacher in a Catholic school or the inner city of Detroit, she promotes education as the only means for a happy and self-fulfilled life.

Later on, she switches careers to work for the United States Treasury, where, during supervisory assignments, she continues to provide guidance and instruction to her employees to be successful in their careers and having a better quality of life. The author herself fulfills her dream of working for the United States Treasury and triumphantly completing her overseas assignment to assist Bulgaria and other Eastern European countries in implementing much-needed tax policies for their newly formed free market economies.

This book is the author's desire to share her life journey and thrive for success, as well as to motivate individuals to fight for freedom and a better life. The author is currently enjoying retirement, catching up on travel restricted under the Bulgarian Communist regime. She dedicates this book to her children and grandchildren, wishing them all very enjoyable and successful lives in the Land of the Free.

CPSIA information can be obtained
at www.ICGtesting.com
Printed in the USA
LVHW090446200322
713745LV00001B/2